POSTCARD HISTORY SERIES

Wilmington

NORTH CAROLINA

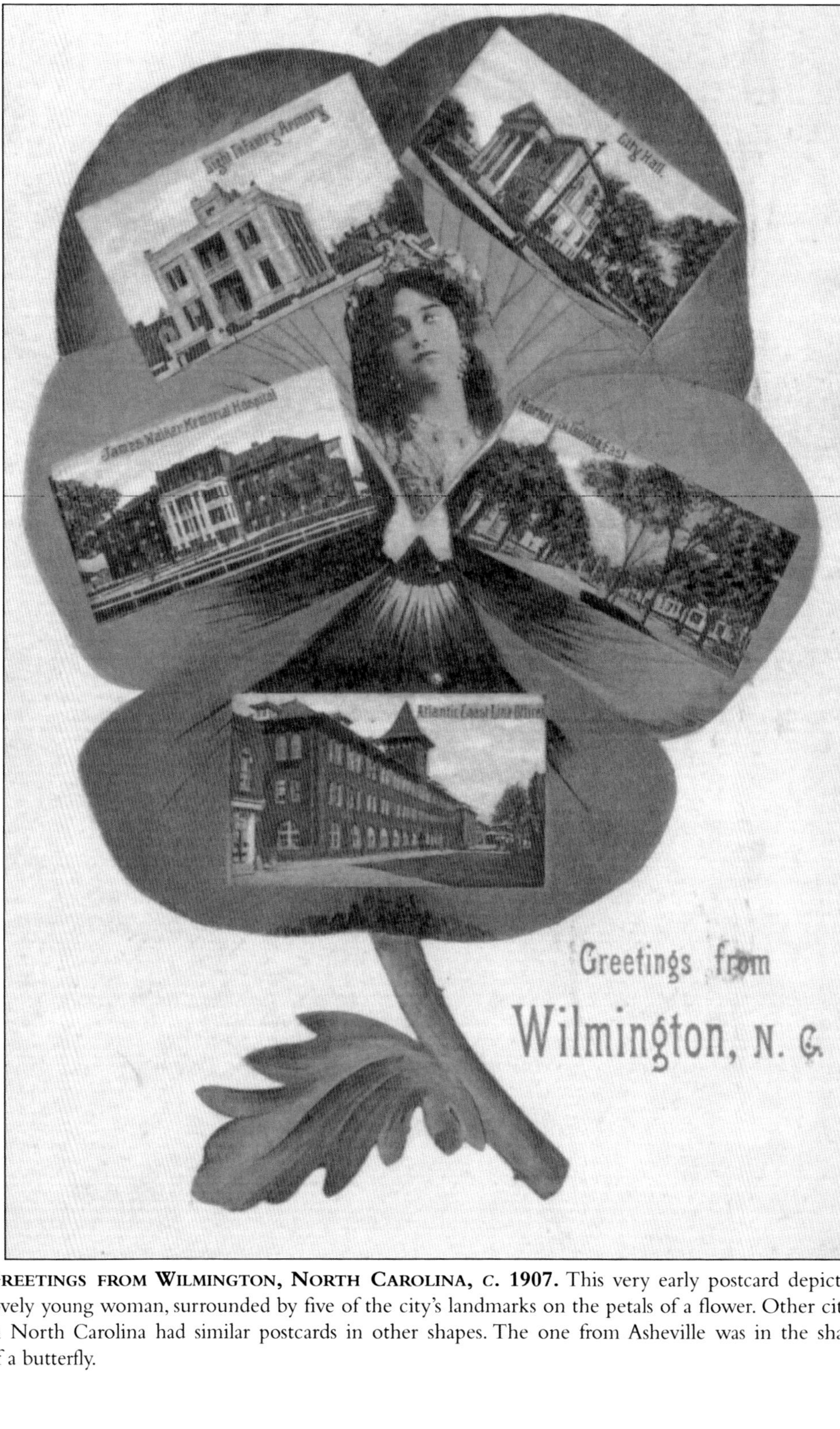

GREETINGS FROM WILMINGTON, NORTH CAROLINA, *C.* 1907. This very early postcard depicts a lovely young woman, surrounded by five of the city's landmarks on the petals of a flower. Other cities in North Carolina had similar postcards in other shapes. The one from Asheville was in the shape of a butterfly.

POSTCARD HISTORY SERIES

Wilmington
NORTH CAROLINA

Ann Hewlett Hutteman

ARCADIA
PUBLISHING

ISBN 978-0-7385-0639-5

Published by Arcadia Publishing
Charleston, South Carolina

Printed in the United States of America

Library of Congress Catalog Card Number: 00-106897

For all general information contact Arcadia Publishing at:
Telephone 843-853-2070
Fax 843-853-0044
E-mail sales@arcadiapublishing.com
For customer service and orders:
Toll-Free 1-888-313-2665

Visit us on the Internet at www.arcadiapublishing.com

Dedication

This book is dedicated to Beverly Tetterton
for 20 years of service as the state and local history librarian
at the New Hanover County Public Library.

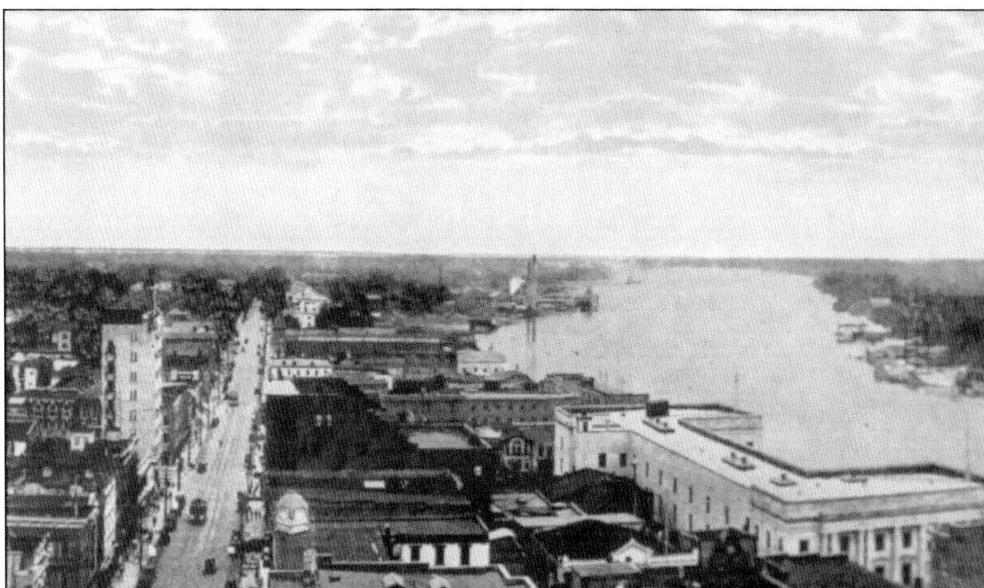

"Bird's-Eye View of Wilmington," Looking South, c. 1920. This scene was taken from the top of the Murchison Building and shows the Cape Fear River, the U.S. Customs House, and a portion of Front Street.

Contents

ACKNOWLEDGMENTS

The majority of the postcards contained in this volume come from the collections of the North Carolina Room of the New Hanover County Public Library. The nucleus of its postcard collection is the Sallie Pearl Stevens Butler Collection and the Wayne Arnold Collection. John Wright Butler contributed his mother's extensive collection to the library in the 1980s. Shortly before his death, avid collector Wayne Arnold of Burgaw donated his postcards. Others in the library collection are taken from the following: the Dr. Robert M. Fales Slide Collection, the James B. McKoy Theater Collection, the Rupert L. Benson Wrightsville Beach Collection, the Thomas Franklin Boyd Collection, William B. Creasey Collection, and Bill Reaves Collection. Without the generosity of these library patrons, this postcard history would not be possible.

Special thanks go to Jonathan Noffke and Blair Jackson of the Bellamy Mansion Museum of History and Design Arts, Tony Rivenbark of the Thalian Hall Center for the Performing Arts, and Ed Combs and Mary Caputo of the Pender County Museum for the use of postcards from their collections. My deep appreciation goes to Hugh Morton, Wilmington native and noted North Carolina photographer; Mrs. Gerald Harrington of Tom and Jerry Card Co.; and Tom Bradshaw of Pender County—all of whom granted permission to allow publication of their postcards.

There are so many people who graciously consented to be interviewed for this book. I tapped the extensive knowledge of Mrs. Susie S. Carson of Southport and Eugene F. Risley Jr. of Carolina Beach, both of whom reviewed the manuscript and gave sage advice. Others who furnished valuable information are as follows: Orrell Parker Jones, George Tregembo, Andrew Kure, Jennie Kure Bagley, B.C. Hedgpeth, Bill Hurst, Harlan McKeithan, Chris Fonvielle, Henry Rehder, Bobby and Lou Greer, Ed Turberg, and Tim Bottoms and Barbara Rowe of the Cape Fear Museum. Also, I appreciate the help of Susan Taylor Block, an experienced author who gave practical advice; Marie Spencer, who reviewed the manuscript for grammar and punctuation; Katherine Dixon Furr, who accompanied me on a fact-finding mission to Southport; and Glenn Tetterton, who with his usual cheerful demeanor, acted as a library courier and chauffeur.

Most of all, I am exceedingly grateful for the cooperation of the staff of the North Carolina Room, New Hanover County Public Library, and especially local history librarian, Beverly Tetterton. She conceived the idea of this postcard history on behalf of the Friends of the Library, edited the manuscript with fervor, and encouraged and supported me in every way. Joseph Sheppard answered my numerous questions with good humor and expertise.

Thank you to my friend, Annie Lucas Richardson, who kept my life organized during this project. Finally, I am grateful to my husband, Harko (Hank) Hutteman, whose patience, encouragement, and loving support made this book possible.

INTRODUCTION

Postcards were first introduced in Europe in the late 1860s, but they did not have pictures or illustrations until the 1890s. They were unknown in the United States until after the 1893 Columbian Exposition in Chicago. On December 24, 1901, the use of the words "post card" was granted by the U.S. government to private printers. The "penny" postcard quickly became one of the most popular and inexpensive means of communication, especially since telephones were not widespread.

The addition of pictures or illustrations greatly enhanced the aesthetics and interest of the postcards. Most people had little experience with cameras, except to have their portraits taken in a studio every few years. Therefore, the photograph of a scene that could be sent through the mail was thought to be remarkable, exotic, and exciting. Between 1907 and 1914, the majority of the picture cards were printed in Germany, which specialized in converting photographs sent from our country into high-quality postcards. There are several in this book that were printed in Germany. The outbreak of World War I stopped trade with Germany, after which postcard production began in earnest in the United States, although at first, the quality was inferior.

Writing was not permitted on the address side; therefore, it is understandable that on some of the early postcards sentences were written on the picture side. On March 1, 1907, the U.S. Post Office approved the divided back postcard, which allowed room for a message on the left side and the address on the right. The messages make interesting reading and give a small glimpse into life in the early twentieth century.

About 1930, "linen" postcards made their debut. They were printed on paper that had a high rag content, with a rough finish. The most modern postcards are known as "chromes." These cards are usually color photographs of high quality and date from the 1940s.

It quickly became apparent to towns and cities all over the nation that postcards were a way to publicize their areas. Local leaders had thousands printed in the hopes of putting the very best possible face on their communities. In some cases, photographs were altered by coloring or cropping the picture for a more attractive scene. Later, individual businesses used the medium to advertise their services. They were particularly useful in the tourist industry.

Collecting postcards became as popular as sending them. They were pasted into albums or books or kept in trunks or shoe boxes for safekeeping. Thankfully, several of these early local collectors have donated their treasures to the New Hanover County Public Library. There is even a word for the serious postcard collector—a deltiologist.

The most difficult task of writing this book was deciding which postcards to include from over 500 in the library's collection. Care was taken to choose a variety that shows how Wilmington and its vicinity evolved from the turn of the last century until the 1960s. Wilmington was North Carolina's largest city from the mid-1800s until about 1910, and there are many postcards that illustrate the importance of the port. The greatest number are of the downtown business district, demonstrating how that area has changed over the years. Our churches, schools, and hospitals are represented. Of course, the beaches are a mecca for tourists, and hopefully, the postcards selected will bring back pleasant memories of summers spent by the sea. Our neighbors, Burgaw and Southport have a close river and railroad connection to Wilmington and these two small towns have been included.

Many of the buildings and landmarks depicted in this book have been victims of the wrecking ball. In that sense, the postcards provide a historical and pictorial record of structures that once contributed to the architectural character of the area. By limiting this book to only postcards, some aspects of our city are not covered, simply because there were no postcards available.

The bold type in the beginning of each entry indicates the title and date the postcard was published. All of the postcards came from the library's collection unless otherwise noted.

It is hoped that the reader will enjoy exploring the rich and diverse history of Wilmington and its neighbors through the medium of postcards.

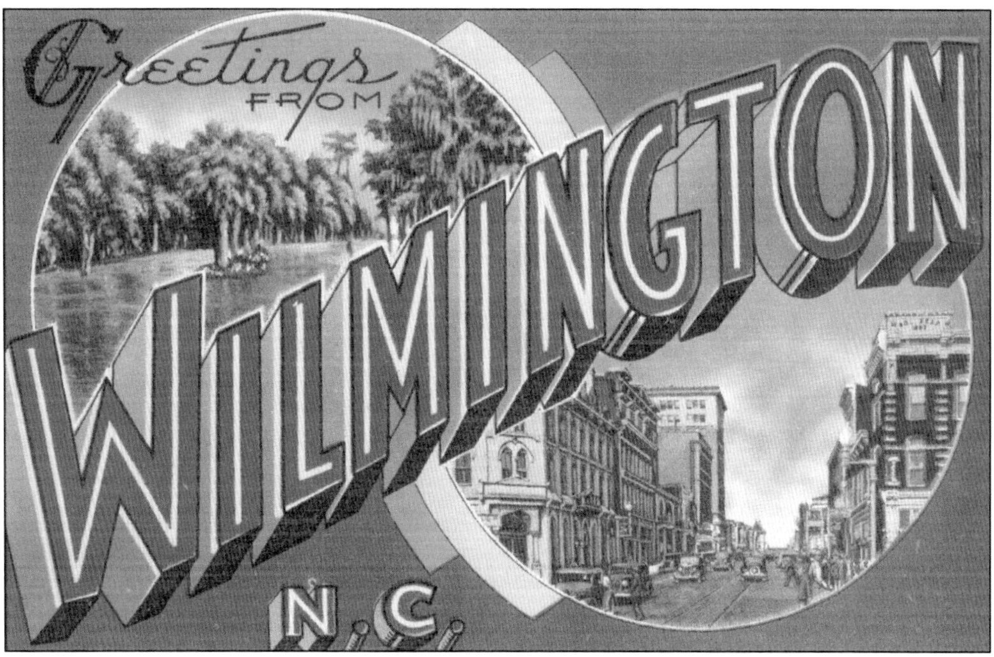

GREETINGS FROM WILMINGTON, NORTH CAROLINA, *C.* 1940S. One of the most popular postcard designs was and still is the "Greetings from . . ." genre. Greenfield Lake and the business district in the 100 block of North Front Street are highlighted in this montage.

One

Waterfront

The Native Americans called the river "Sapona," which begins by the joining of the Haw and Deep Rivers in Chatham County, North Carolina. It flows southeasterly toward the Atlantic Ocean and the cape, which would eventually give the river its permanent name. Variously called the River Jordan by the Spanish, and the Charles and Clarendon by the English, the name, Cape Fear, is entirely appropriate. At the mouth of the river, the treacherous Frying Pan Shoals jut out 28 miles into the Atlantic Ocean. These dangerous underwater sandbars have caused numerous shipwrecks, which made sailors "fear" the entrance to the river; hence, the Cape of Fear.

Wilmington was founded 1739–1740 at the junction of the Cape Fear and Northeast Cape Fear Rivers. First called New Carthage, the town was the second permanent settlement on the river after Brunswick Town. For a time, it was known as New Liverpool, then New Town or Newton before being named for Spencer Compton, the Earl of Wilmington, a patron of Royal Governor Gabriel Johnston (1698–1752). The site of the town is approximately 30 miles from the mouth of the river.

The port and the industrial area that developed along the waterfront had enormous economic importance. Foreign and domestic ships came into port and made Wilmington a cosmopolitan center.

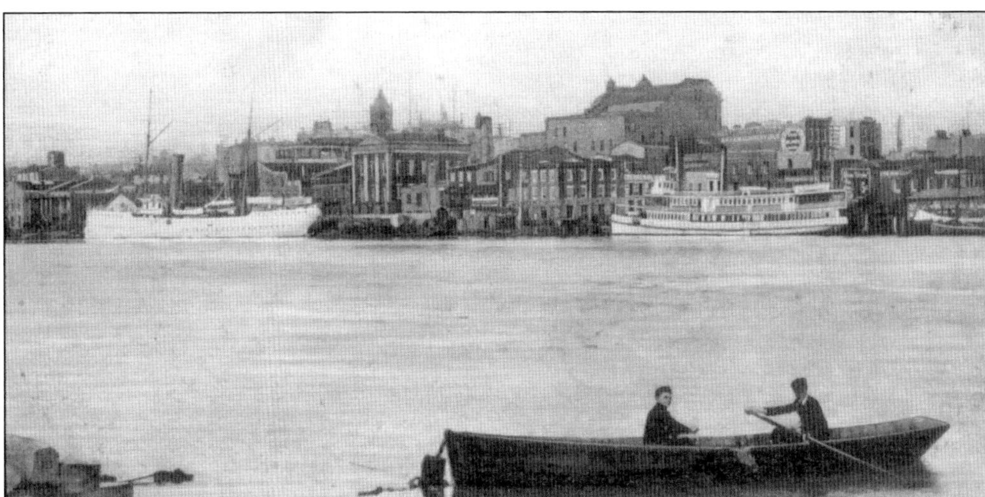

Wilmington Harbor, c. 1910. This view is of the Wilmington harbor, between Market and Princess Streets. At center, the two-story Greek Revival–style building facing the river is the United States Customs House, designed by John Norris and built in 1840. At left, the U.S. revenue cutter *Seminole* is docked at the government wharf. The other large vessel is the steamer *Wilmington*, moored at her dock at the foot of Market Street.

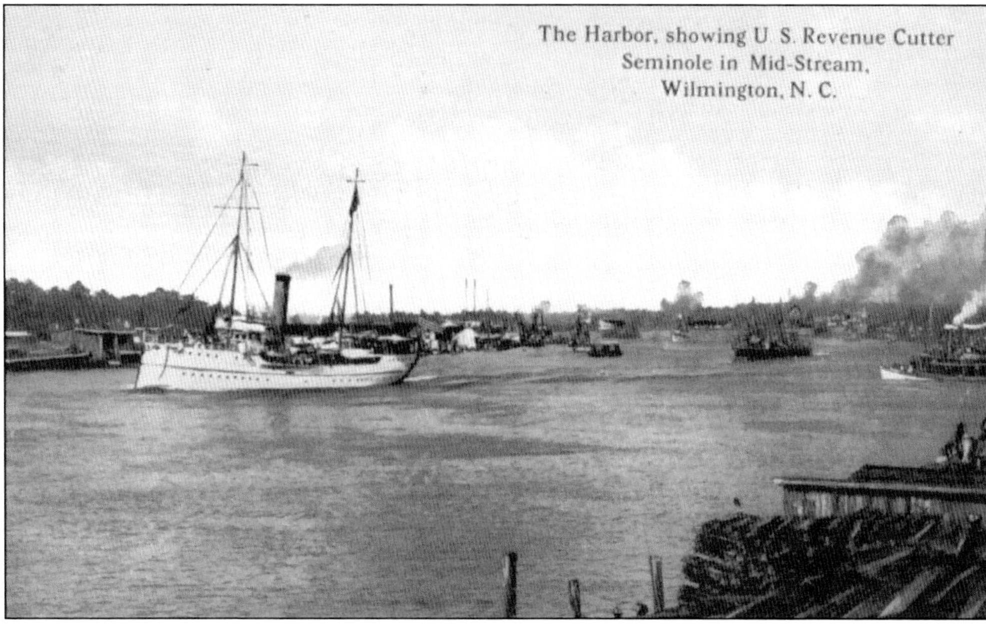

THE U.S. REVENUE CUTTER *SEMINOLE*, C. 1915. The U.S. Revenue Service was founded in 1790 by Alexander Hamilton, the first Secretary of the Treasury, to collect import tariffs. One of the first ten authorized ships was assigned to North Carolina. The *Seminole* was one of a number of cutters that have called the port of Wilmington home.

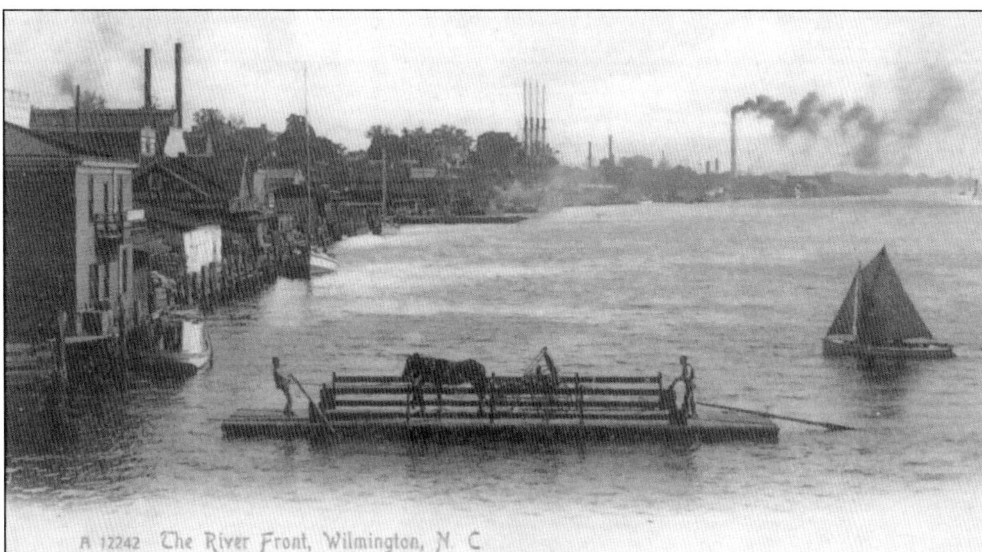

FERRY CROSSING CAPE FEAR RIVER, C. 1906. From colonial days, ferries carried man, beast, and products across the Cape Fear River from Eagles Island on the western bank to a dock at the foot of Market Street. The causeway leading into Wilmington from the west crossed low-lying, marshy land and was usually in such disrepair that its deplorable condition was noted frequently in early county court minutes. The ferry approached the dock, next to the JaWaHa Building at far left. The tall smokestack in the background is that of the Tidewater Gas Works, located at the foot of Castle Street.

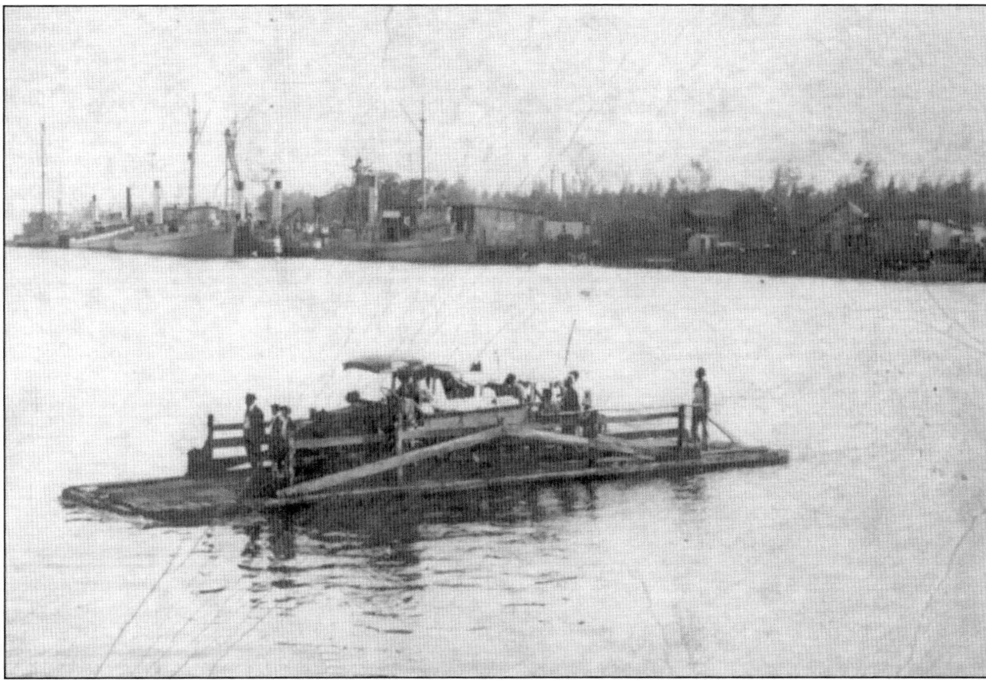

FERRY CROSSING CAPE FEAR RIVER, *C.* 1905. An early ferryboat is in mid-river, with Eagles Island in the background. The island was named for Richard Eagles, a native of Bristol, England, who was granted the property in 1737. In the mid-nineteenth century, the island was the center of the naval stores and lumber industries.

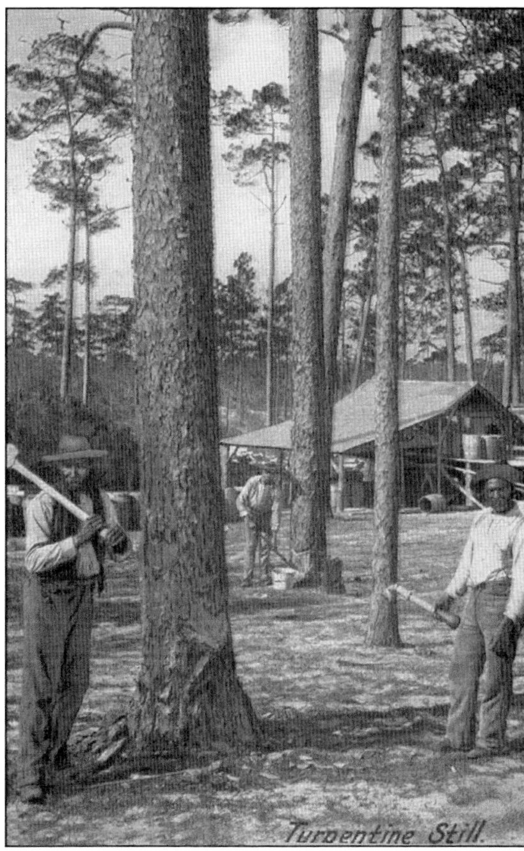

TURPENTINE STILL, *C.* 1909. From colonial times, naval stores comprised an important industry for Southeastern North Carolina, reaching its zenith prior to the Civil War. The large local stand of virgin forests provided the raw material for tar, pitch, resin, and turpentine, products that were necessary to waterproof wooden ships and to tar rigs of sailing vessels. Workers would tap the resin, which had been prepared by hacking the bark of the tree that in turn produced a sap, which was then distilled into turpentine. The hacking season usually lasted from the middle of March to November.

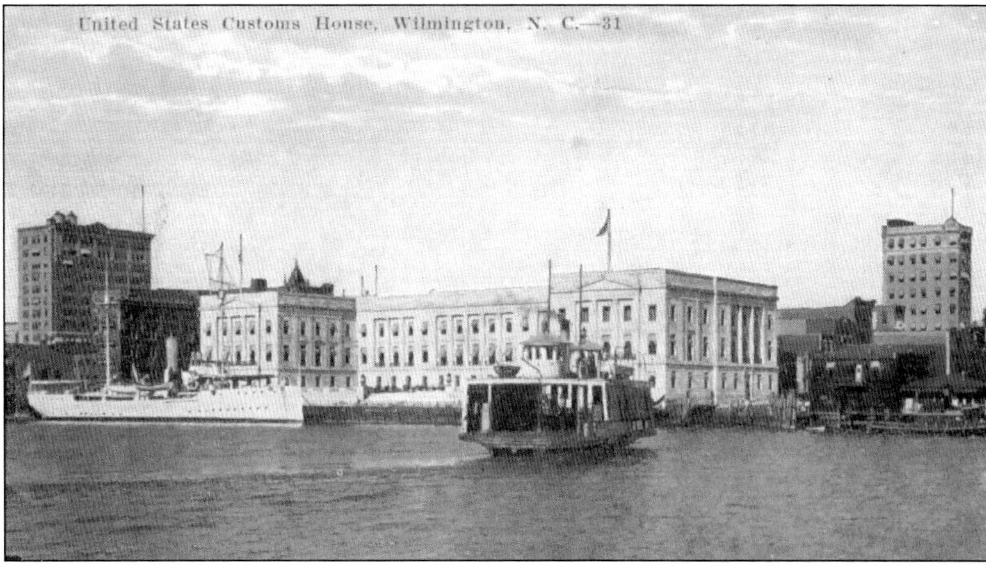

WATERFRONT, C. 1924. The ferryboat *John Knox* is seen in front of the U.S. Customs House with the city skyline in the background. The ferryboat was named for John Knox, who was the chairman of the Brunswick County Commissioners for many years. The U.S. revenue cutter *Seminole* is tied up at the government wharf.

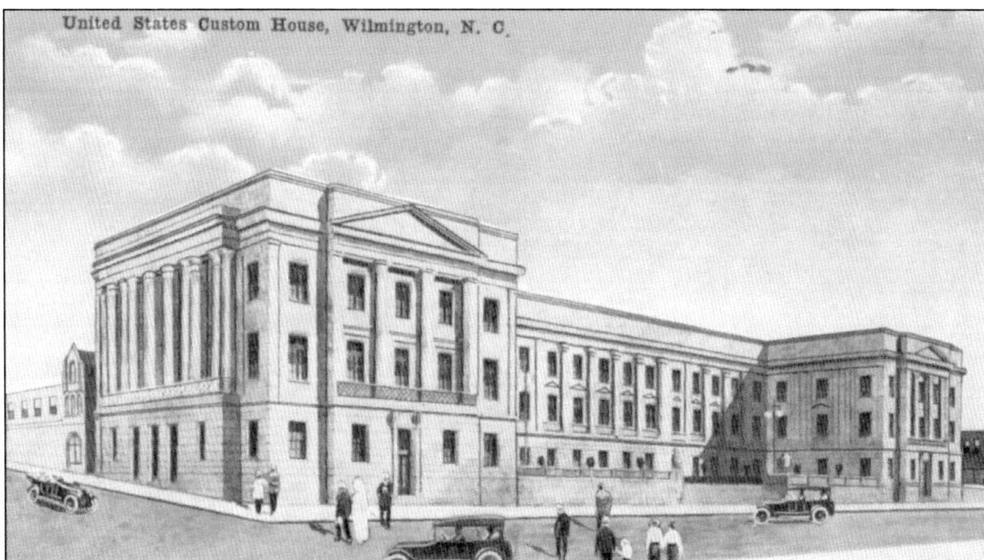

UNITED STATES CUSTOMS HOUSE, C. 1920. One of the most impressive buildings in the city is the U.S. Customs House, which was designed by John Wetmore, an architect for the U.S. Treasury Department. The cornerstone was laid on December 9, 1916, on the same site as the 1840 Customs House. Delayed by WW I, the Neoclassical Revival structure was ready for occupancy in 1919. Known as the Alton A. Lennon Federal Building after a late local congressman, the building in recent years has been the location for a number of projects of Wilmington's thriving film industry, including *Matlock*, a television series starring North Carolina native Andy Griffith.

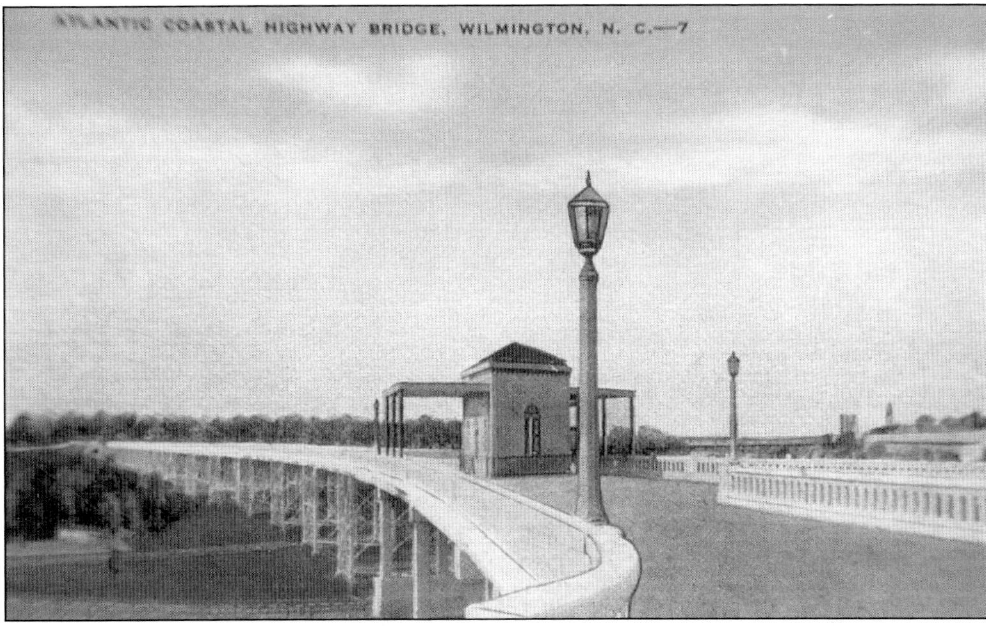

ATLANTIC HIGHWAY BRIDGE, c. 1940. The Northeast Cape Fear River Bridge opened to traffic on December 10, 1929. At the same time, another bridge was dedicated, which crossed the Northwest Cape Fear River. Costing in excess of $1 million, the project replaced the ferries that had plied the river since the city's founding. It marked the first time in the area's history that vehicular traffic from the south was able to drive into Wilmington. At some later date, the light poles in the photograph were removed and are now located on the property of a motel on Market Street.

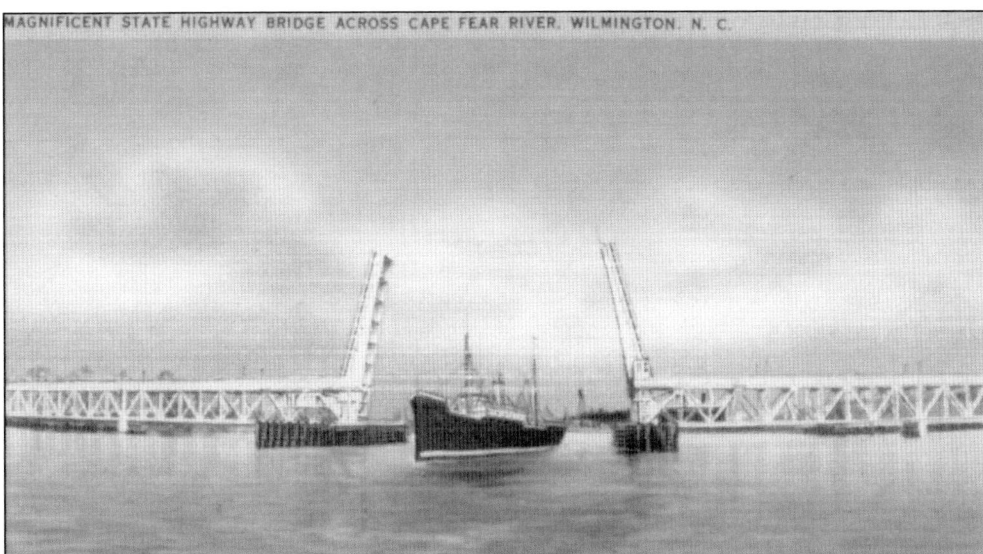

NORTHEAST CAPE FEAR RIVER BRIDGE, c. 1940. The Northeast Cape Fear River Bridge opens its span for a freighter, heading down the river from Navassa with a cargo of fertilizer. Several fertilizer factories were located on the western bank of the river and north of the bridge.

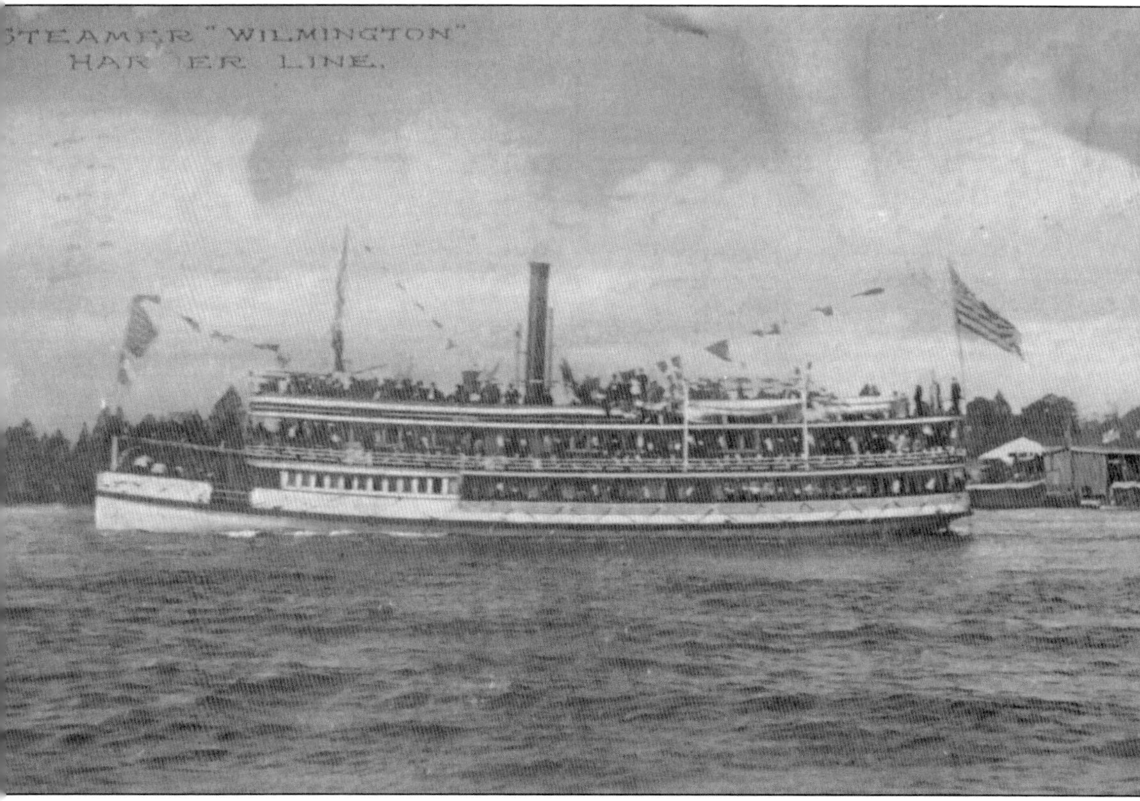

STEAMER *WILMINGTON*, HARPER LINE, 1912. The steamer *Wilmington* was owned and operated by Captain John W. Harper (1856–1917). Built in 1881, Captain Harper purchased the boat in Wilmington, Delaware. Already named the *Wilmington*, she arrived in her new home-port on April 28, 1891, and was greeted by a tumultuous welcome from local citizens who lined the river bank. The iron steamer was 130 feet long, had a beam of 23 feet, and drew 6 feet of water. She had three decks, with a wide promenade that wrapped completely around the main deck. During the summer months, the swift boat could transport passengers from Wilmington to a wharf on the river at Carolina Beach in about an hour. In all, she made two trips daily from Wilmington to Smithville (Southport), transporting about 2,000 passengers a day in peak season. For years, Captain Harper had the contract for carrying the mail on his steamers, and he also contracted and furnished transportation for the garrison at Fort Caswell. The belle of the Cape Fear River, the *Wilmington* was not just a steamboat, but something of a Lower Cape Fear institution.

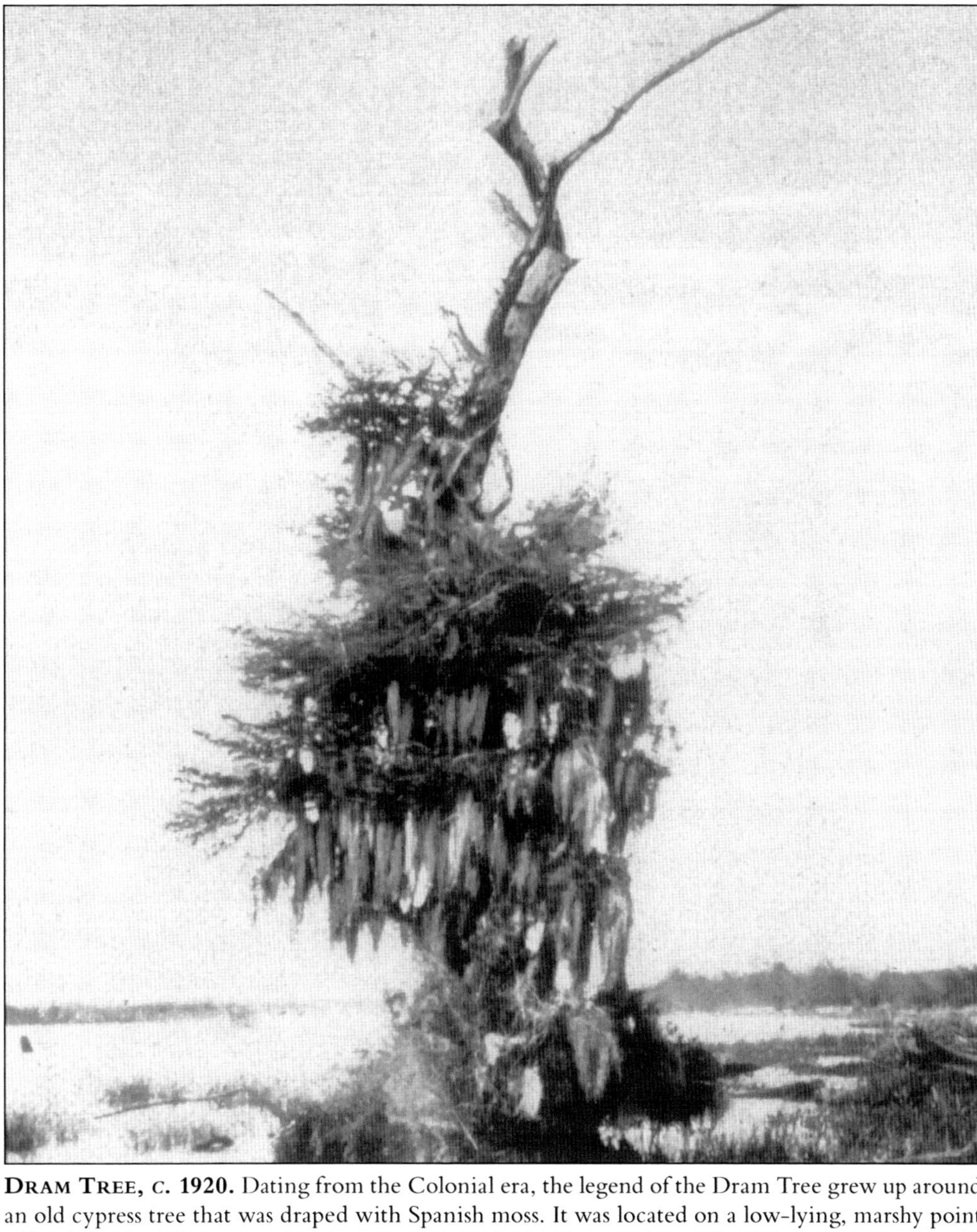

DRAM TREE, *C.* 1920. Dating from the Colonial era, the legend of the Dram Tree grew up around an old cypress tree that was draped with Spanish moss. It was located on a low-lying, marshy point of land that jutted out into the river, just south of what is now the residential area of Sunset Park. When vessels entered and left the port, they stopped briefly at the Dram Tree to give thanks for a safe voyage or to pray for a safe return. At those times, a dram of rum was given to all on board to toast the occasion. Sadly, the tree was lost in the early 1940s, when the Newport News Shipbuilding and Dry Dock Company was dredging the river to expand an old WW I shipyard.

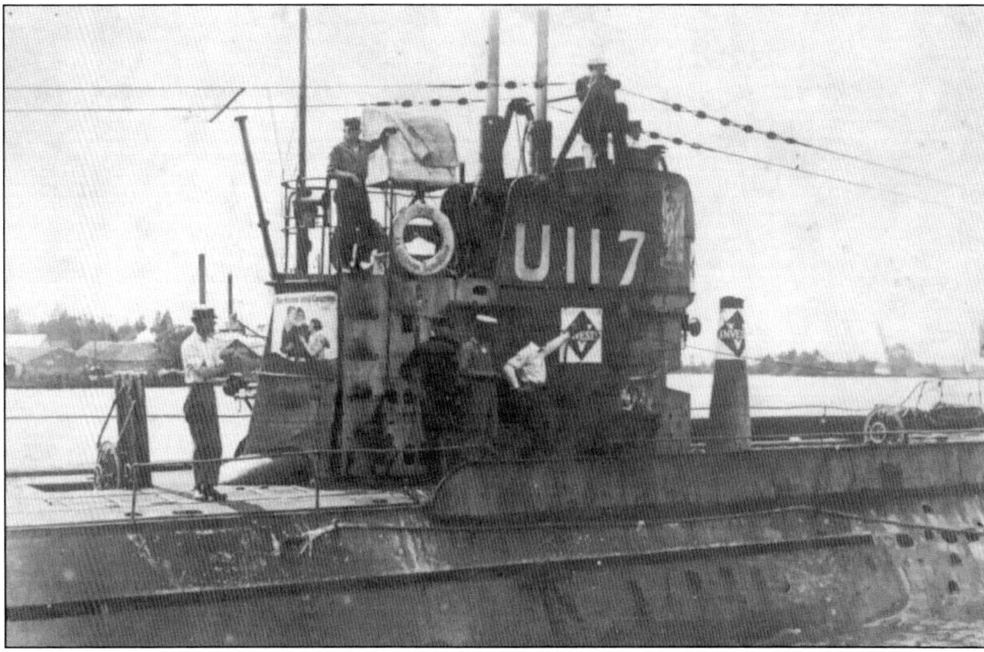

GERMAN SUBMARINE IN PORT OF WILMINGTON, 1919. German submarine U-117 was brought into the port on May 19, 1919. WW I had ended in an Allied victory the previous November and such boats were displayed throughout the nation as war trophies.

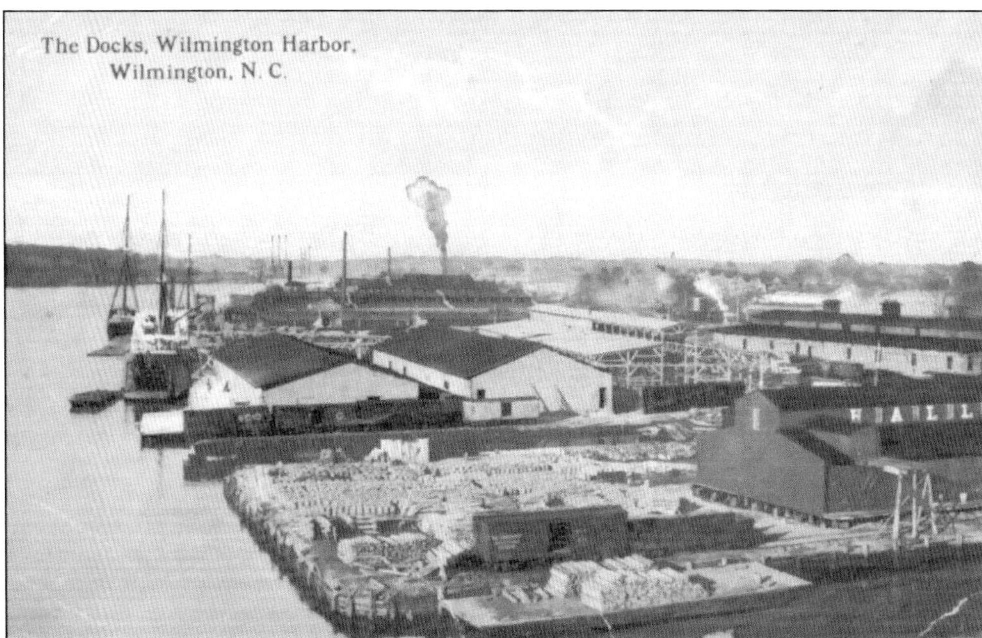

THE DOCKS, WILMINGTON HARBOR, 1912. Wilmington's harbor has always been a busy place, welcoming ships from the four corners of the earth. In the foreground are the docks of the Hall & Pearsall Lumber Yard. Note the masts of sailing vessels tied up to the wharves at left center.

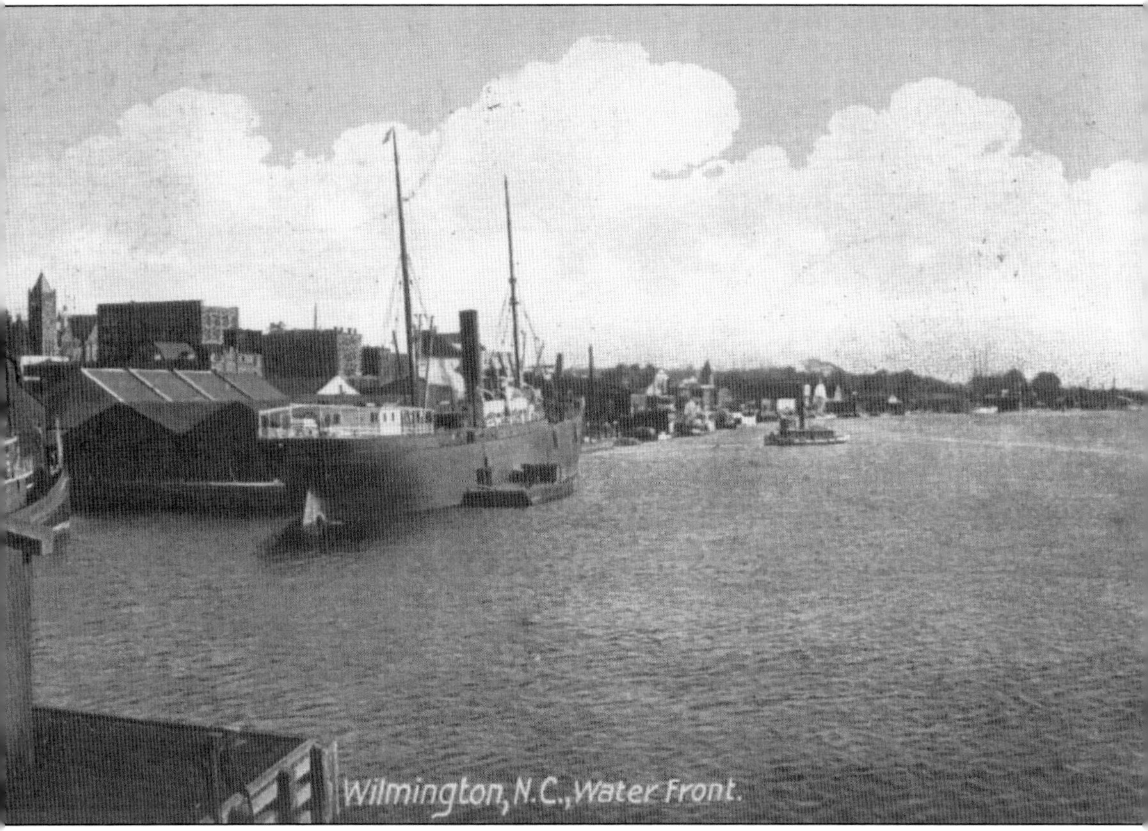

WATERFRONT, LOOKING SOUTHEAST, *c.* 1907. This panoramic view of the busy Wilmington waterfront is testament to the economic importance of the Cape Fear River. From Colonial times the waterfront was the scene of all major commerce in the area. Wharves lined nearly every foot of both sides of the river. Warehouses of all sizes, shapes, and building materials were located short distances from the docks. Ships stores were conveniently located at short intervals along the length of the waterfront. When this photograph was taken, one could have seen every imaginable sailing vessel of the time, from small packets to the above freighter, which is tied up at the Champion Compress Company dock.

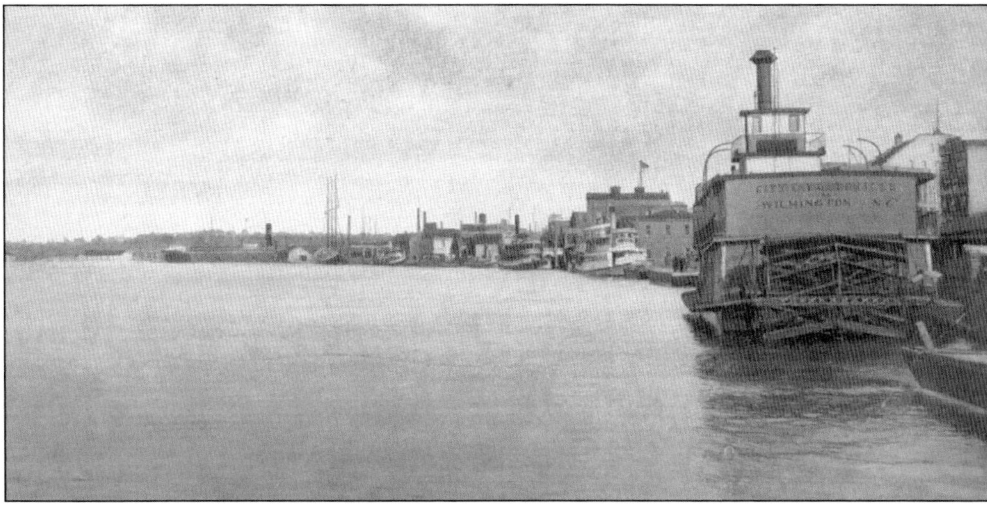

WATERFRONT, LOOKING NORTH, c. 1910. At right, the river steamer *City of Fayetteville* is moored at a dock awaiting a return trip up the Cape Fear River to Fayetteville. The steamboats were common sights, frequently carrying passengers and goods inland and returning with raw materials to be shipped out of the port of Wilmington.

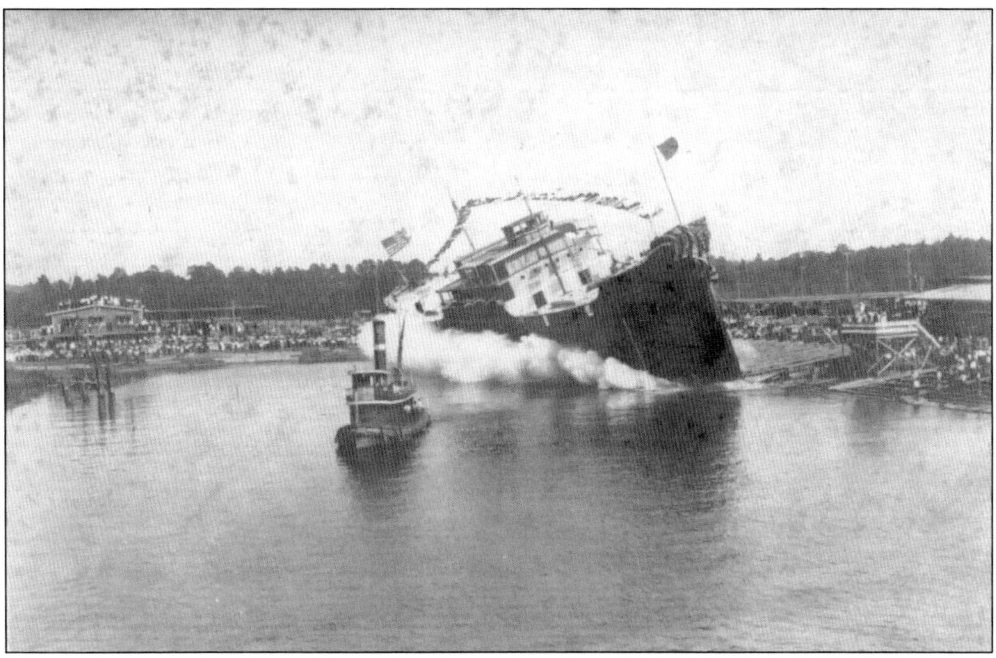

LAUNCHING A CONCRETE SHIP, c. 1919. In May 1918, a shipyard was started on the south side of town by the Liberty Shipbuilding Corporation of Boston. The first concrete ship to be built in North Carolina was launched "sideways" on July 30, 1919, and named the *Cape Fear.* Some of the spectators were drenched when the *Cape Fear* slid into the water. It was only the second such vessel constructed on the South Atlantic seaboard.

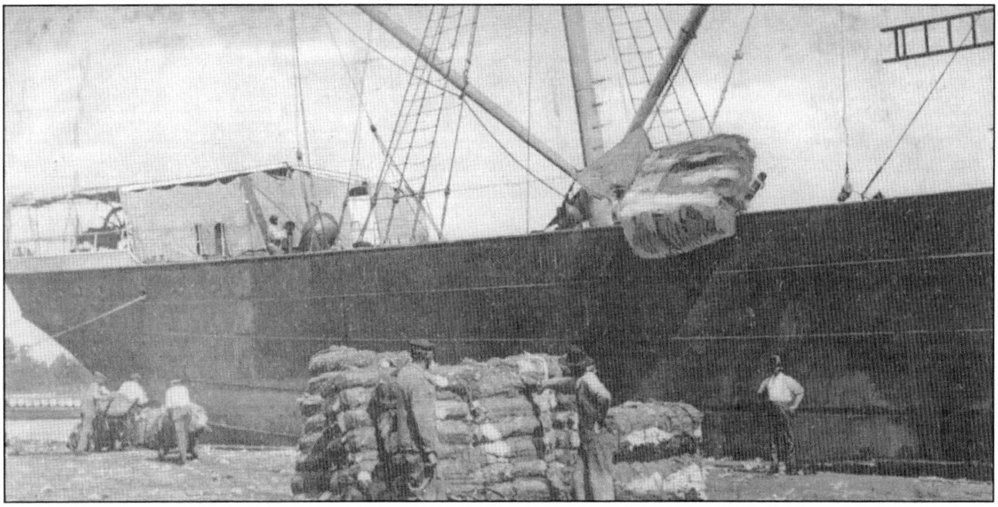

English Steamer Loading Cotton, 1910. Cotton was a chief cash crop in the South for generations. An English steamer loads a full cargo of cotton at the wharf of the Champion Compress Company. The company was organized in 1879, when Alexander Sprunt & Son and the E.J. Pennypacker Company merged. They built a huge structure on the river between Nutt and Red Cross Streets, which could store 20,000 bales of cotton. The company's docks had room for three to four ocean steamers, or four to five sailing packets at the same time.

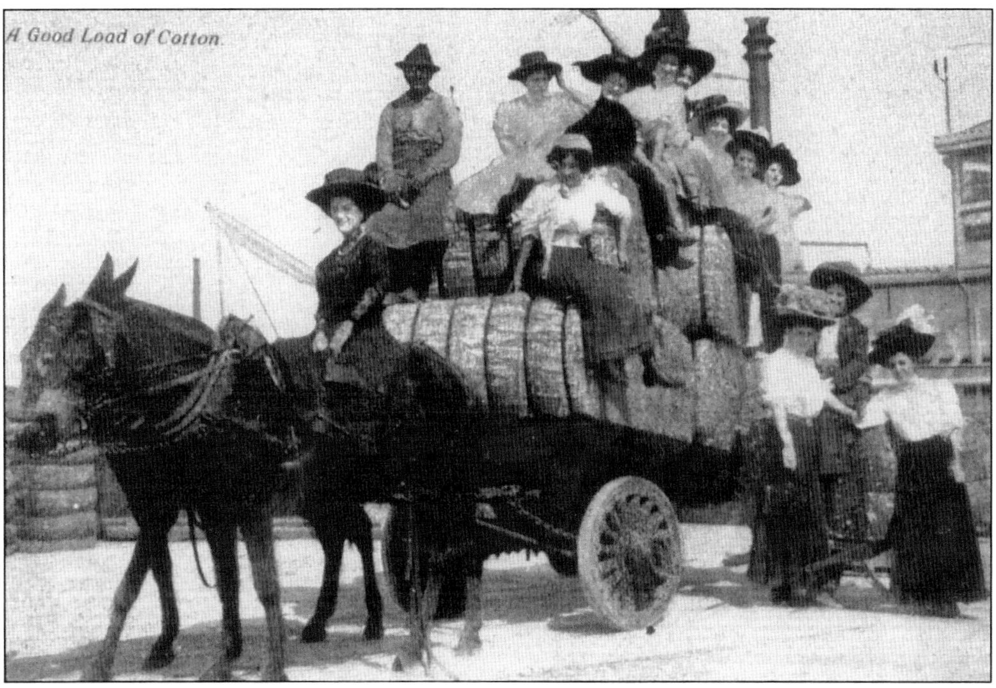

A Good Load of Cotton, 1910. A group of ladies rides in a horse-drawn wagon containing a number of cotton bales. The production of cotton was aided greatly when Eli Whitney invented the cotton gin in 1793, replacing the slow, labor-intensive hand method of separating the cotton lint from the seed.

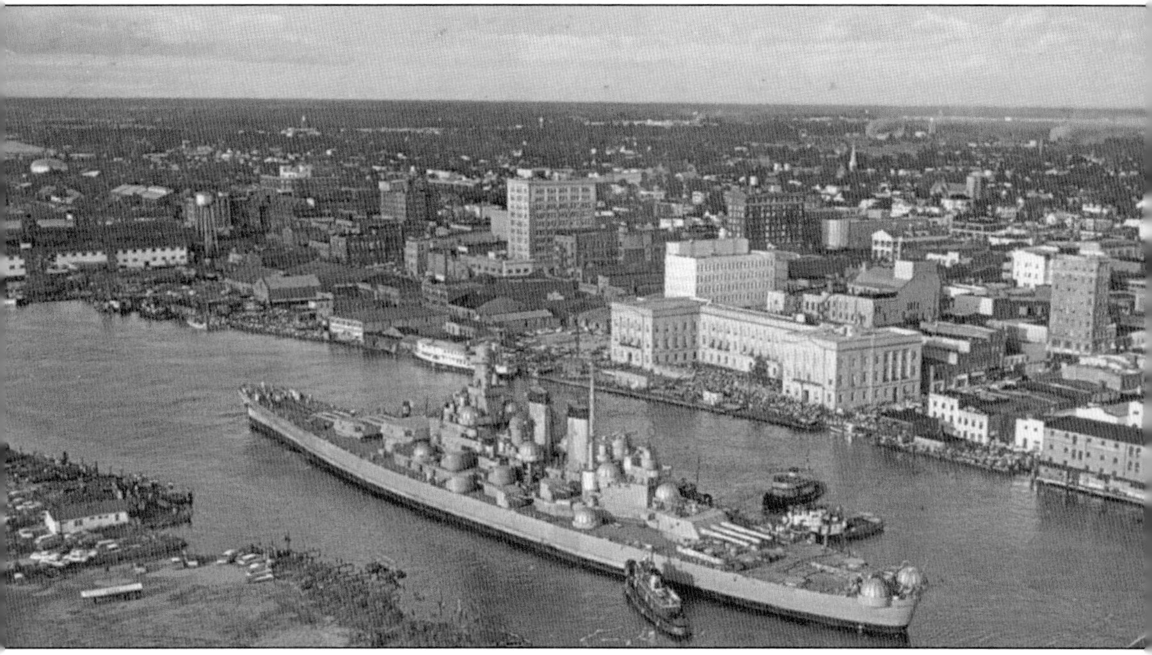

THE USS *NORTH CAROLINA*, 1961. The battleship was commissioned on April 9, 1941, just eight months before the Japanese attack on Pearl Harbor. Nicknamed "the Showboat," the battleship was awarded 12 battle stars for performing heroically in the Pacific, from Guadalcanal in 1942 to the Japanese surrender in 1945. In 1947, the battleship was decommissioned, assigned to the Atlantic Reserve Fleet, and permanently moored in Bayonne, New Jersey. In 1958, the U.S. Navy announced that the ship would be sold and scrapped. The following year, James S. Craig Jr. conceived the idea to buy the battleship from the U.S. Government, bring her to Wilmington, and place her in a permanent berth as a fitting memorial to the 10,000 North Carolina men who perished in WW II. The idea caught on, and North Carolina Governor Luther Hodges appointed a Battleship Commission to raise funds for the project. Under the capable direction of Hugh Morton, the commission completed the task. Finally, October 2, 1961, arrived and the mighty ship, which was taller than a 15-story building and longer than two city blocks, made her final journey up the Cape Fear River. Her new home was on Eagles Island, directly across the river from downtown Wilmington. Thousands lined the banks of the river to see the huge ship guided up the river under the command of river pilot Captain B.M. Burris Sr. of Southport, North Carolina. Unfortunately, James S. Craig Jr. never saw the battleship in her permanent home. He was badly burned in an airplane accident at the local airport on September 24, 1961, and died on October 14, 1961, the day the great ship was first opened to the public. (Courtesy of Hugh Morton.)

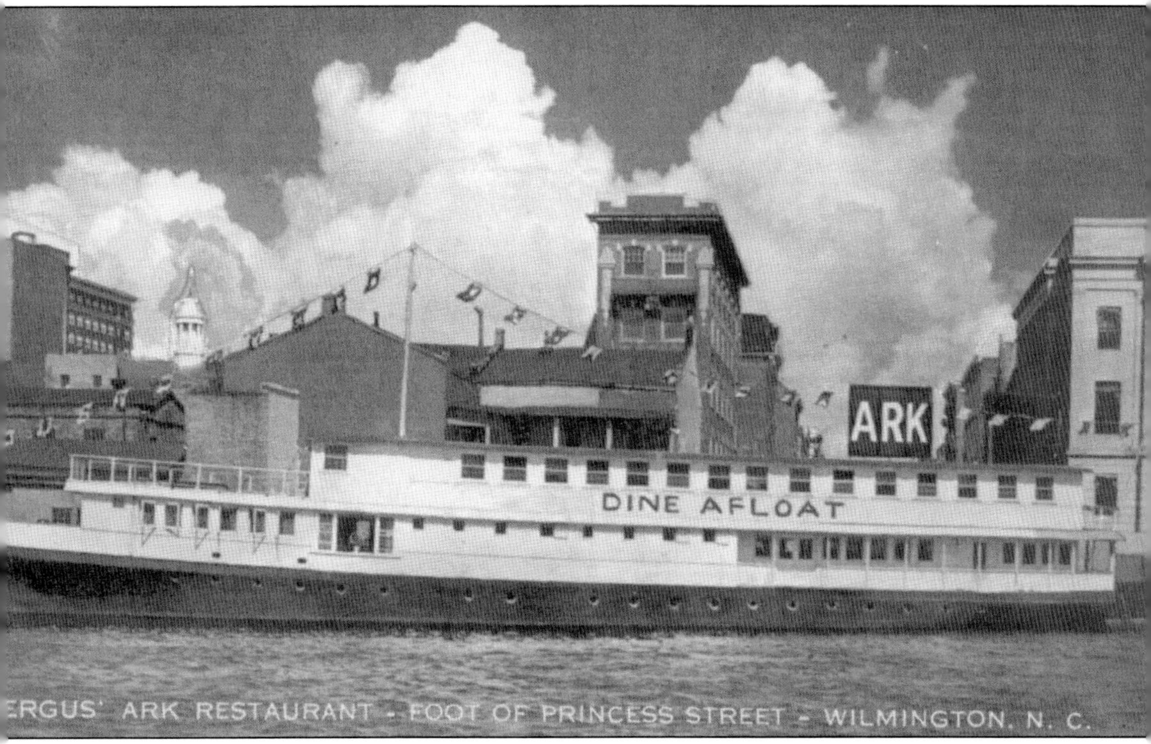

FERGUS' *ARK* RESTAURANT, *C.* 1952. In 1951, Eldridge Fergus (1914–1998) purchased a boat with a concrete hull and made plans to open a floating restaurant. Built in Wilmington in 1922, the boat had served as an army troop transport, a banana boat, a gambling boat, and a Coast Guard quarter vessel. This unique restaurant, the *Ark*, was docked at the foot of Princess Street and her menu specialized in seafood. She was located directly across from the permanent berth of the USS *North Carolina*. The trickiest part of navigating the battleship to its mooring was the turn, which had to be made to enter the slip. The river at that point is only 550 feet wide and the ship was 728 feet long. As the numerous tugboats began to push the battleship into her berth, the bow got stuck in the mud, which caused the stern to hit the *Ark* on the port side. It crushed the wall in the *Ark's* kitchen causing about $10,000 in damages. The owner claimed that the *Ark* was the only vessel to be hit by a U.S. battleship in U.S. waters. After repairs to the restaurant were made, Mr. Fergus had a purple heart painted at the point of impact.

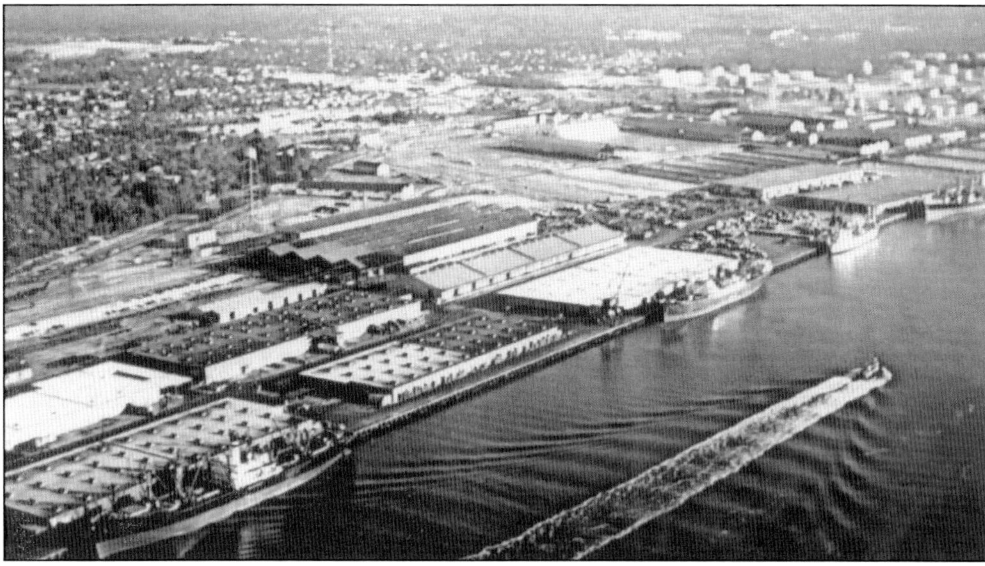

NORTH CAROLINA STATE PORTS AUTHORITY, C. 1965. In 1945, the North Carolina General Assembly established the State Ports Authority to oversee the construction and operation of modern ocean terminals. Two terminals were opened at Wilmington and Morehead City in 1952. Located on the south side of the city, Wilmington's docks have been expanded and improved several times.

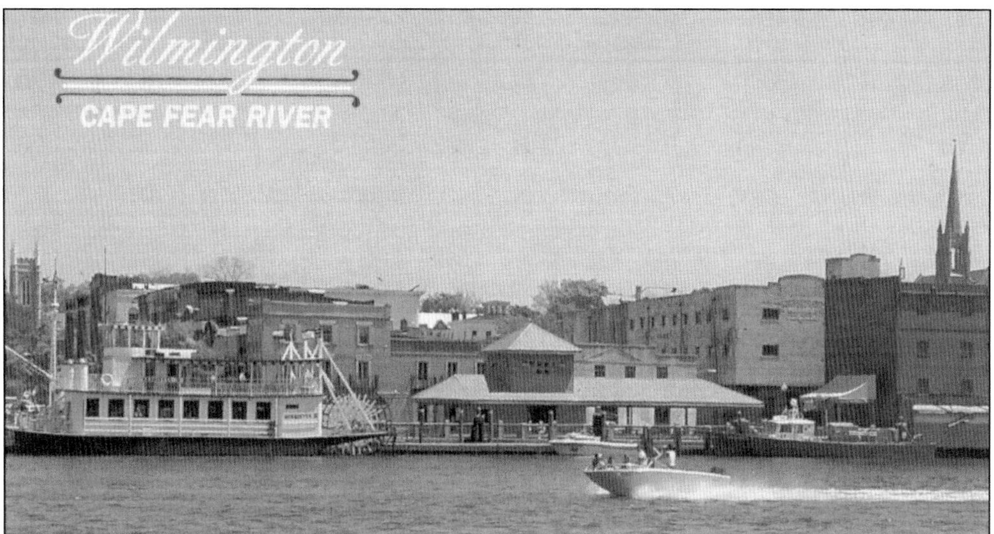

WATERFRONT, C. 1990S. The *Henrietta II*, a paddlewheeler moored at the foot of Market Street, takes tourists and locals for river excursions. Nearby, the Cape Fear Coast Convention and Visitors Bureau operates an information booth. At right, the J.W. Brooks Building, a former grocery warehouse, has been turned into upscale condominiums and shops. Plans have been developed for a riverwalk to span the waterfront from the Coastline Convention Center to Castle Street. The waterfront has been transformed from a dingy, unattractive work area into an inviting and charming place for people to spend their leisure time. (Courtesy of Tom & Jerry's Card Co.)

Two

Downtown

Downtown Wilmington is loosely defined as the area bordered by North Front Street, Fifth Avenue, Orange Street, and Red Cross Street. Historically, it has been the main business, governmental, and economic center of the city. There was a time not long ago when a trip downtown was an event, with shoppers and workers crowding the sidewalks. Although there were several other shopping districts in the city, the best business address was North Front Street.

After the general offices of the Atlantic Coast Line Railroad moved to Florida in 1960, the area began to decline as businesses moved out to various shopping centers, culminating in the opening of Independence Mall on Oleander Drive in 1977. The mall robbed downtown of its largest department store, Belk-Beery. Empty stores lined the streets and some of the important buildings were razed. In the late 1980s, the area made a dazzling comeback and is now a thriving tourist area. Shops and restaurants line the sidewalks while one-way traffic on North Front Street is routed through a pleasant street, filled with flower beds and trees. Wilmington's downtown renaissance is in full swing.

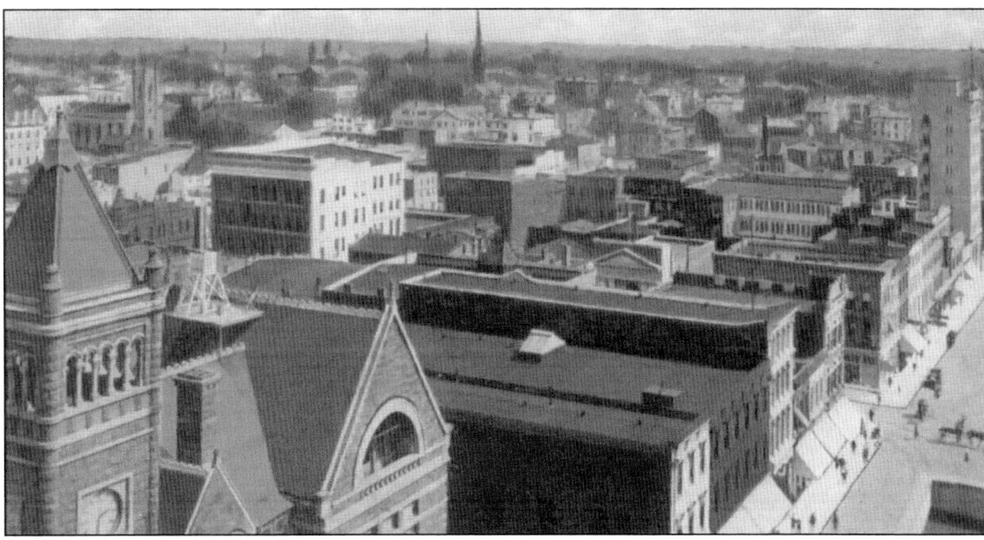

A Bird's-Eye View of Downtown Wilmington, c. 1915. Looking southeast, this view was taken from the Murchison Bank Building on the corner of Front and Chestnut Streets. The tower of the old brownstone post office is bottom left. The Tidewater Power Co. Building is at left center, with the tower of St. James Episcopal Church and the spire of First Presbyterian Church in the background. The nine-story Atlantic Trust Building is at right. (Courtesy of Bellamy Mansion Museum.)

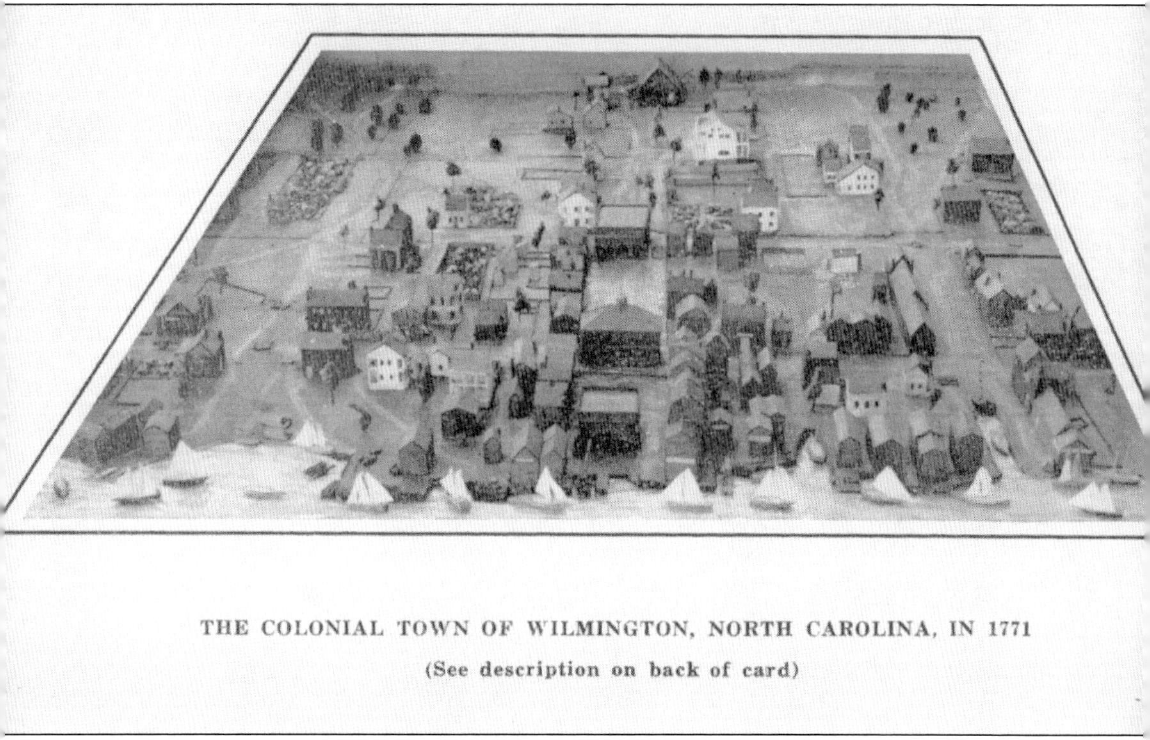

MODEL OF THE COLONIAL TOWN OF WILMINGTON, 1771, *C.* 1940. The model was conceived and executed in the late 1930s by local historian Miss Elizabeth F. McKoy (1887–1984), who was particularly interested in Colonial-era land transactions. Using her extensive knowledge and the Sautier Map of Wilmington, 1769, Miss McKoy created this interesting model. On Market Street, in the center of the model, there is first (looking from the river) the Market House, with the old courthouse at the center of the intersection with Front Street. The building at the intersection of Second Street is the combined Town Hall and Fish Market. The familiar outline of the Burgwin-Wright House (Cornwallis House) is at Third and Market Streets. At the top of the model is the original St. James Episcopal Church (erected 1751–1770) in the middle of the street. For a number of years, the model was on display in the lobby of City Hall and the Wilmington Public Library. Since 1979, it has been a part of the artifact collection of the Cape Fear Museum.

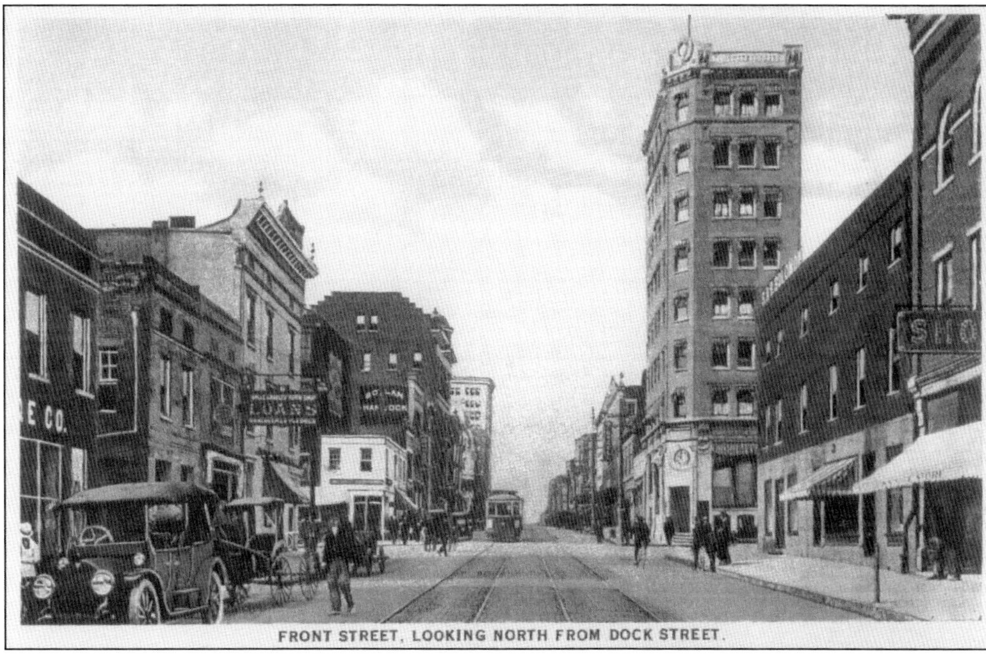

FRONT STREET, LOOKING NORTH FROM DOCK STREET, *c.* 1920. The intersection of Market and Front Streets was once known as Exchange Corner, because the original Market House was in the middle of Market Street. The side of the Masonic Temple and Murchison Building can be seen in the distance. On the right side of the street, the corner structure was the S. & B. Solomon Wholesale Dry Goods Store. The tall building is the Atlantic Trust Building. Front Street was a major route for city streetcars.

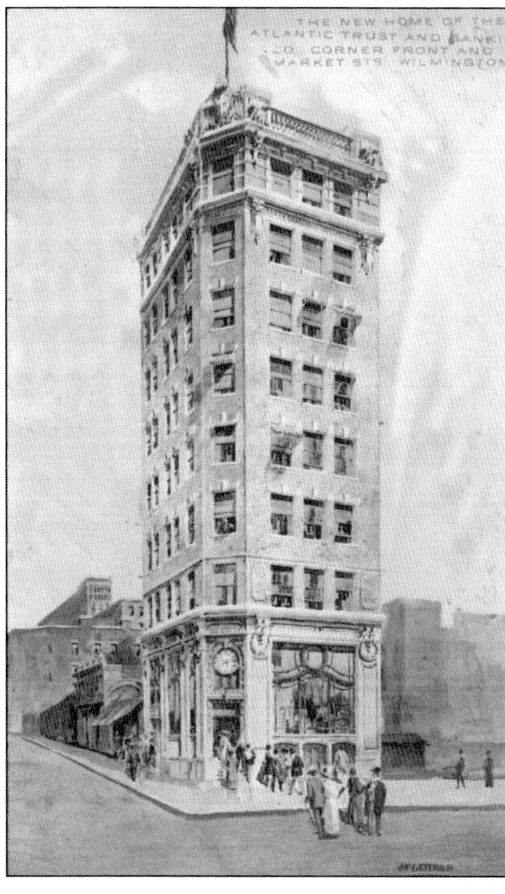

THE ATLANTIC TRUST AND BANKING COMPANY BUILDING, 1912. Located on the northeastern corner of Front and Market Streets, the structure was the first in the city higher than five stories. J.F. Leitner was the architect for the nine-story building, which has fine Neoclassical Revival detailing. It drew much interest and comment from local citizens when it was completed in 1912.

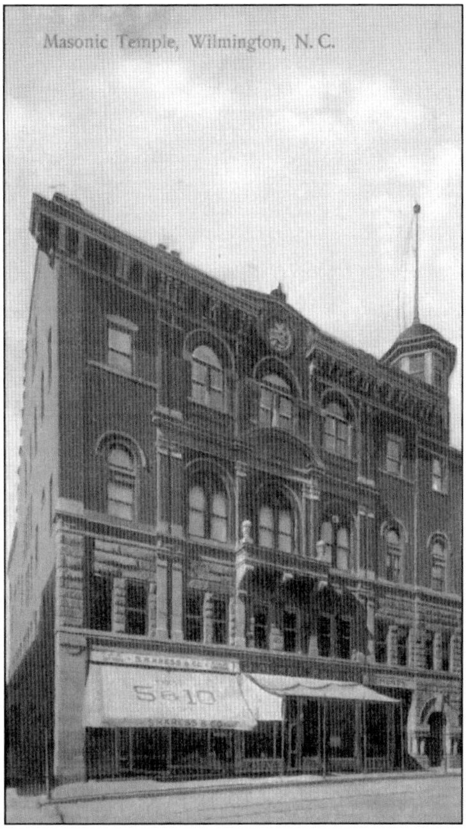

Masonic Temple, c. 1910. Completed by November 1899, the Masonic Temple was designed by noted Masonic architect Charles McMillen. From about 1902, the S.H. Kress Five and Ten Cents Store was a ground-floor tenant of the brownstone building. Offices occupied the second story. The Masonic Lodge was on the third floor. The fourth contained "a beautiful ballroom with an arched ceiling and parlors, reception rooms, café and theater." In the 1990s, Hollywood actor Dennis Hopper purchased the building and still retains ownership of an apartment there.

North Front Street, Looking North, c. 1940s. During World War II, the 0 block of North Front was a main retail shopping street. In the distance is the People's Bank and the tallest building in town, the Murchison Bank Building. Across the street, Kingoff's Jewelers is the structure second from right, with its 1930s Two Dial Post Clock. The Bailey Theater marquee advertises first-run films. In the late 1940s, the theater was one of the first city businesses to be air-conditioned.

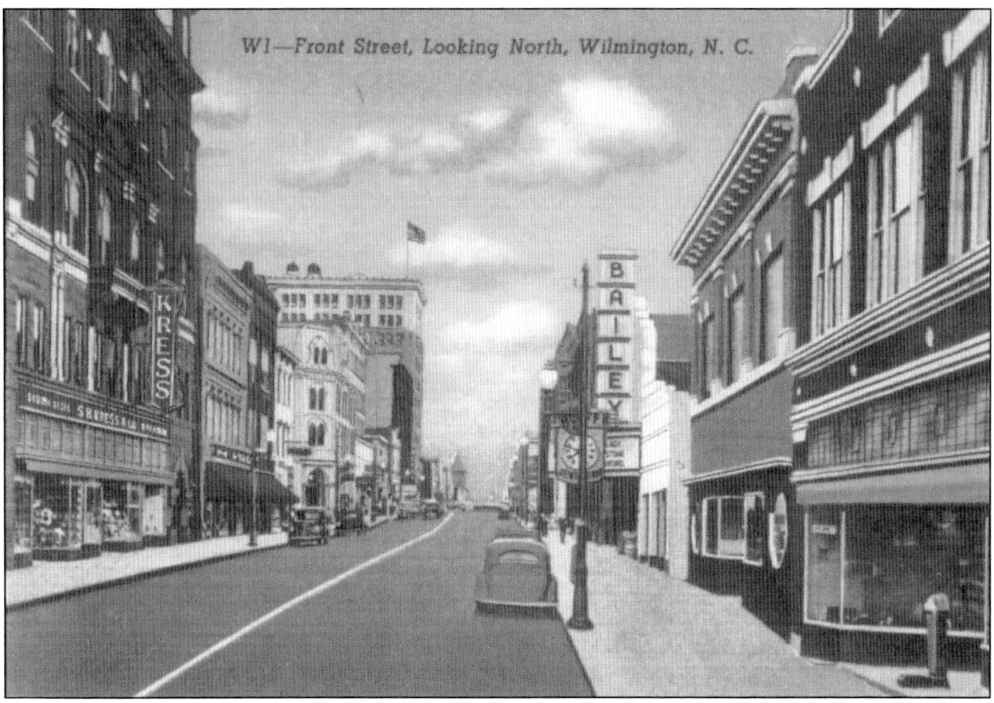

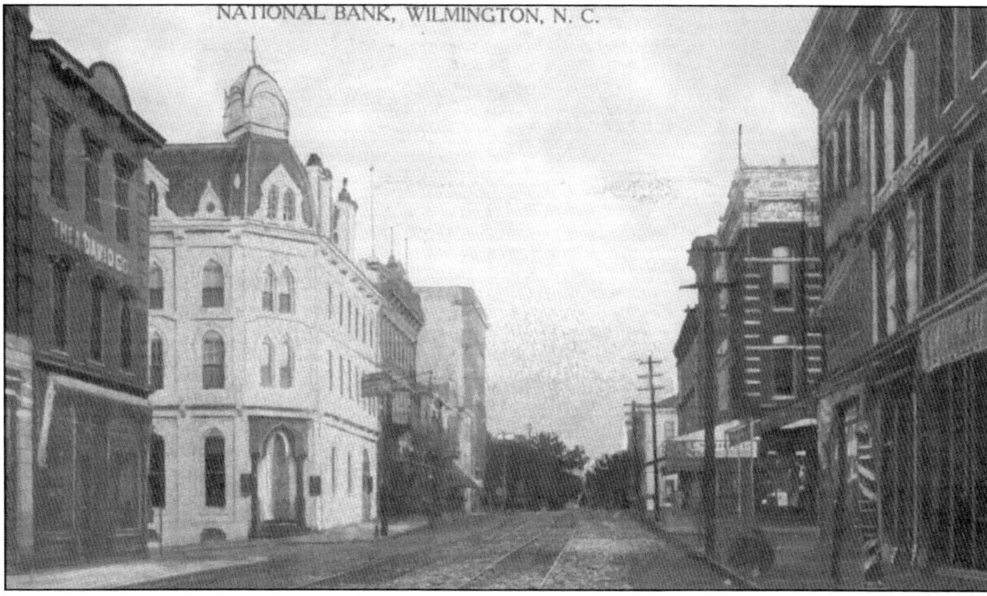

NORTH FRONT STREET, LOOKING NORTH, *C.* 1909. The western terminus of the electric beach car line was at the intersection of North Front and Princess Streets. At left, is the A. David Men's Clothing Store. On the northwest corner, the handsome structure with the mansard roof was occupied by the Atlantic National Bank. Built in 1873, it was designed by noted Philadelphia architect Samuel Sloan. Sadly, the elegant building was razed in 1959 to make way for the Wachovia Bank Building.

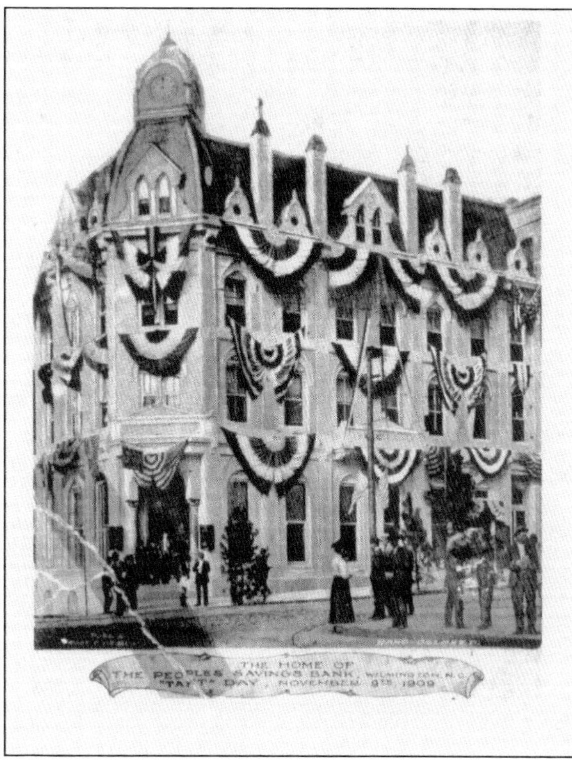

PEOPLE'S SAVINGS BANK, "TAFT," NOVEMBER 9, 1909. By 1909, the People's Savings Bank had offices in the building, which is festooned with bunting for the visit of U.S. President William Howard Taft on November 9, 1909. The corpulent President Taft was a commanding figure, and Wilmington and vicinity went all out to make the visit a memorable one. Schoolchildren, dressed in red, white, and blue, formed an American Flag on the hill on Market Street between Third and Fourth Streets. That day, the crowd in downtown Wilmington was estimated at over 20,000 people.

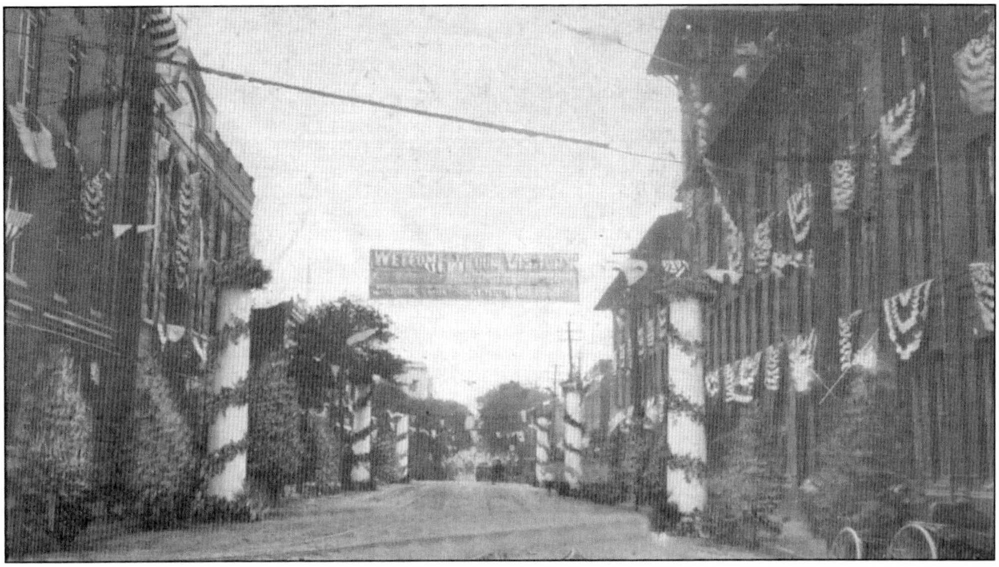

WELCOME TO PRESIDENT TAFT, NOVEMBER 9, 1909. When President Taft stepped from his private train, local officials greeted him at the railroad station. The photograph is a view of the street decorations along the President's route, taken in front of the Atlantic Coast Line Offices on North Front Street near Red Cross Street. Before radio and television furnished a daily voice or image of the U.S. President, most citizens had never seen him nor heard him speak. No one who attended the event ever forgot the grand occasion.

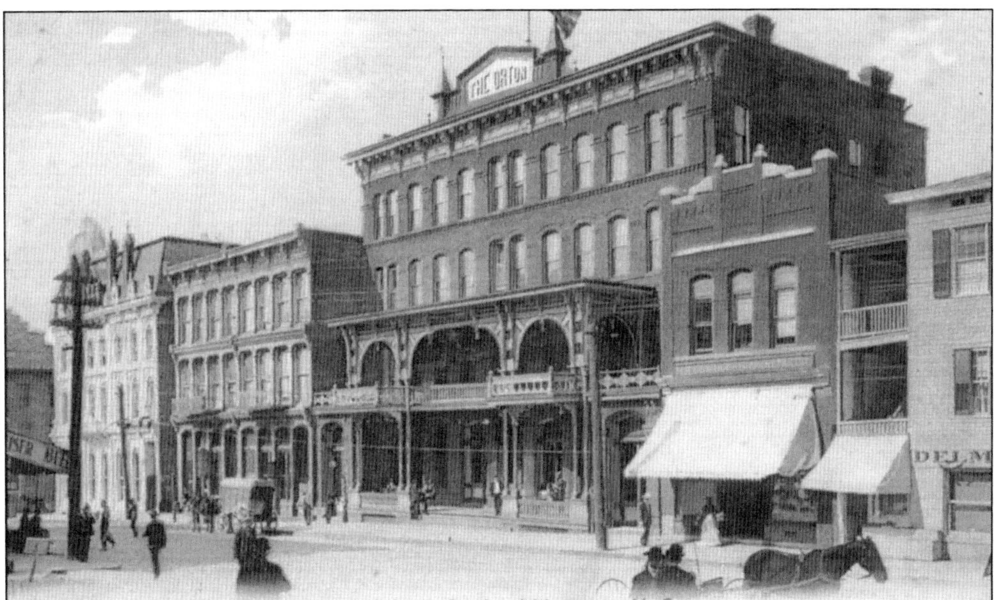

ORTON HOTEL, 1905. In 1888, Colonel Kenneth M. Murchison built the Orton Hotel, designed by J.A. Wood, naming it after his Brunswick County plantation. Ladies always entered by the right side entrance and rarely went into the lobby, because it was usually crowded with "drummers" (traveling salesmen). The hotel restaurant was well known for its fine cuisine and splendid service.

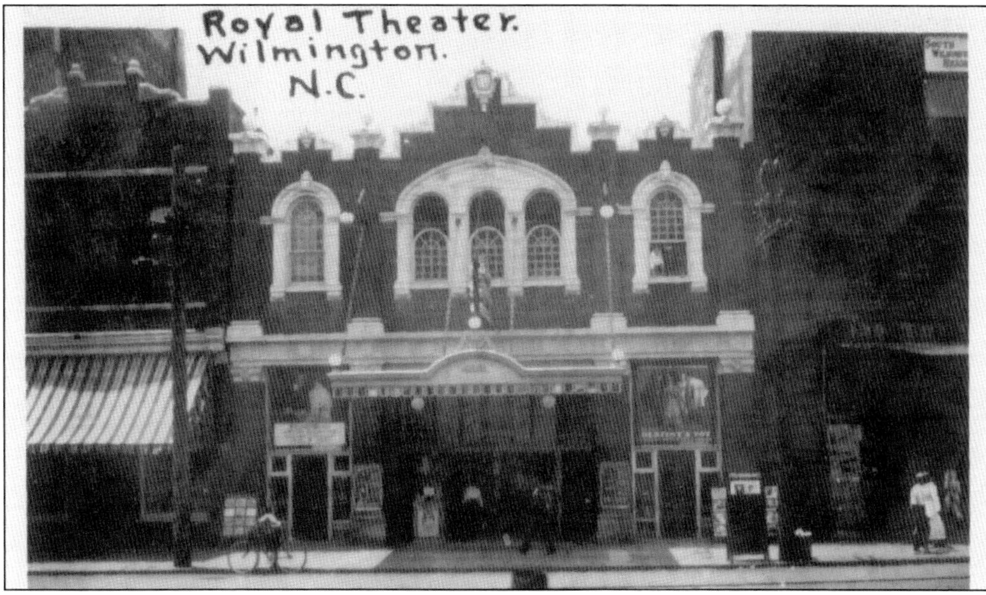

Royal Theater, c. 1917. Architect Buret Stephens designed the Royal Theater, located one door north of the Orton Hotel. Constructed in 1915, the theater was the first business in town to have an animated electric sign. Author Lewis Philip Hall described the scene as follows: "This sign hung over the sidewalk with the name Royal in electric lights. Around the edges of the sign rabbits hopped one behind the other—or so it seemed." The Royal was destroyed in the Orton Hotel fire on January 21, 1949.

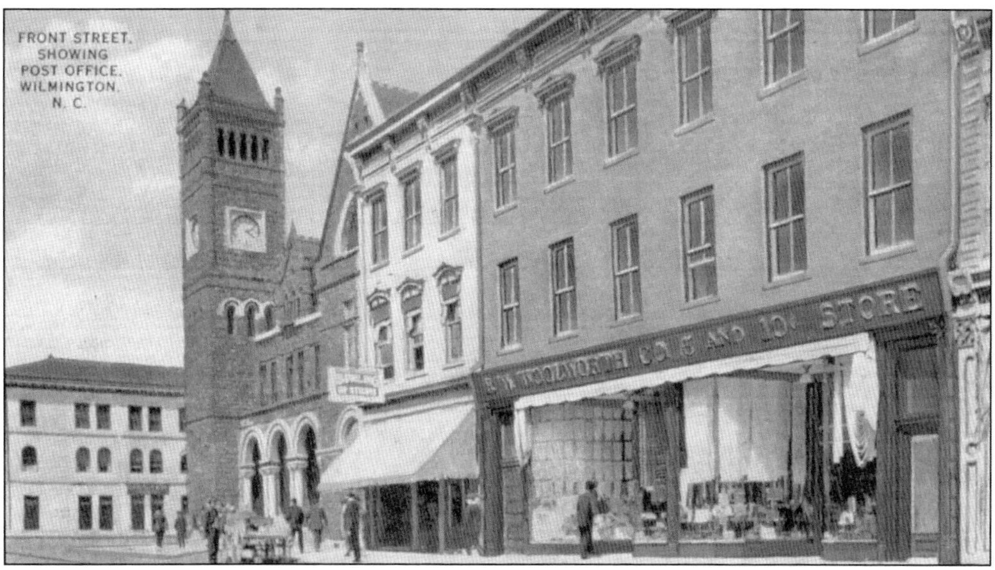

North Front Street, East Side, 100 Block, c. 1917. Customers of the F.W. Woolworth Five and Ten Cents Store often visited the lunch counter in the store, after purchasing notions, school supplies, or countless other items. Later, the store expanded into the building next door to the left. During the 1940s, the store had an elevator that came up through the sidewalk, which helped get merchandise to the basement for storage. The front facade of the brownstone post office is seen at center. (Courtesy of Bellamy Mansion Museum.)

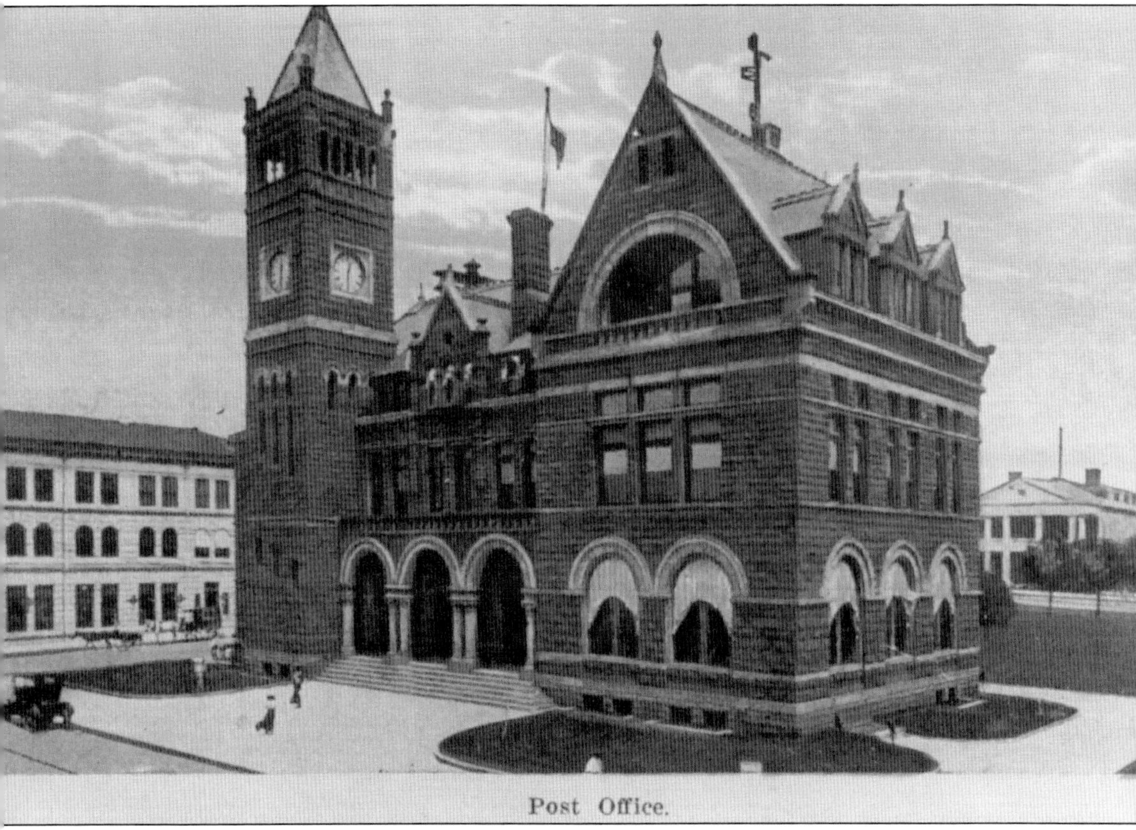

UNITED STATES POST OFFICE, *c.* 1915. Located on the southeastern corner of Front and Chestnut Streets, the brownstone post office was constructed in 1889–1891. Designed by W.A. Feret, supervising architect of the U.S. Department of the Treasury, it had a handsome clock tower and fine Romanesque detailing. When the postal authorities announced plans for a new building, a controversy erupted over the demolition of the building and the style of the new one. The building was torn down in 1936 to make way for a new facility.

Opposite: **NEW POST OFFICE, 1937.** After the brownstone post office was demolished, a new federal building was erected on the same site. Completed in 1937, the WPA project housed in addition to the post office, the local offices of the Internal Revenue and other federal departments. The Neoclassical Revival structure was designed by architect R. Stanley Brown, who used tobacco leaves instead of acanthus on the capitals of the entry columns. It seemed more appropriate to use the leaves of a chief cash crop of North Carolina on a building in the Old North State.

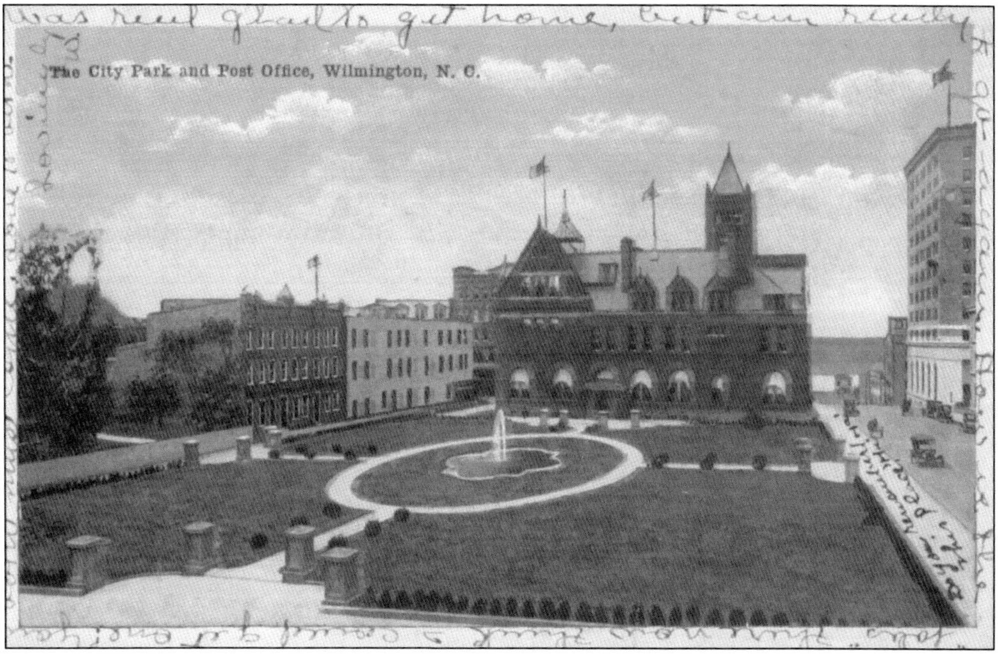

CITY PARK AND POST OFFICE, 1917. The city park behind the brownstone post office was a favorite gathering place for local citizens. In the 1920s, the *Wilmington Morning Star's* offices were located across from the park on Chestnut Street. Before radios were readily available, crowds would congregate in the park to hear the latest scores of World Series games, which were shouted through a megaphone by a newspaper employee reading the national wire. Many residents remember hearing the news of Charles Lindbergh's successful trans-Atlantic solo flight from the same source.

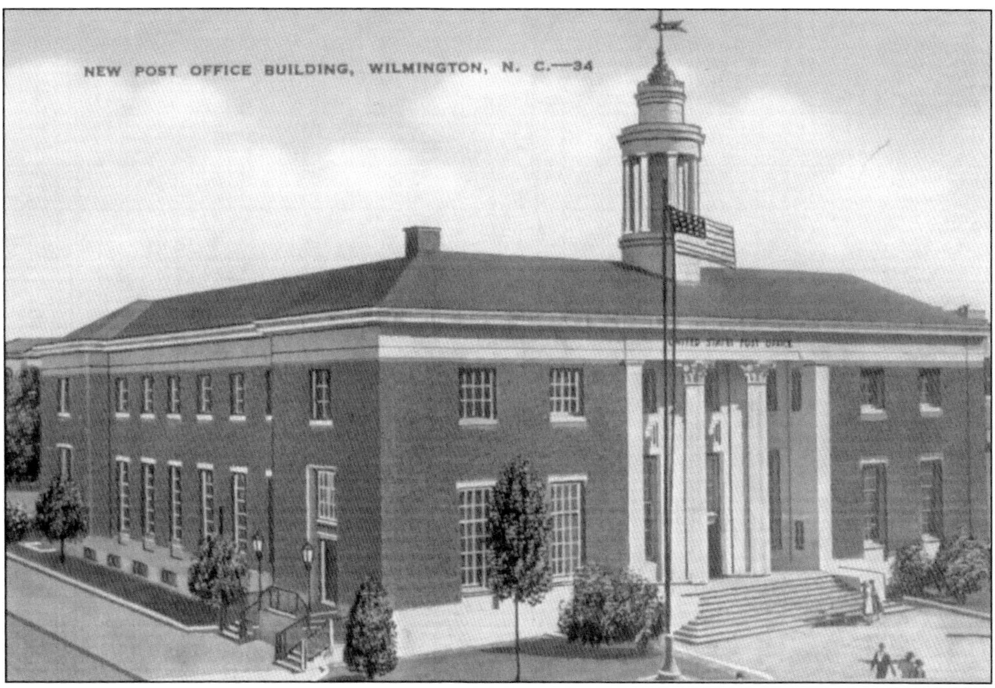

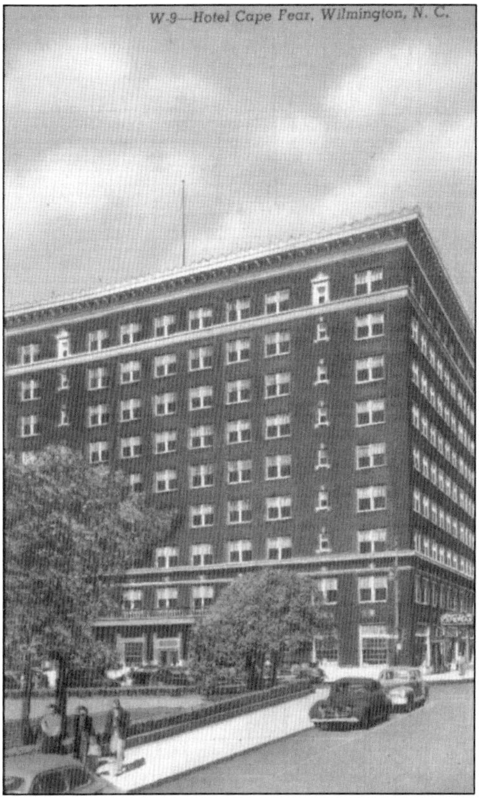

HOTEL CAPE FEAR, 1949. Opened on January 10, 1925, the hotel is the last surviving downtown hotel built before WW II. G. Lloyd Preacher, the architect, had previously designed the Fort Sumter Hotel in Charleston, South Carolina. In the 1980s, the nine-story structure on the northwestern corner of Second and Chestnut Streets was renovated into apartments for senior citizens.

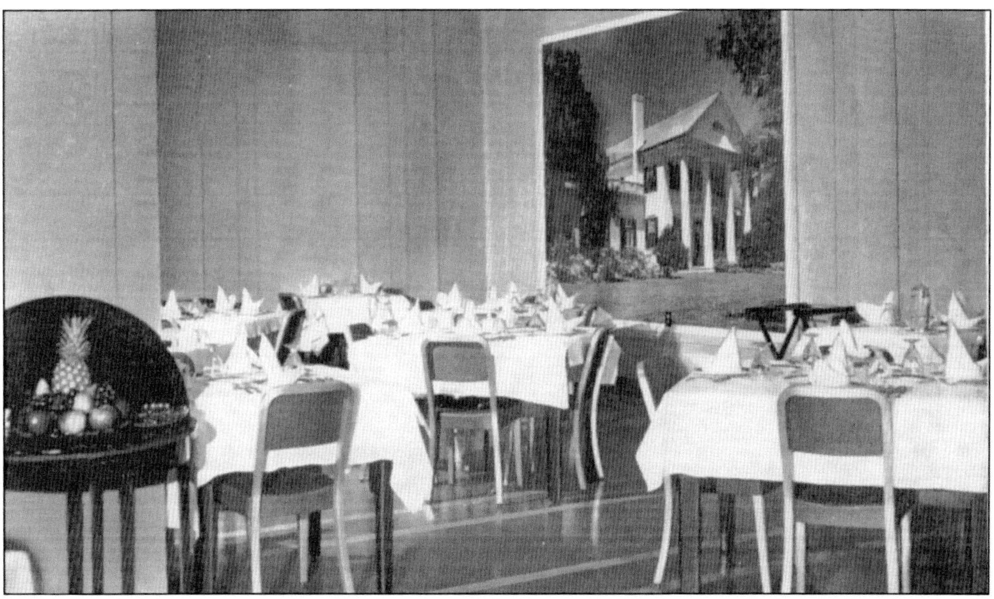

HOTEL CAPE FEAR DINING ROOM, 1950. The dining room was taken over by the U.S. Army in 1942 to use as a Women's Army Corp.(WAC) mess. It was reopened to the public the following year. For a number of years, Wilmington's civic clubs held their weekly luncheon meetings in a room on the hotel's mezzanine.

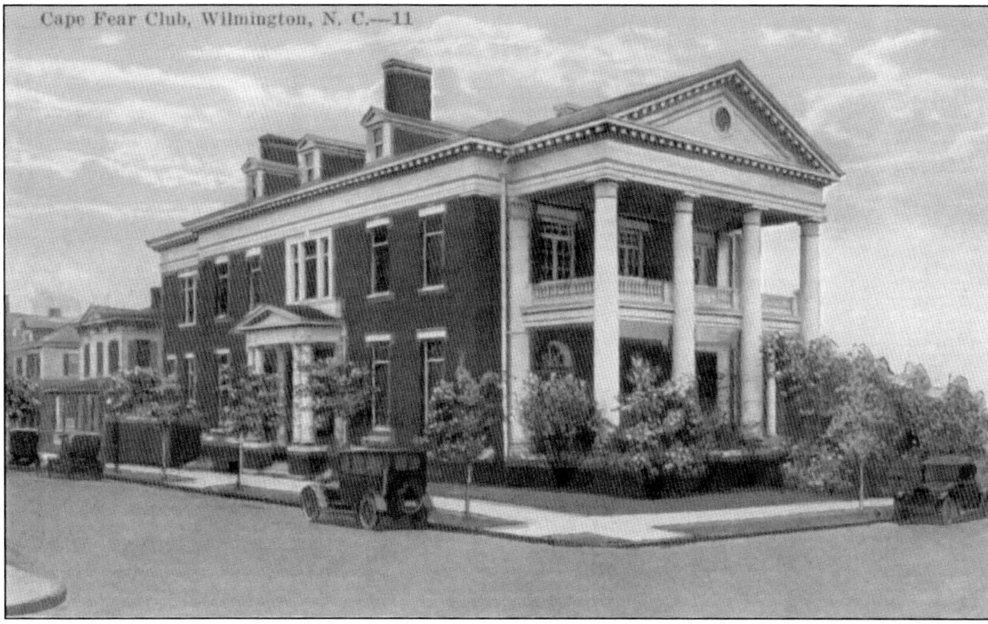

CAPE FEAR CLUB, *c.* 1930. Located on the southeastern corner of Second and Chestnut Streets, the Cape Fear Club is one of the oldest gentlemen's social clubs in the South. Organized in 1852, Governor Edward B. Dudley was the first president. The club became inactive during the Civil War and was reorganized in 1866. C.H.P. Gilbert was the architect of the Neoclassical Revival structure, which was built in 1912–1913.

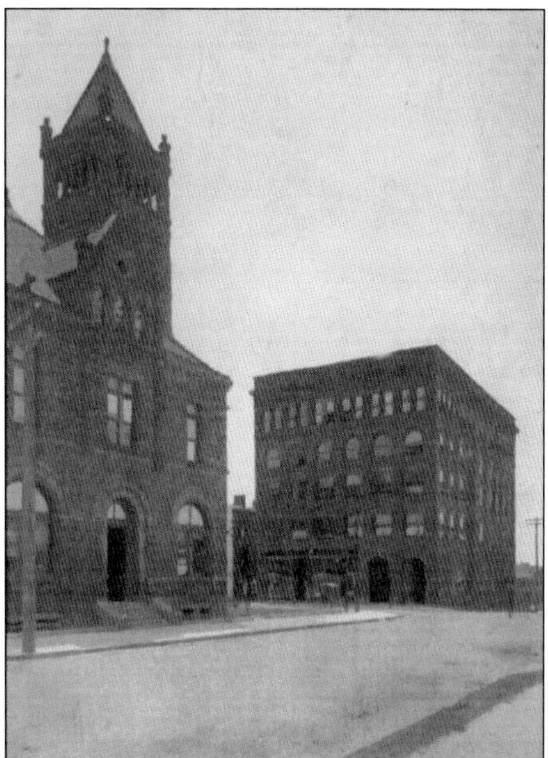

SOUTHERN (HEYER) BUILDING AND BROWNSTONE POST OFFICE, 1906. Completed in 1904, the five-story Southern Building was designed by Charles McMillen for owner, Matthew J. Heyer (1854–1913). At various times, Will Rehder Florist; Julian K. Taylor Clothiers, and Nisbet's Ladies Shop occupied the ground-floor stores. The upper floors contained the offices of attorneys, insurance firms, dentists, doctors, and real estate agencies. Miss Elizabeth Chant and Miss Irene Price, prominent local artists, taught art there at one time. At left is the Chestnut Street side of the brownstone post office.

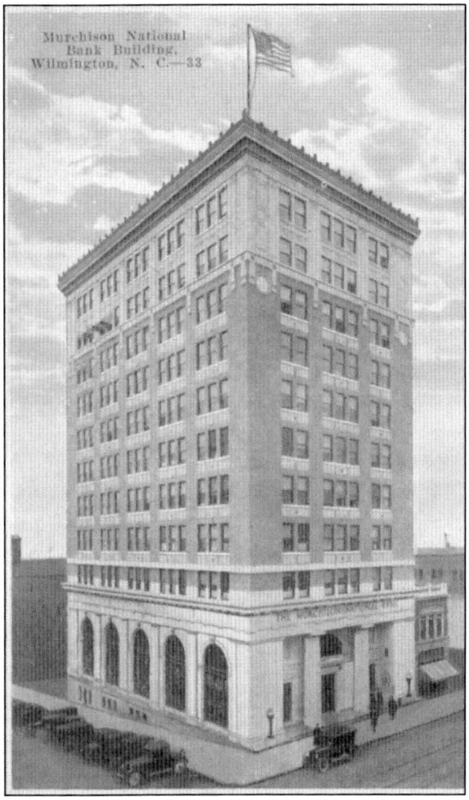

MURCHISON NATIONAL BANK BUILDING, c. 1920s. At 11 stories, the Murchison Building is the tallest building in town. It first housed the Murchison National Bank on the ground floor, giving the building its name. Constructed in 1913–1914 with rich Neo-Classical Revival detailing, it was designed by Wilmington native Kenneth Murchison of New York. The *Wilmington Star-News* had its offices and plant on the ground floor from 1935 to 1970. For about 50 years, one of the city's early beauty parlors, Alida's Beauty Salon, operated by Alida Kuhl Jordan, was tucked away in a space on the mezzanine. In 1972, the building was renamed after its ground floor tenant, First Union National Bank.

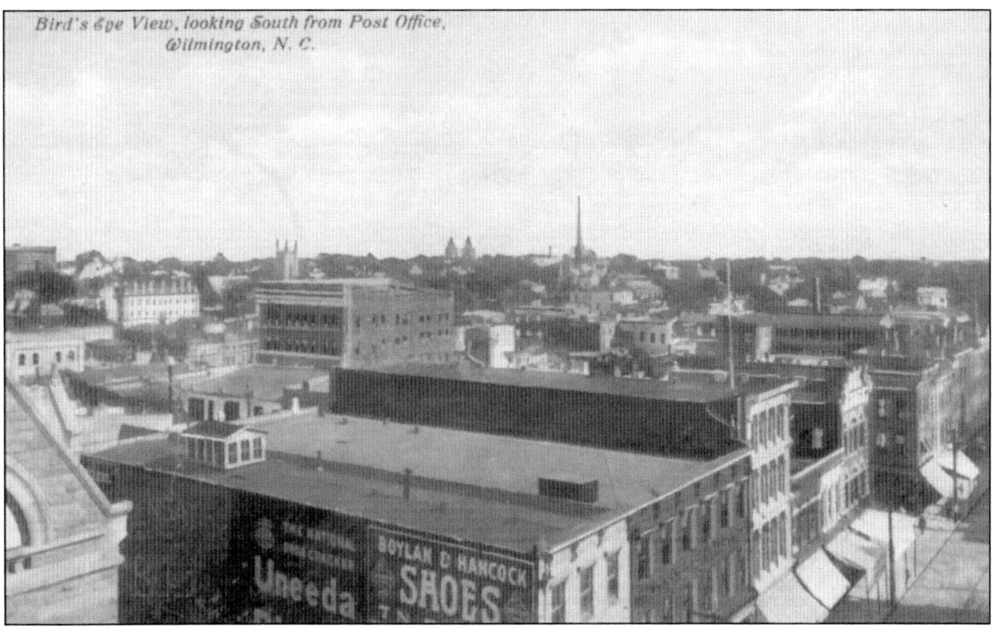

"BIRD'S EYE VIEW," LOOKING SOUTHEAST, c. 1915. This photograph was taken from the roof of the Murchison Building, a popular place to take city-wide views. It shows a downtown crowded with buildings in contrast to today's numerous empty lots, most of which are used for parking.

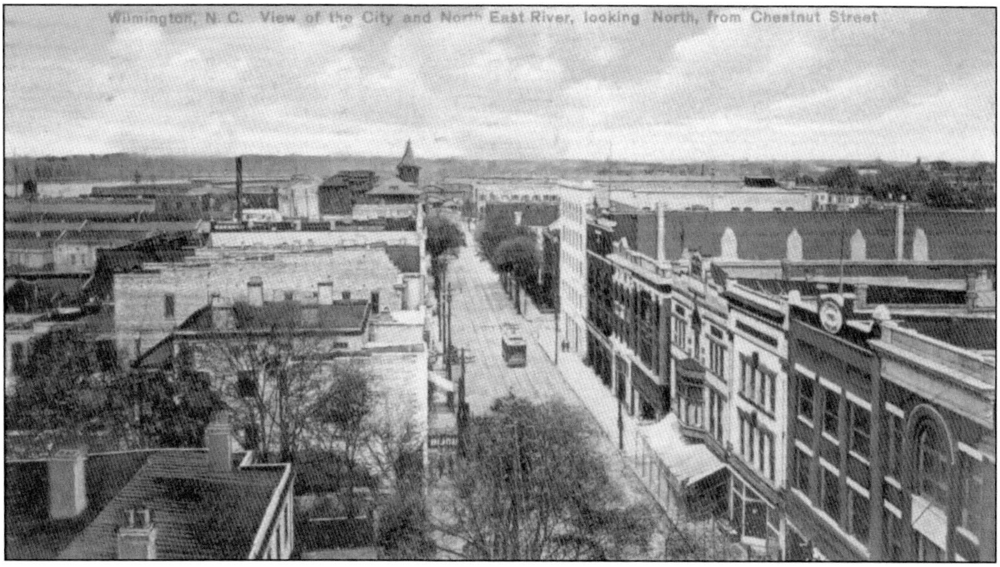

North Front Street, Looking North, c. 1910. This view of the 200 block of North Front Street was taken from the top of the Murchison Building, looking toward the Atlantic Coast Line Offices at the end of the street. Belk-Williams Department Store occupied two stores in the middle of the block on the right-hand side of the street. Note the Bijou Theater sign at center and the streetcar.

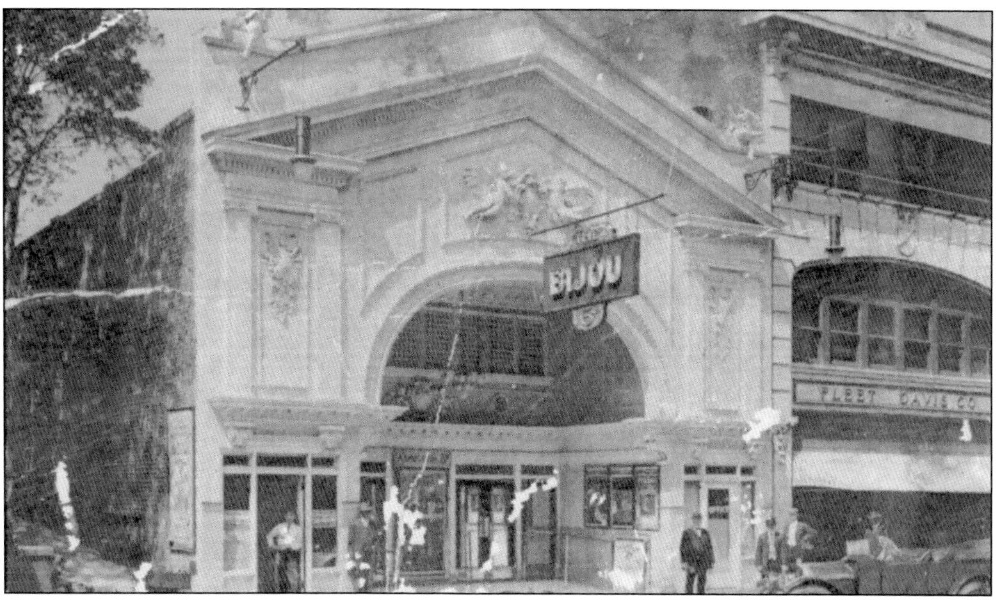

Bijou Theater, 1914. Reputed to be the first movie theater in North Carolina, the Bijou had humble beginnings in a carnival tent at 211 North Front Street. By 1912, the owners, J.H. "Foxy" Howard and Percy Wells, were successful enough to construct a permanent home for their moving pictures. Wilmingtonians were entertained at movies with such favorite western stars as Hoot Gibson, Tom Mix, and Buck Jones. On Saturdays, "cliffhanger" series were presented, including "The Perils of Pauline," whose heroine's terrible troubles were not solved until the following week.

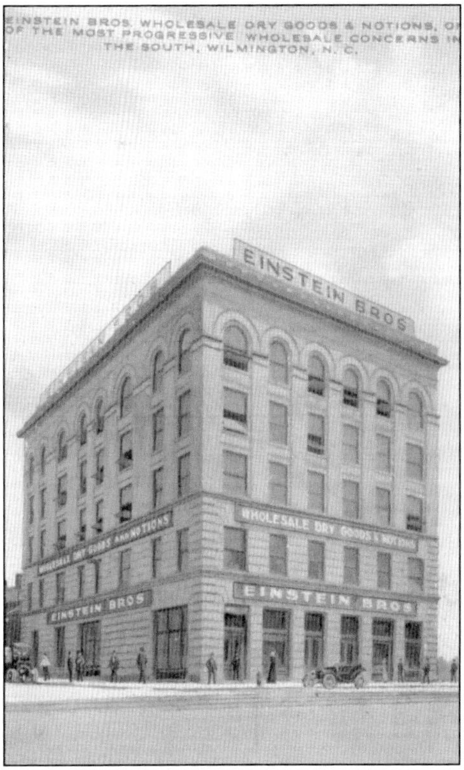

EINSTEIN BUILDING, 1914. In November 1909, Einstein Brothers, Inc. moved their wholesale dry goods and distributing firm from Kinston, North Carolina, to Wilmington. Located in a five-story building at the corner of North Front and Grace Streets, the company erected six signs on the building, which the *Wilmington Dispatch* called, "the largest sign contract for any single building in North Carolina." The business continued to operate in the city until 1923.

NORTH FRONT STREET, 200 BLOCK, LOOKING SOUTH, 1911. Later, Efird's Department Store occupied the building on the southeastern corner of North Front and Grace Streets, which was formerly the Einstein Building. People of a certain age will remember when large stores, such as Efird's, had no cash registers. Customers paid in cash and the clerk placed the cash and sales ticket into a small brass cylinder. The cylinder was placed in a pneumatic tube and sent to a central cashier. The customers waited for their change to return by the same system.

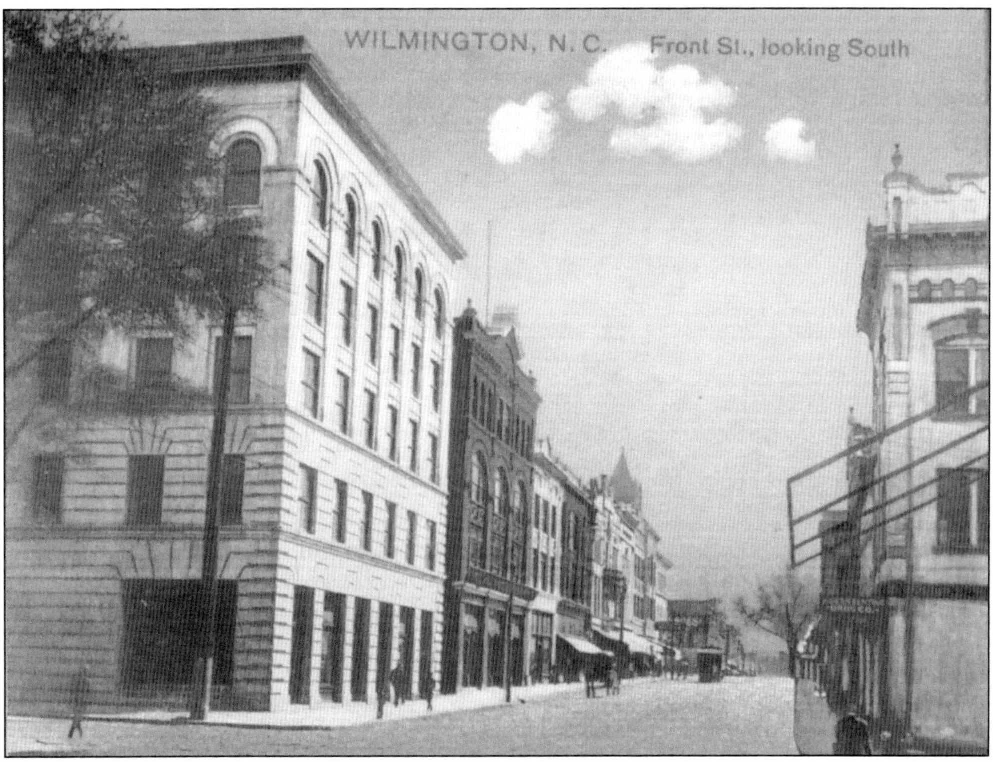

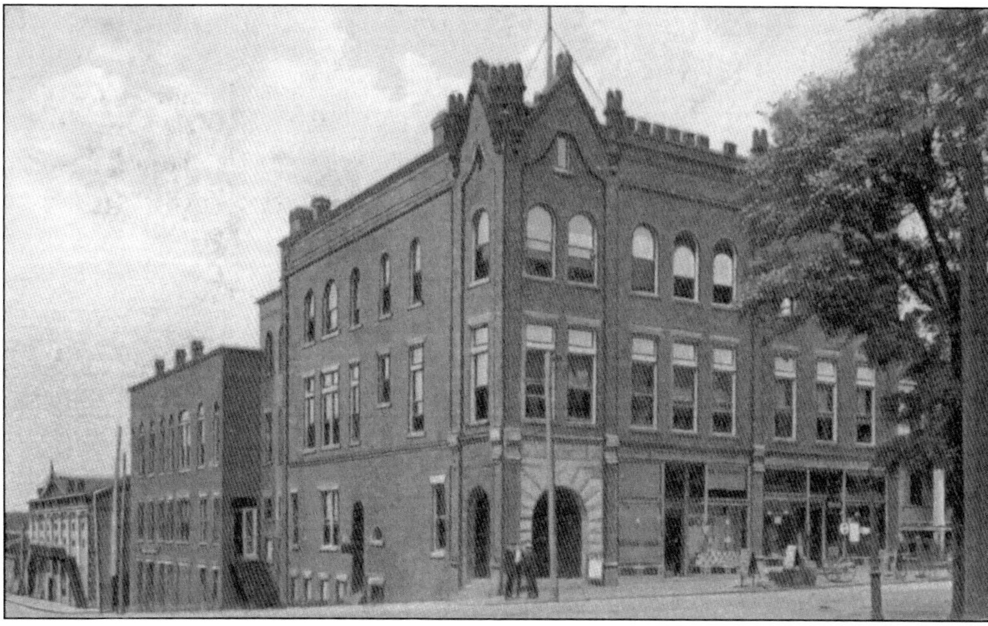

YMCA BUILDING, 1907. In 1891, the first YMCA Building was constructed on the northwestern corner of Front and Grace Streets. The "Y" had a swimming pool in the basement, probably the first pool in the city. Members wore no bathing suits, swimming naked in the pool unless spectators were present for races. The building was sold in 1911 to Joseph J. Loughlin, who renovated the building for use as the Brunswick Hotel, which continued to welcome guests at the location for the next 50 years.

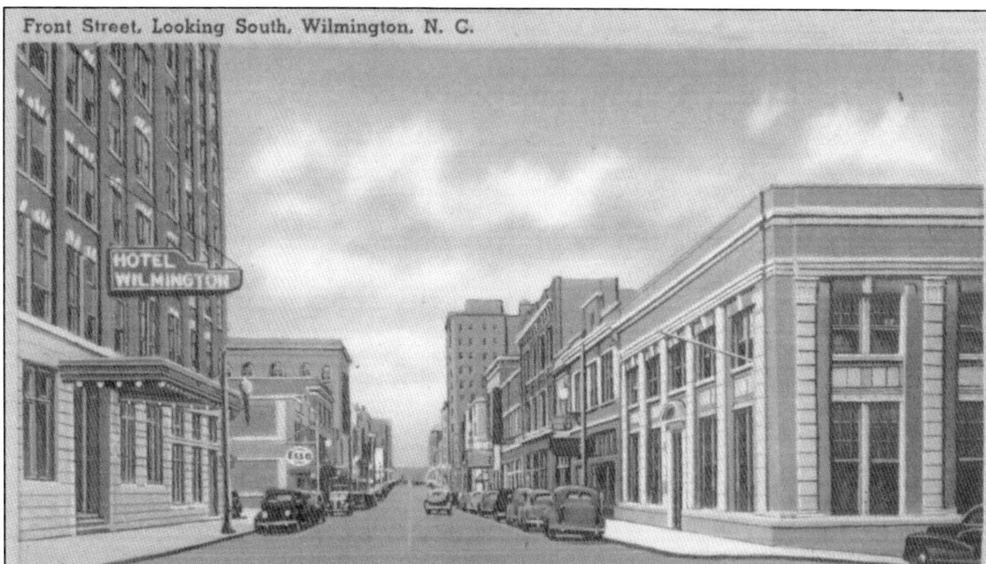

NORTH FRONT STREET, 300 BLOCK, LOOKING SOUTH, C. 1940S. Designed by Henry E. Bonitz, the building (at right) is the Alexander Sprunt & Son Building, constructed in 1919–1920. One of the largest cotton exporters in the South, the Sprunt firm was founded in 1866 and also operated the Champion Compresses and Warehouses on the river. At left is the Hotel Wilmington.

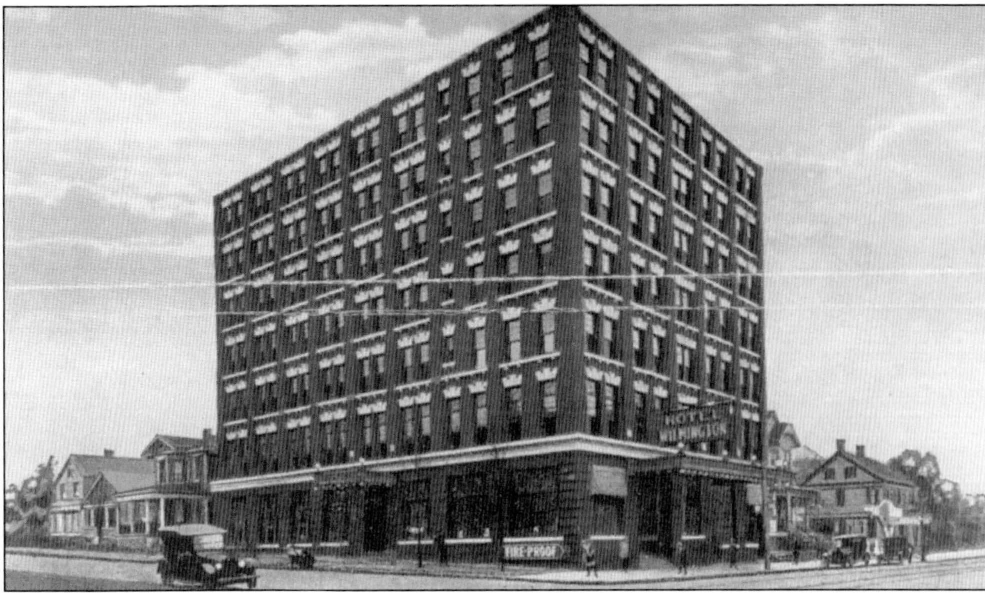

WILMINGTON HOTEL, *C.* 1920. Opened in the summer of 1914 and located on the southeastern corner of North Front and Walnut Streets, the Wilmington Hotel was owned by T.A. Green of Spartanburg, South Carolina, and C. Gresham of Charlotte. The seven-story structure's lobby had "floors of white marble tile and the columns were made of brown marble. All of the rooms were painted in glittering white." In 1929, E.I. and E.B. Bugg of Durham purchased the property. The hotel was torn down in March 1975.

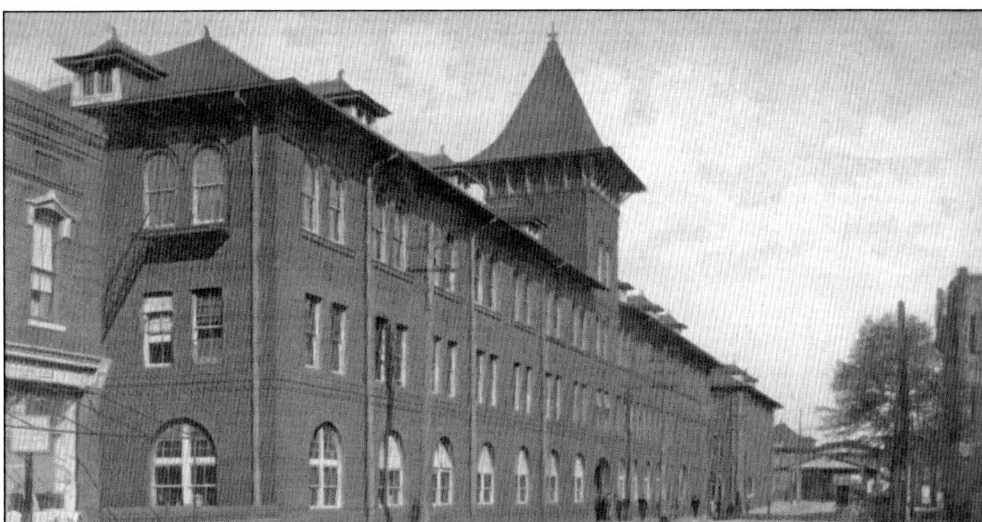

ATLANTIC COAST LINE RAILROAD, GENERAL OFFICES, 1910. In 1880, the Wilmington & Weldon Railroad constructed their first office building on the northwestern corner of North Front and Red Cross Streets. Some years later, that railroad was absorbed into the Atlantic Coast Line Railroad System, which took over the W & W's structure and purchased additional land on the western side of North Front Street. Eventually, there were four buildings on this site, which housed the A.C.L. General Offices. This photograph was taken before the concourse and passenger terminal were constructed at the end of the street.

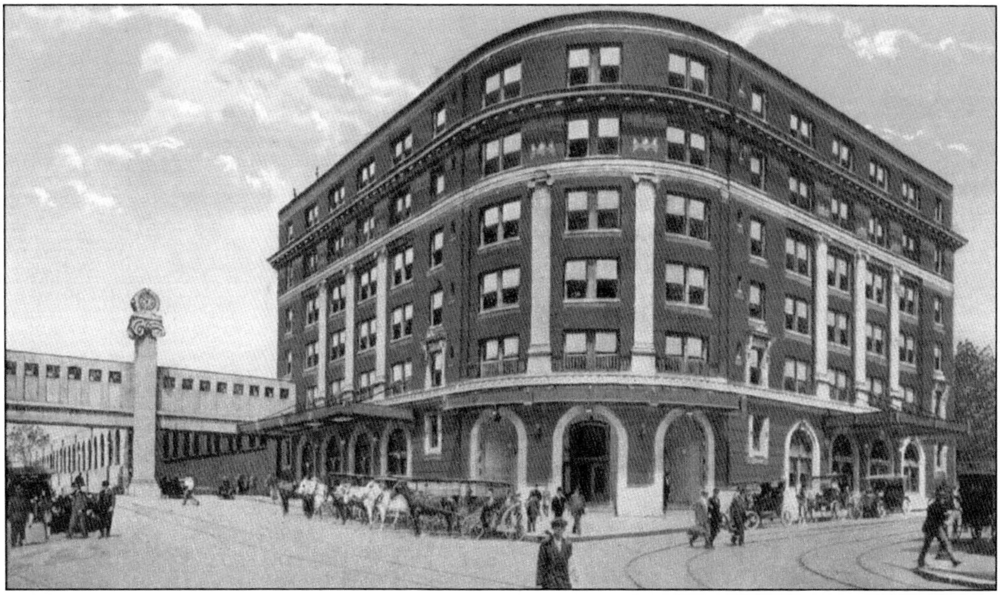

ATLANTIC COAST LINE DEPOT, *c.* 1915. Joseph F. Leitner, the official architect of the Atlantic Coast Line Railroad, designed the 1913 Union Station. Passenger waiting rooms were located on the left side of the building. The impressive concourse led to where the trains were boarded. It was always an exciting, anticipatory walk, whether going to New York City or to Goldsboro, North Carolina, to attend a New Hanover High School football game on a special train. (Courtesy of Bellamy Mansion Museum.)

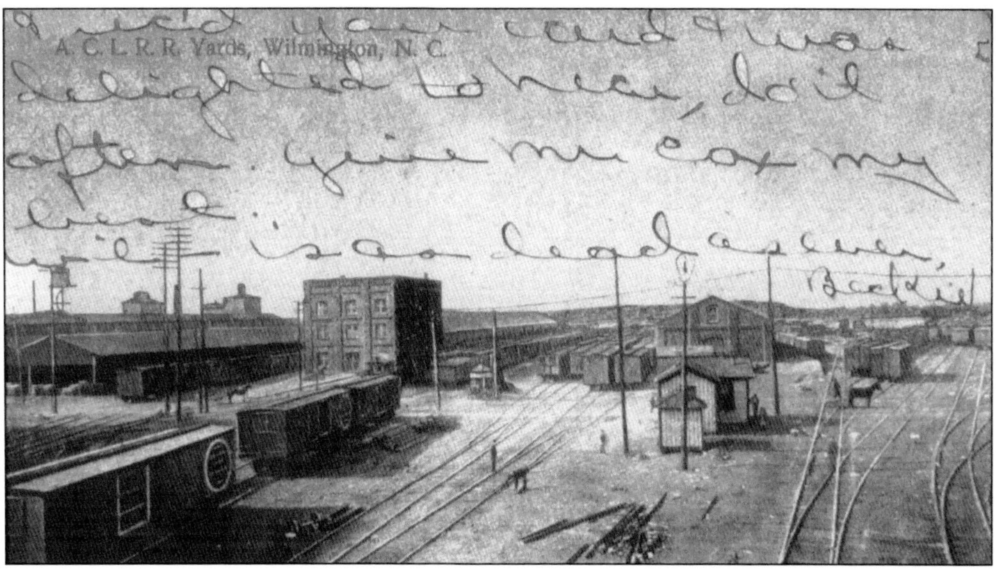

ATLANTIC COAST LINE RAILROAD YARDS. It was the railroad that brought prominence to the port of Wilmington, where land transportation meets maritime transit. The A.C.L. freight yards took up a large area on North Water and Nutt Streets near the river. Constructed in 1900, the three-story A.C.L. Freight Office (at center) is only one of four railroad structures still standing. The Wilmington Railroad Museum has occupied the building for a number of years.

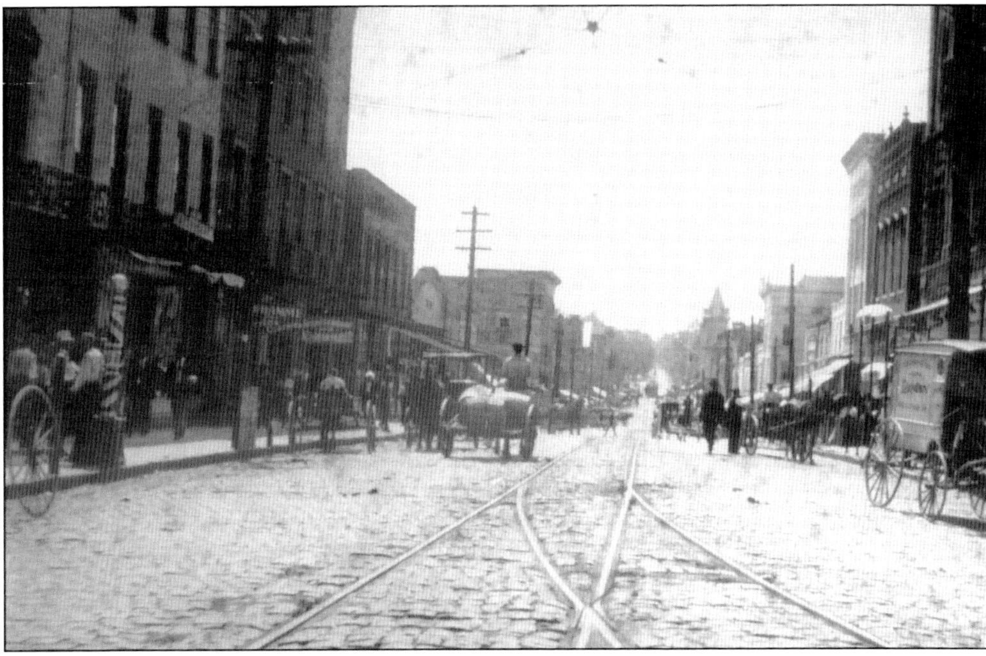

NORTH FRONT STREET, LOOKING SOUTH, 1910. This photograph is from the middle of the 0 block of North Front Street. The tower of the city market is in the background. Note the brick pavement and the streetcar tracks. The sign of F. Hamme, Hatter, is seen at left.

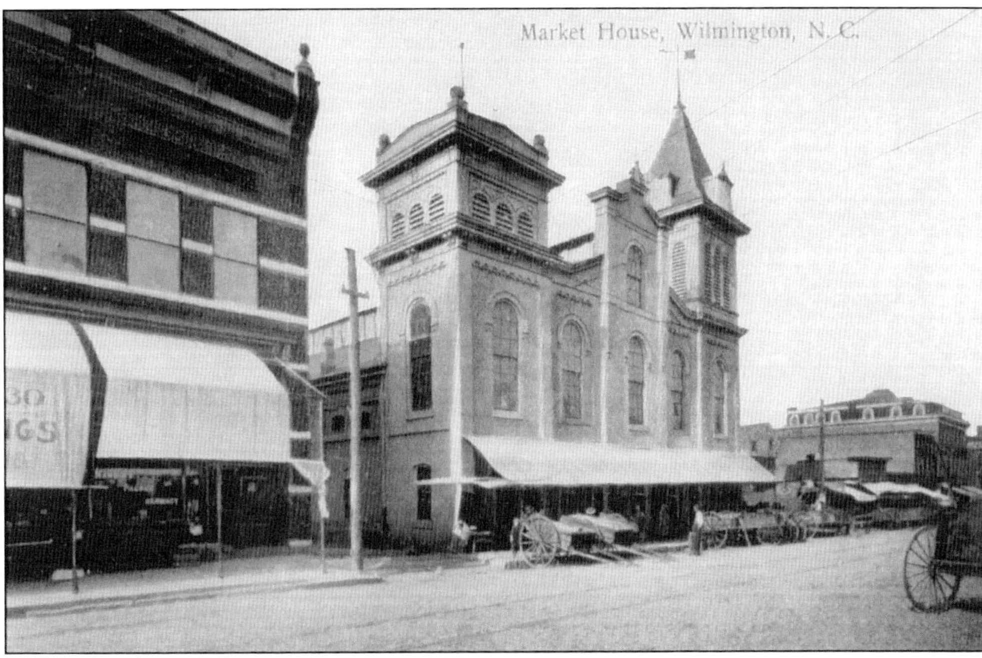

CITY MARKET, C. 1905. In 1881, the city market replaced the old market, which was located in the middle of Market Street between Water and Front Streets. The new market at 120–124 South Front Street was a two-story structure that had two massive towers on the front and an auditorium on the second floor. Sometime between 1920 and 1930, the towers were removed.

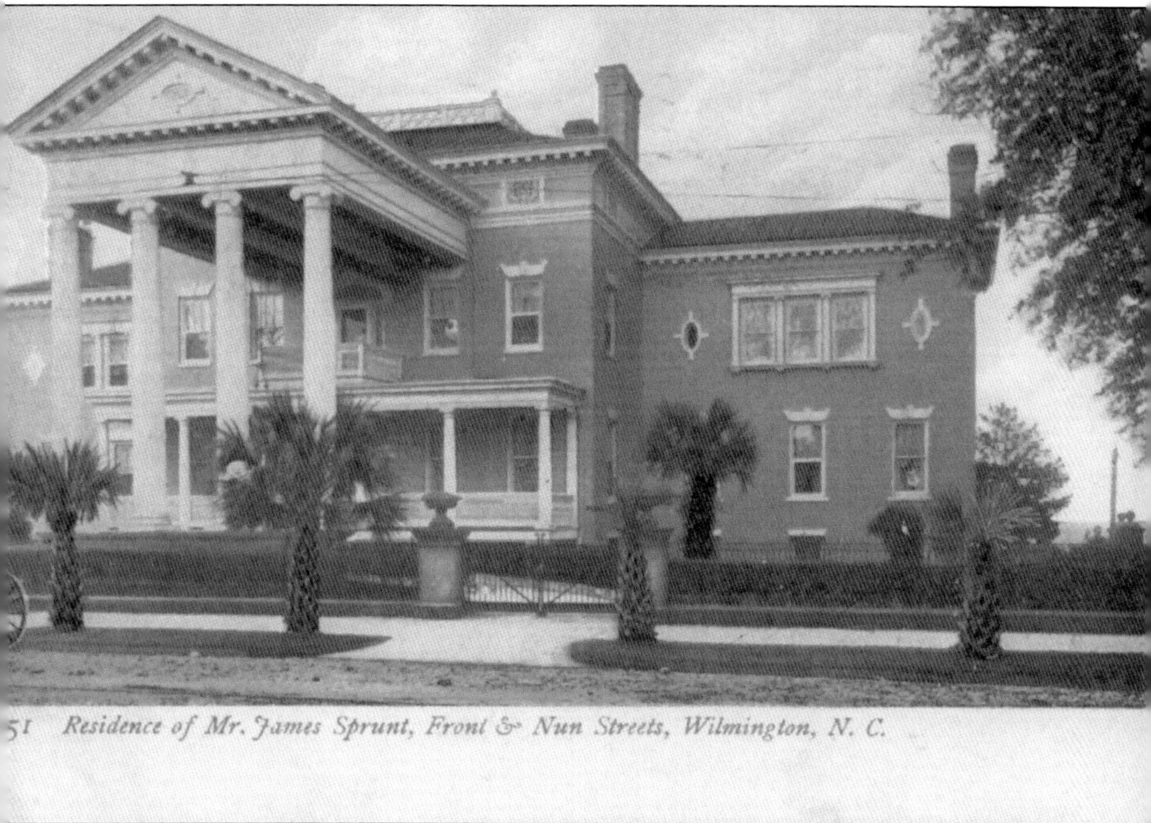

GOVERNOR DUDLEY MANSION, 1910. At the turn of the last century, South Front Street between Ann and Castle Streets was one of the best residential areas in town. In 1836, Edward B. Dudley (1789–1855) became the first popularly elected governor of North Carolina. The center portion of the house is thought to have been constructed by Governor Dudley about 1825. After Dudley's death, the property was owned by several prominent local families, including multimillionaire Pembroke Jones. Dr. James Sprunt and his wife, Luola Murchison Sprunt, purchased the house in 1895 and added the two wings, the massive portico, and the porches. The Sprunts also planted the palmetto trees. After J. Lawrence Sprunt inherited the property, the portico was removed. The Wilmington Lodge of the Independent Order of Elks bought the house in the 1940s. When the Elks moved to new quarters on Oleander Drive, the mansion became the first home of the Historic Wilmington Foundation, while owned by Thomas H. Wright Jr.

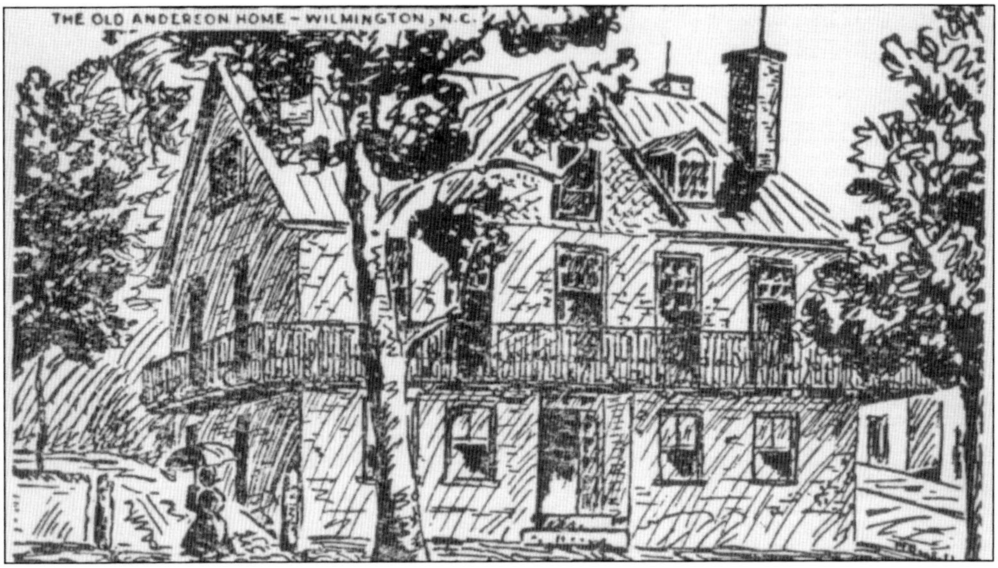

SMITH-ANDERSON HOUSE. In the 1950s, prominent local artist Claude Howell did a series of pen-and-ink drawings of a number of Wilmington landmarks, which were published as postcards. This one is of the Smith-Anderson House, built *c.* 1740. The Georgian-style house, with Greek Revival alterations, is thought to be the oldest surviving structure in Wilmington.

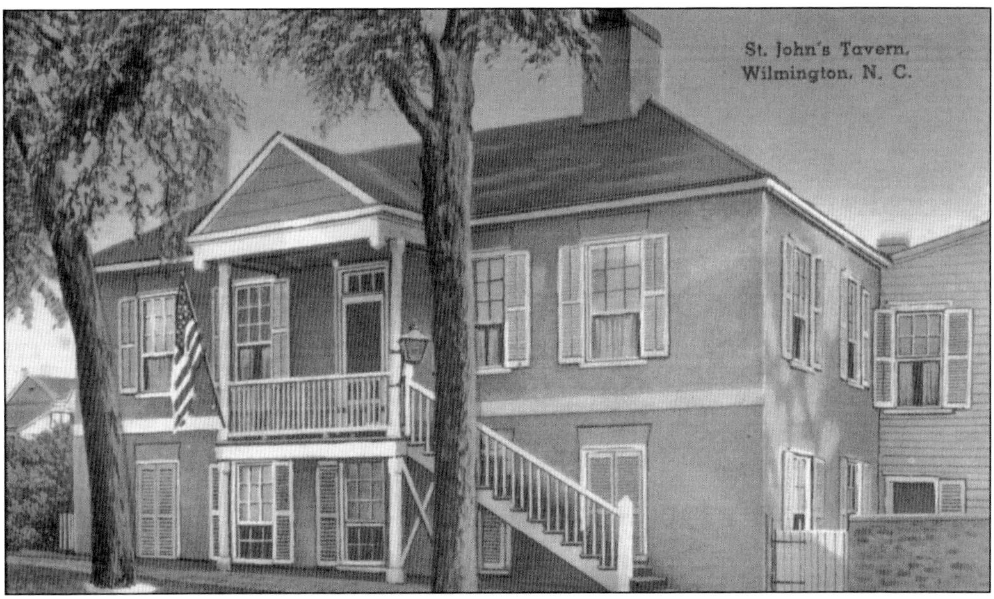

ST. JOHN'S TAVERN, *C.* 1943. The building at 114 Orange Street was the home of St. John's Masonic Lodge from 1803 until 1825. A silversmith named Thomas W. Brown purchased the property from the Masons, and it remained in his family until 1943. During WW II, James McKoy and Gar Faulkner established St. John's Tavern, an upscale restaurant. It became a very popular place to dine for local citizens and the vast number of new residents helping in the war effort. Since 1962, the Georgian-style structure has been the home of St. John's Art Museum.

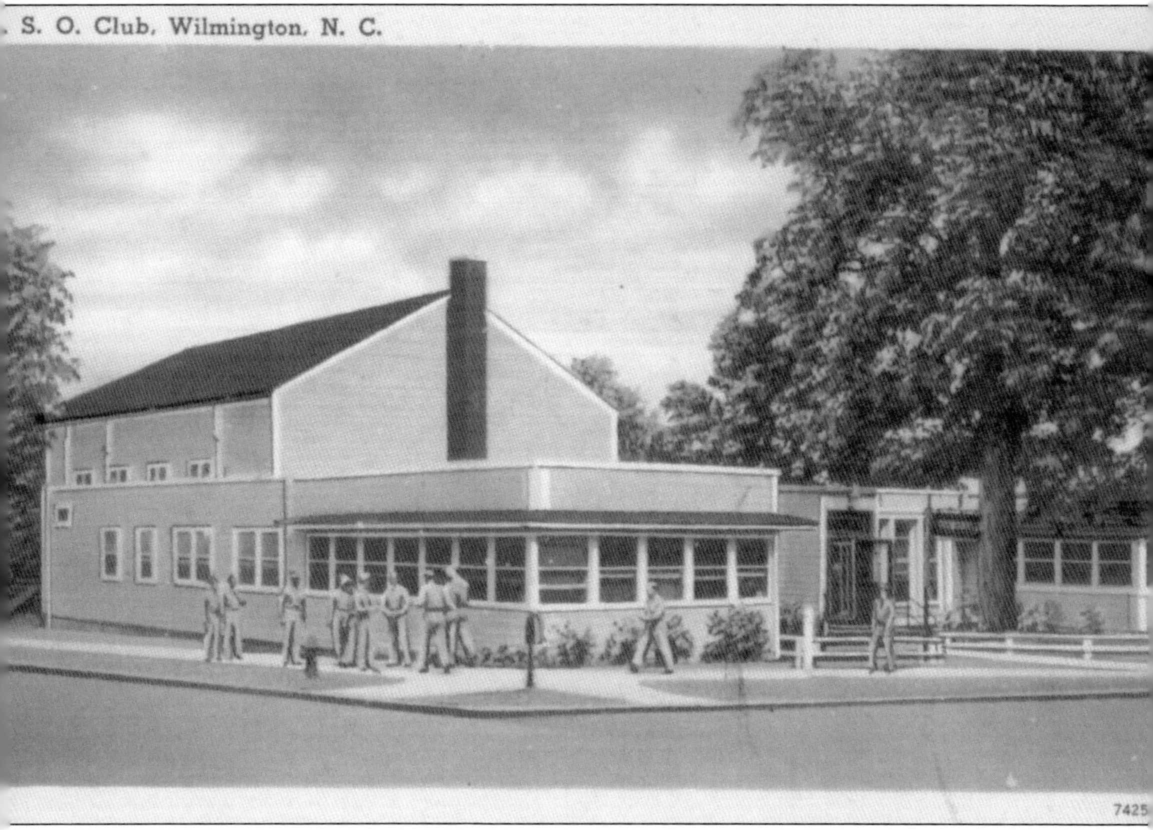

USO Club, c. 1942. Located on the southwestern corner of Second and Orange Streets, the building was constructed according to standardized architectural plans furnished by the Constructing Quartermaster Department of the U.S. Army. Completed by Christmas 1941, the structure contained a spacious lobby, two lounges, a canteen, and soda fountain. The auditorium had a wooden dance floor, which could accommodate 500 dancers. Big bands played from the large stage, which had disappearing footlights. Thousands of military personnel who trained at Camp Davis and other nearby bases took advantage of the facilities during WW II. Many local girls met their future husbands at functions held at the club. After the war, the U.S. government deeded the building over to the city and county. It has been used as a community arts center for many years. During the late 1990s, there was some discussion about demolishing the old building, but a group of active WW II enthusiasts and historic preservationists have managed to save the USO from the wrecking ball. The frame building is one of three surviving original USO structures in the United States.

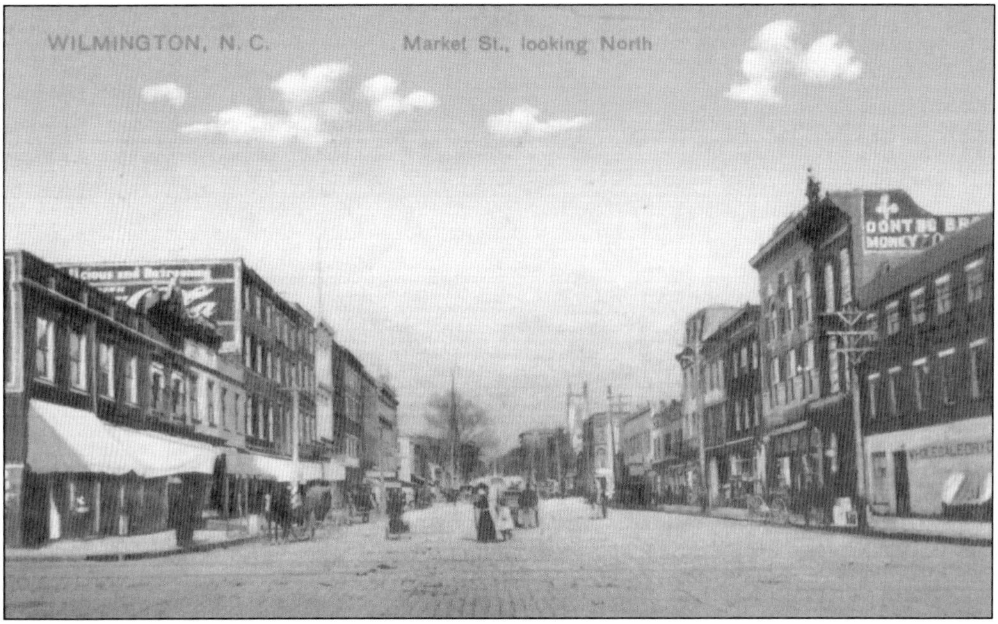

MARKET STREET, LOOKING NORTH, *c.* 1910. Wilmington's main east-west thoroughfare is Market Street, named for the first market house, which was located in the middle of the street between Water and Front Streets. The site of the colonial port was at the foot of the street, which ends at the Cape Fear River.

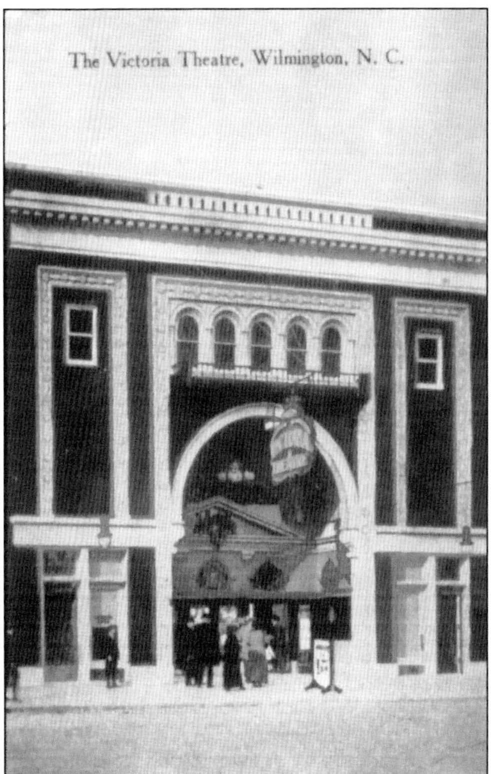

VICTORIA THEATER, *c.* 1915. In 1912–1913, the Bonitz Hotel, located on the northwestern corner of Second and Market Streets, was torn down to make way for the construction of the Victoria Theater. Owned by Jacob M. Solky, it opened on January 12, 1914, with four vaudeville attractions and two of the latest movies. It was a lavish theater for its time, having the best lighting facilities in town and nine sets of curtains and scenes. By the 1940s, the name had been changed to the Carolina. It was the last of the local movie theaters to have performers from the vaudeville circuit.

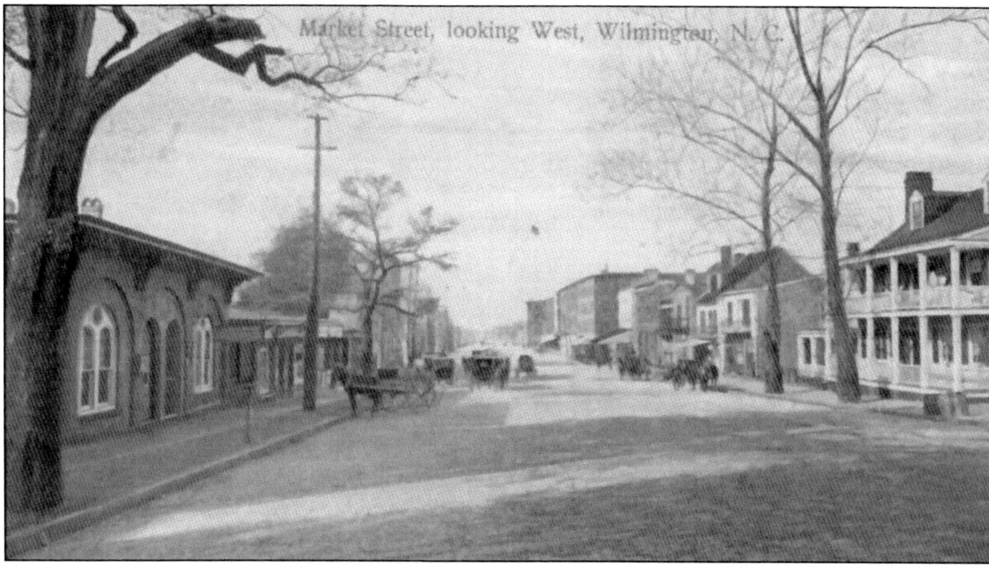

MARKET STREET, LOOKING WEST, *C.* 1910. At one time, the low, brick building (at left) contained offices for several doctors. Later, a bicycle shop occupied the structure. The house with the double piazzas (at right) was built by Captain Samuel Potter (*c.* 1811–1856). The famous legislator Henry Clay (1777–1852) addressed a huge crowd on April 10, 1844, from the second-floor piazza. The *Wilmington Chronicle* declared, "Never was such a scene, or anything approaching to it, witnessed in Wilmington."

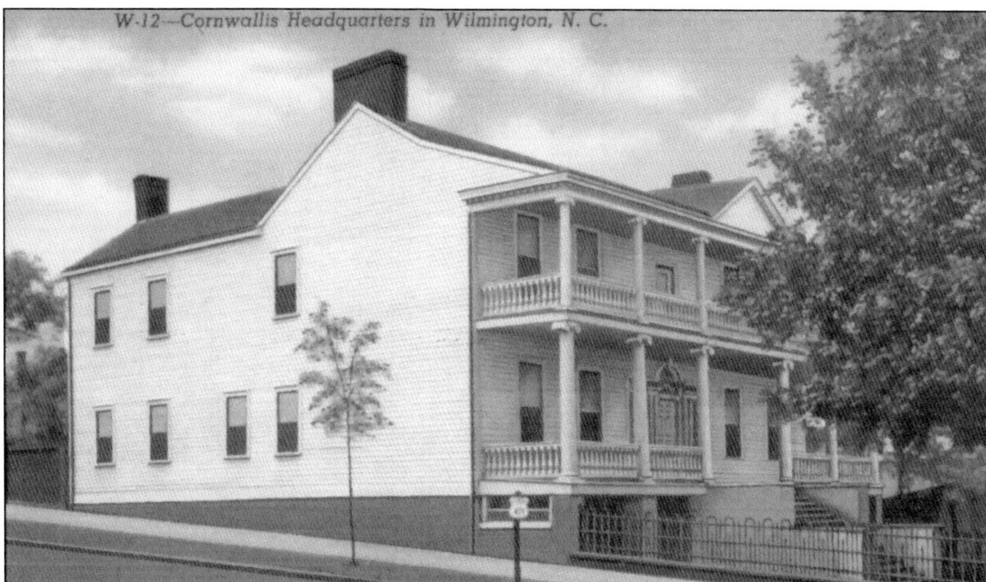

BURGWIN-WRIGHT HOUSE, *C.* 1940S. Located on the southwestern corner of Third and Market Streets, the house was built in 1770–1771 by John Burgwin (1731–1803), a lawyer, merchant, and large landowner. According to local tradition, Lord Cornwallis, Commander-in-Chief of British forces in the Carolinas during the American Revolution, resided here during his stay in Wilmington in the spring of 1781. The house was sold to Judge Joshua Grainger Wright in 1799 and remained in his family until 1869.

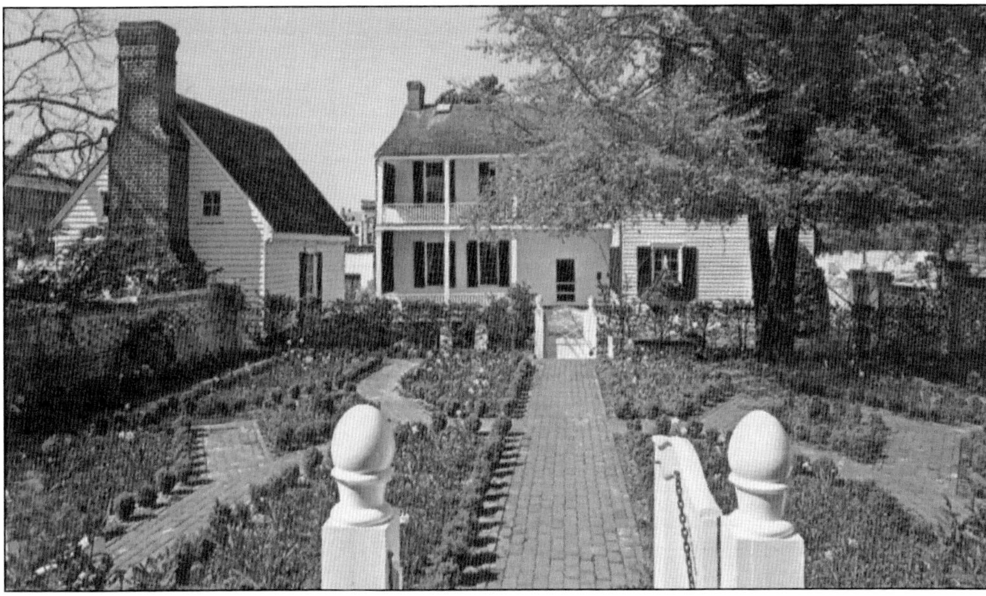

Burgwin-Wright House Garden, c. 1955. In the lovely formal garden, the detached kitchen (at left) reminds us of measures taken to minimize fire hazards, which was a constant threat to colonial buildings. The North Carolina Society of Colonial Dames purchased the house in 1937 and maintain it as their headquarters and house museum. (Courtesy of Hugh Morton.)

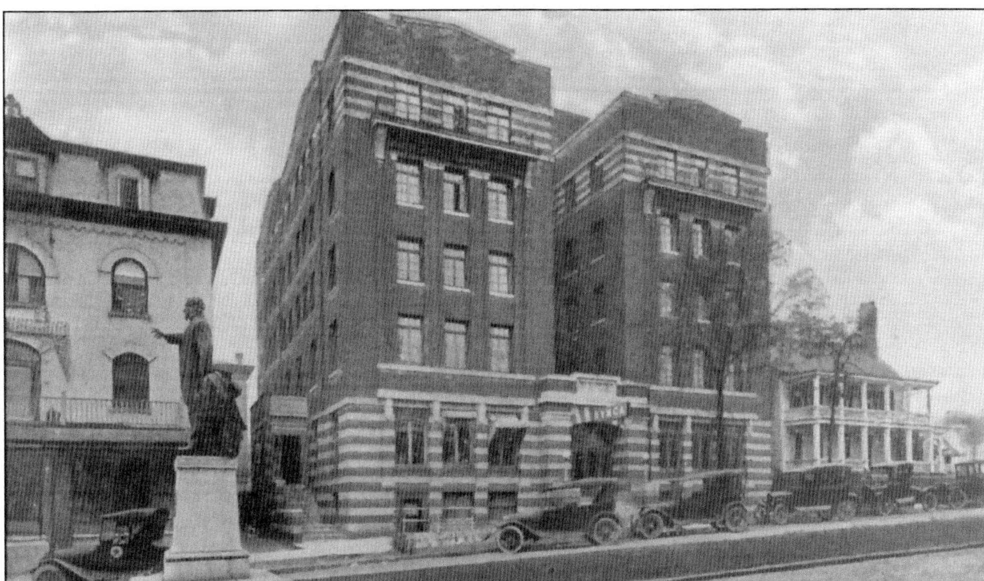

YMCA and George Davis Monument, c. 1920s. Constructed in 1912–1913, the red-brick YMCA Building had a gymnasium and swimming pool on the lower floors. The upper floors contained rooms, which were rented by the day or month. The structure was razed in 1970 after the "Y" moved to modern quarters at 2710 Market Street. At left is the Colonial Apartments, built in 1903–1904 for Oscar Pearsall on the northeastern corner of Market and Third Streets. Next door to the YMCA (at right) is the residence of Dr. John B. Cramner (1874–1954), who practiced medicine in Wilmington for 49 years. The George Davis Monument is in the foreground.

GEORGE DAVIS MONUMENT, c. 1914. The monument is located in the middle of the plaza of Market Street at Third Street. Executed by noted sculptor Frank H. Packer of New York, it was erected by the Cape Fear Chapter #3, United Daughters of Confederacy and was unveiled on April 20, 1911. It honors Wilmington native George Davis (1820–1896), an attorney who served the Confederate States of America as a North Carolina senator and attorney general.

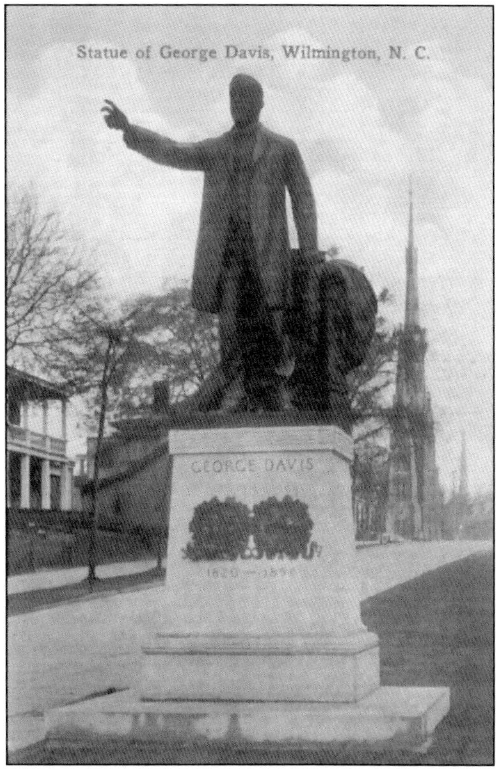

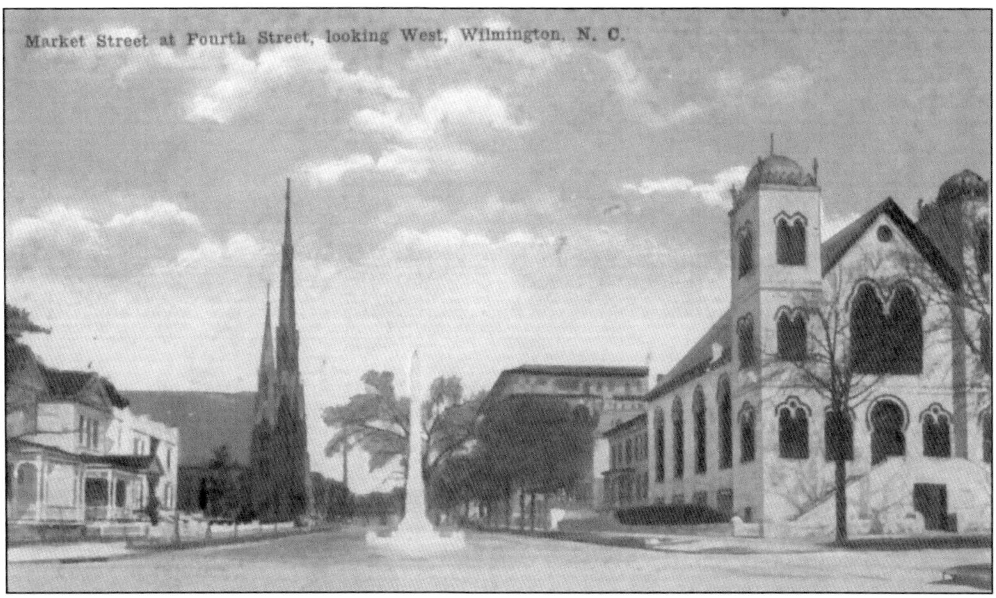

INTERSECTION OF FOURTH AND MARKET STREETS, LOOKING WEST, 1911. At center is the Cornelius Harnett obelisk, which was erected in 1906 to honor colonial heroes of the Lower Cape Fear. A Wilmington native, Harnett (1723–1781) was an American Revolutionary patriot who died while imprisoned by the British. Erected in 1875–1876, the Temple of Israel (at right) is the oldest Jewish house of worship in North Carolina. The church at left center is the First Baptist Church.

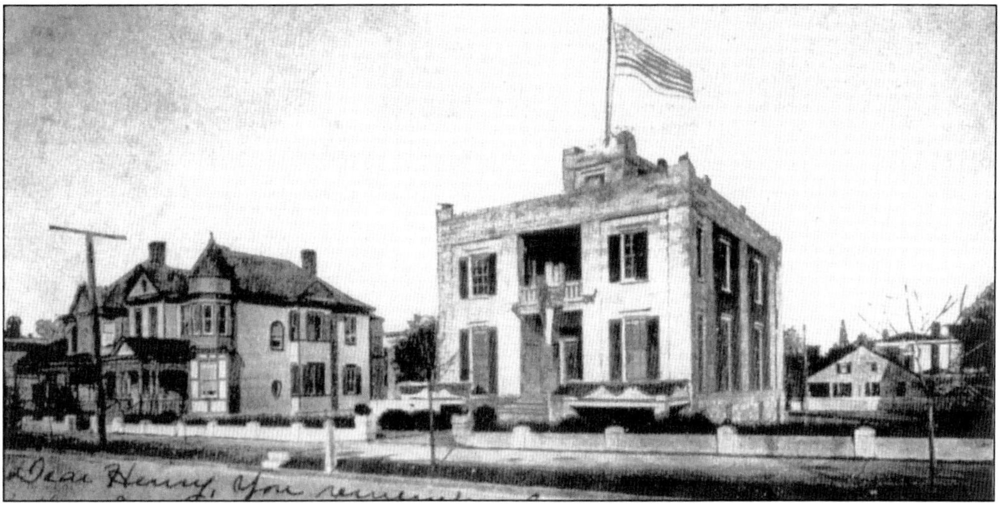

WILMINGTON LIGHT INFANTRY ARMORY. A successful businessman, John Allen Taylor (1798–1873) built the house (at center) *c.* 1847 in an unusual Classical Revival–style with a marble facade. From 1892 to 1951, it was the headquarters of the Wilmington Light Infantry (WLI), a local military reserve unit, organized in 1853. The cannons on the roof and the cannonballs on the fence are captured armament from the Spanish-American War. In 1951, the WLI gave the building to the city for the use of the Wilmington Public Library. After the library moved in 1981 to its present location, the building served as administrative offices for several city agencies. First Baptist Church bought the property in the 1990s.

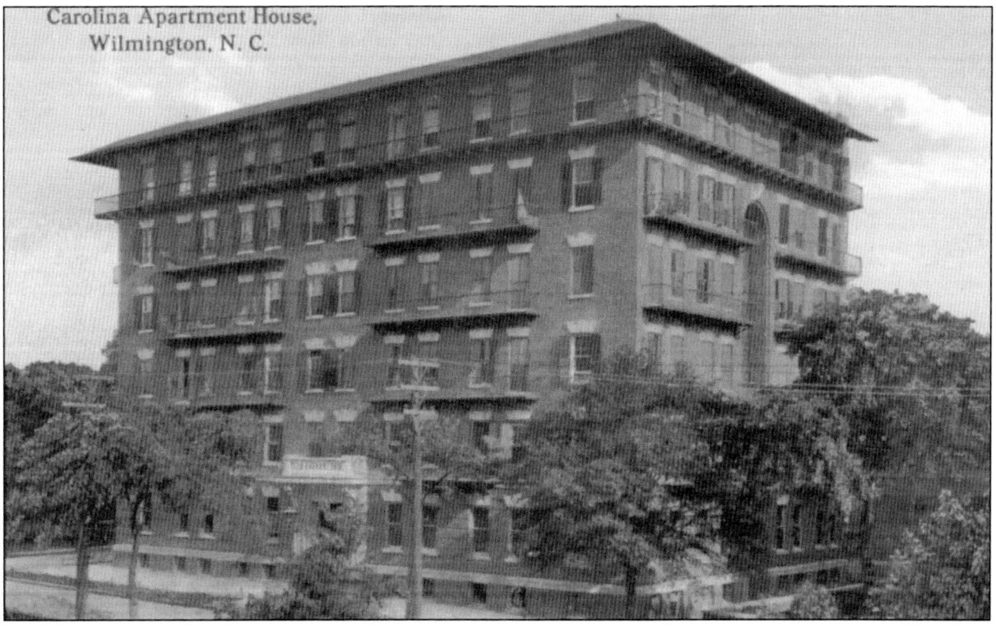

CAROLINA APARTMENTS. In 1906–1907, local businessman Thomas H. Wright constructed the apartments located on the southwestern corner of Fifth Avenue and Market Street. Architect Robert Louis Sharpe designed the building, taking his inspiration from the elegant apartments that line New York's Fifth Avenue. The apartments' most famous tenant was the artist Claude Howell (1915–1997), who was born in the building and lived there most of his life.

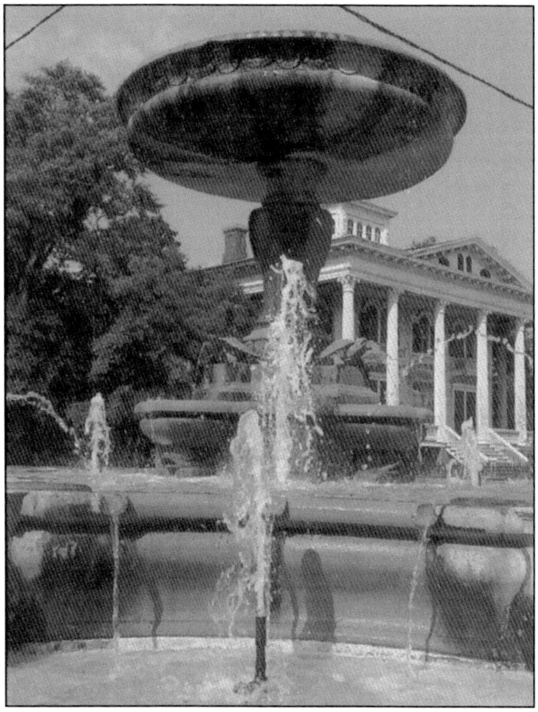

KENAN MEMORIAL FOUNTAIN, C. 1965. In 1921, William Rand Kenan Jr. gave the city the Kenan Memorial Fountain in memory of his parents, William R. and Mary Hargrove Kenan. Designed by Carrere and Hastings of New York, the fountain gives the intersection at Fifth Avenue and Market Street the flavor of a European city. (Courtesy of Tom & Jerry's Card Co.)

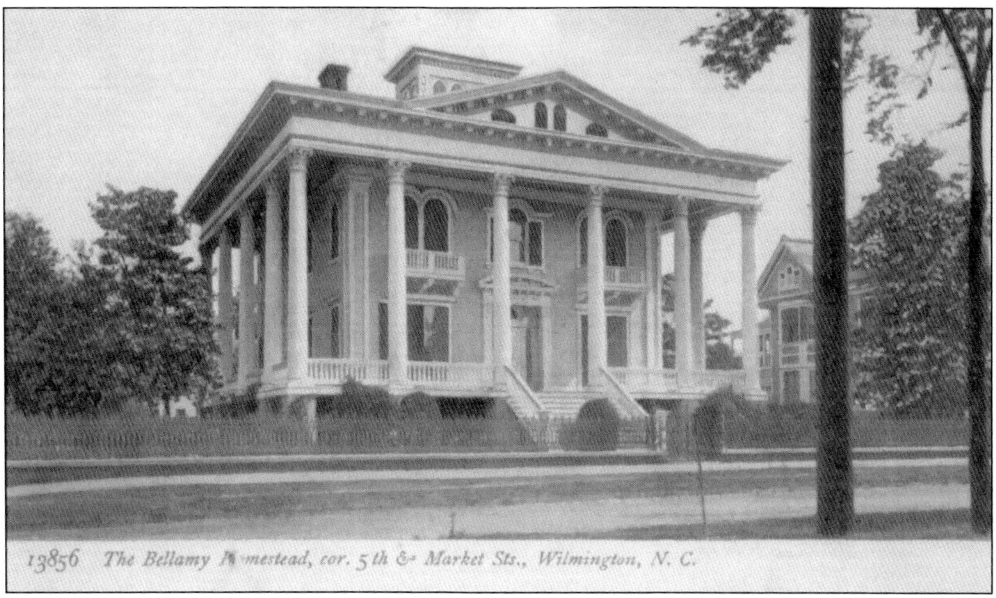

BELLAMY MANSION, 1906. The stately "Bellamy Homestead" was built in 1859 for Dr. John Dillard Bellamy, a wealthy plantation owner originally from South Carolina. The mansion was designed by Rufus Bunnell of Vermont. The house has elements in the styles of Greek Revival, Italianate, and Classical Revival. During the Civil War, the belvedere on top of the house was used as a lookout especially in the days after the Confederate defeat at Fort Fisher. Subsequently, the mansion billeted Union officers during the federal occupation. The house is now the Bellamy Mansion Museum of History and Design Arts.

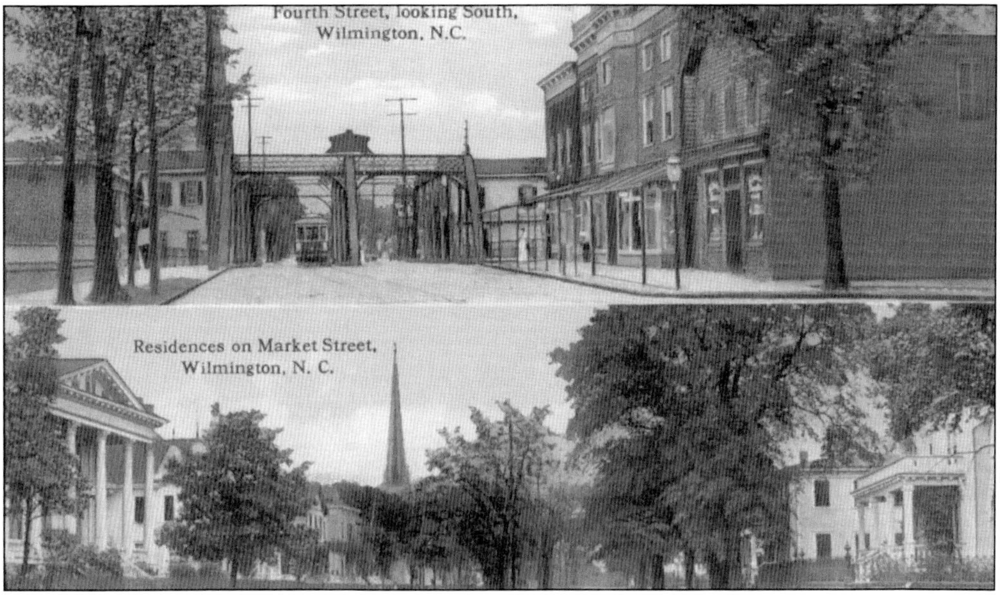

SCENES OF MARKET STREET AND NORTH FOURTH STREET, 1918. The bottom panel of this postcard is a photograph taken from the intersection of Fifth Avenue and Market Street, looking north. The house at the far right was once owned by John Dawson, a former mayor. Looking south, the top panel shows the steel railroad bridge on North Fourth Street, a business district removed from downtown. The building at right next to the bridge is the J.H. Rehder Department Store.

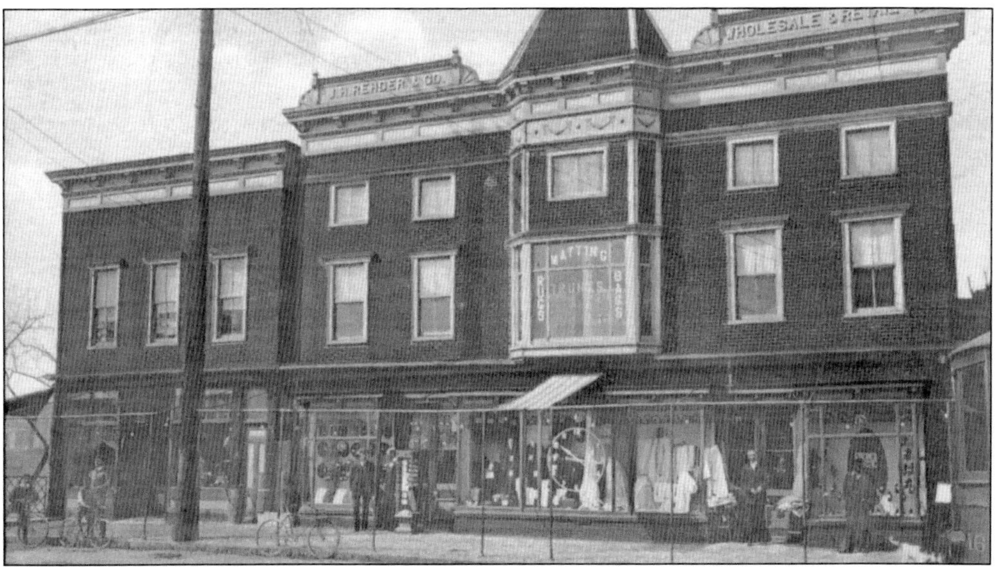

J.H. REHDER DEPARTMENT STORE, 1917. In the early 1890s, John H. Rehder (1866–1938) opened a department store on North Fourth Street in partnership with Carl W. Polvogt. In 1898, Rehder bought out Polvogt's interest and expanded the store. The department store carried a high-quality line of clothing. Many young girls purchased their first pair of silk stockings from the firm. Another of Rehder's business interests was publishing postcards, several of which are included in this book.

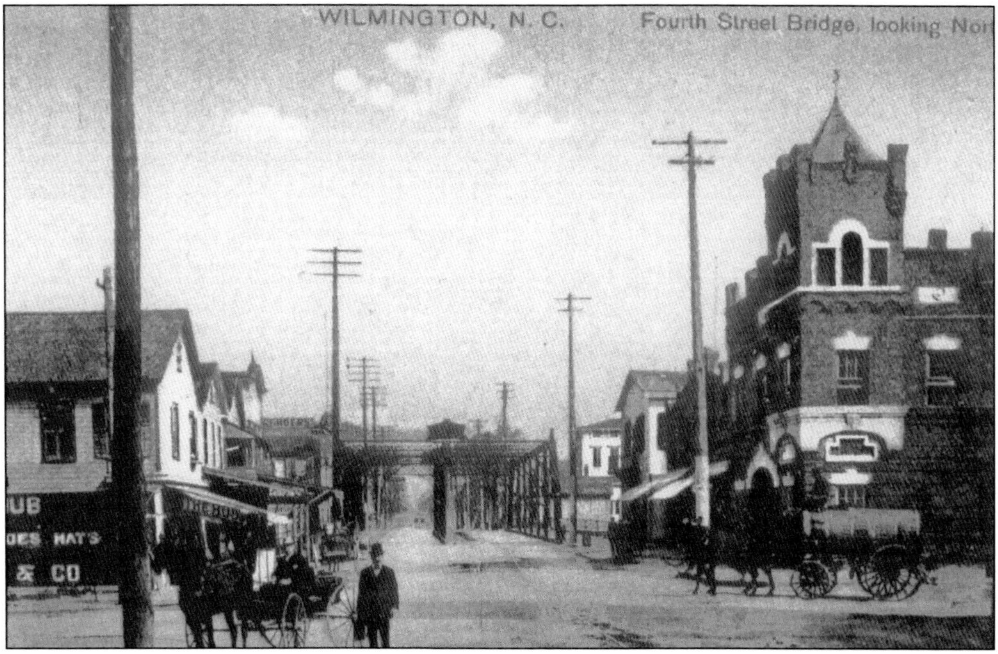

FOURTH STREET BRIDGE, LOOKING NORTH, 1910. This photograph of North Fourth Street was taken from the intersection of Fourth and Campbell Streets, with the railroad bridge at center. The building with the tower (at right) is the Consolidated Market and Firehouse #3. Completed in 1908, Henry Bonitz designed the firehouse with horse-drawn equipment and a stable in mind.

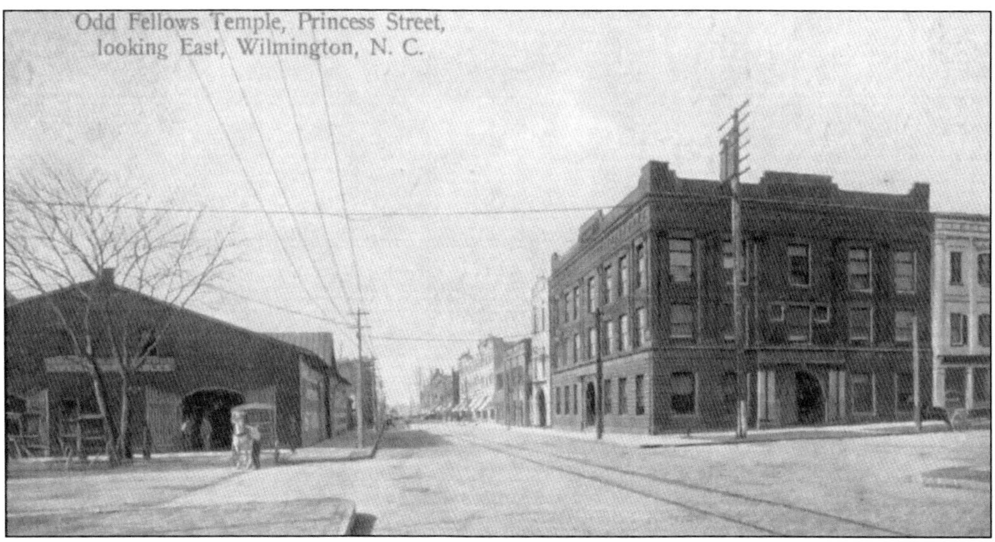

ORRELL LIVERY STABLE AND ODD FELLOWS BUILDING, 1909. When this photograph was taken in the pre-automobile age, the Orrell Livery Stable was still operating on the southwestern corner of Third and Princess Streets. Across the street, the three-story Odd Fellows Building, constructed in 1904, contained the offices of many prominent attorneys on the two lower floors. Designed by Charles McMillen, the structure was built of red Philadelphia brick trimmed with granite. Cape Fear Lodge, IOOF occupied the third-floor hall.

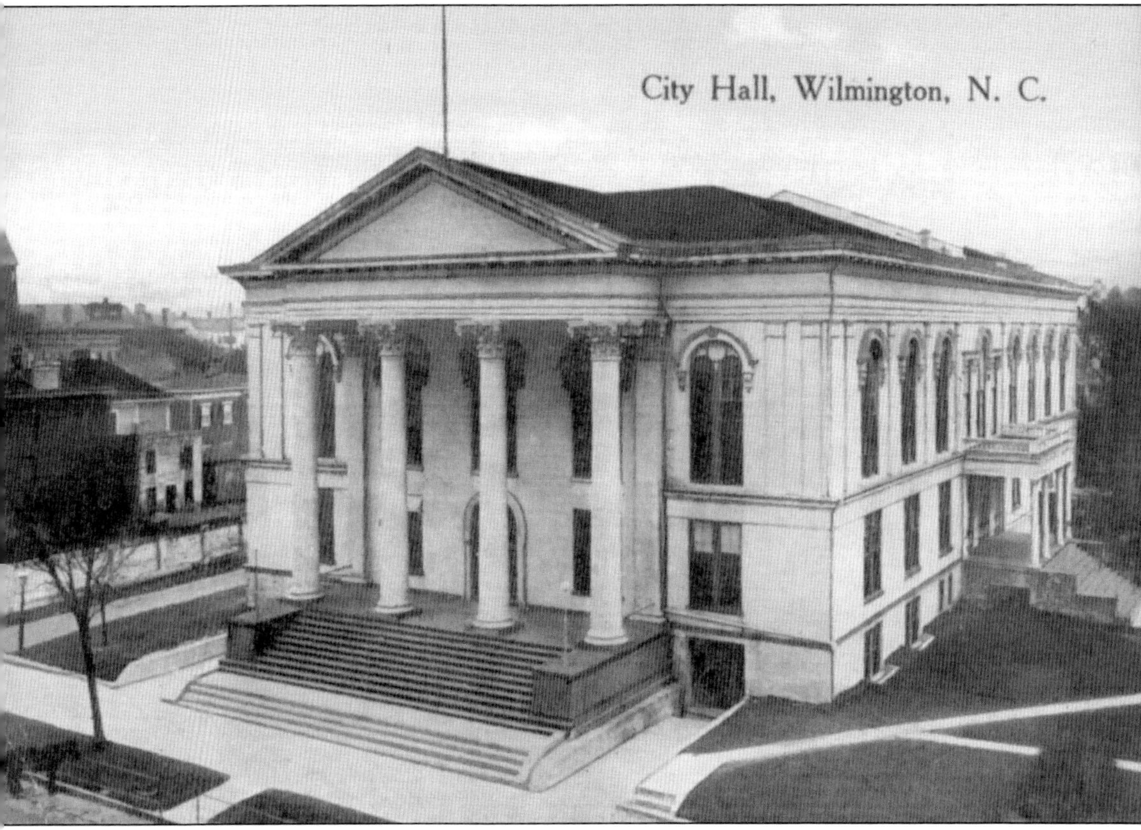

CITY HALL, C. 1910. When Wilmington's City Hall was built in 1855–1858, the city's population was just over 5,000 people. The mammoth Italianate and Classical Revival–style structure was unusual for a port city of that size. The city's aldermen included in the building Thalian Hall, a superb Victorian theater, named after a local amateur theater group. The building was designed by New York architect John M. Trimble, with James F. Post as local supervising architect. For a time, the city library was located on the front of the second floor and the police department was on the north side of the ground floor. In 1909, President William Howard Taft addressed area citizens from a platform erected on the front steps.

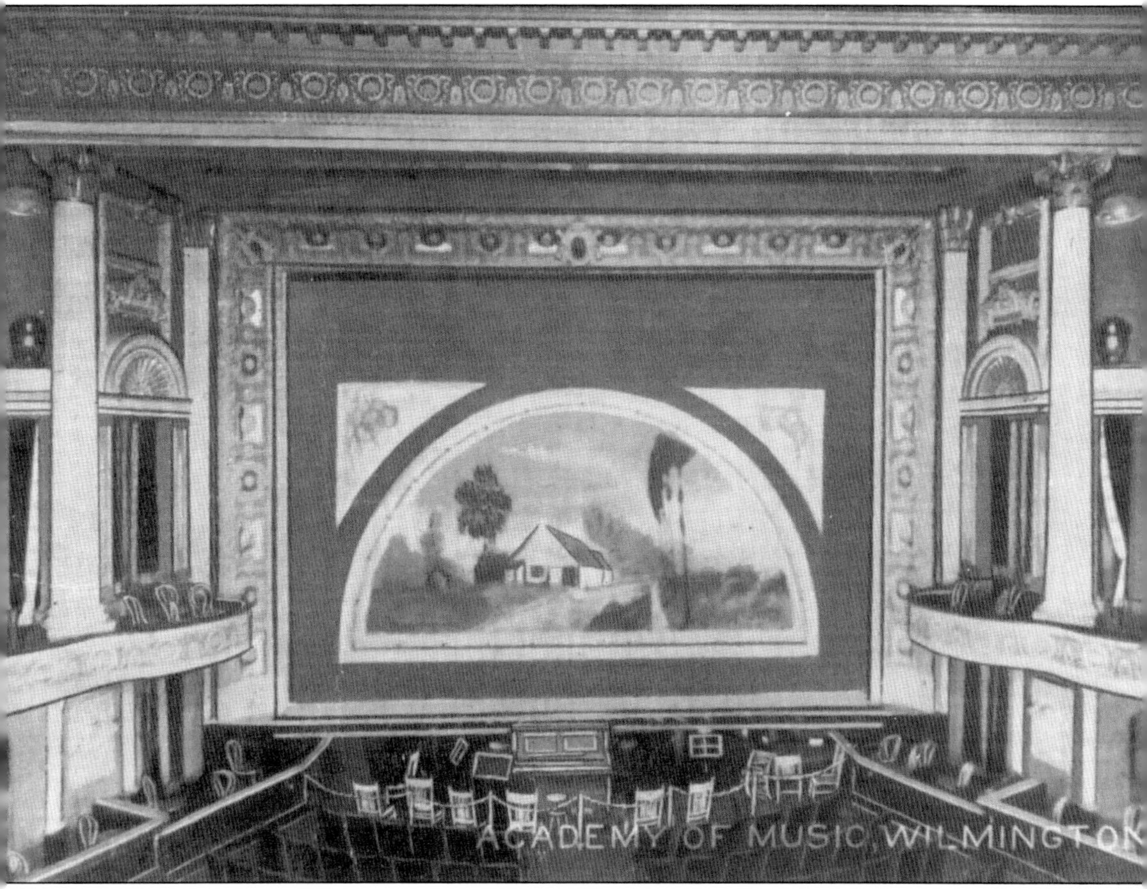

THALIAN HALL, *C.* 1910. During its long history, the theater has had several names: the Opera House, the Academy of Music, and Thalian Hall. Designed by well-known New York theatrical architect John Trimble, it opened in April 1858. The theater seated 1,500 and was the largest theater south of Richmond. Richly frescoed, the interior has been refurbished a number of times and served as a model for the restoration of Ford's Theater in Washington, D.C. The hall has been used as a community center, hosting local events that include recitals, school programs, memorial services, and charitable fairs. A number of famous actors, actresses, orators, and vocalists have appeared here, including Marion Anderson (1925), William Jennings Bryan (1912), John Philip Sousa and his band (1897, 1902, 1908), General Tom Thumb (1868, 1875), Oscar Wilde (1882), novelist Charles Dickens's son (1888), and Tyrone Power (1958). (Courtesy of Thalian Hall Center for the Performing Arts Archives.)

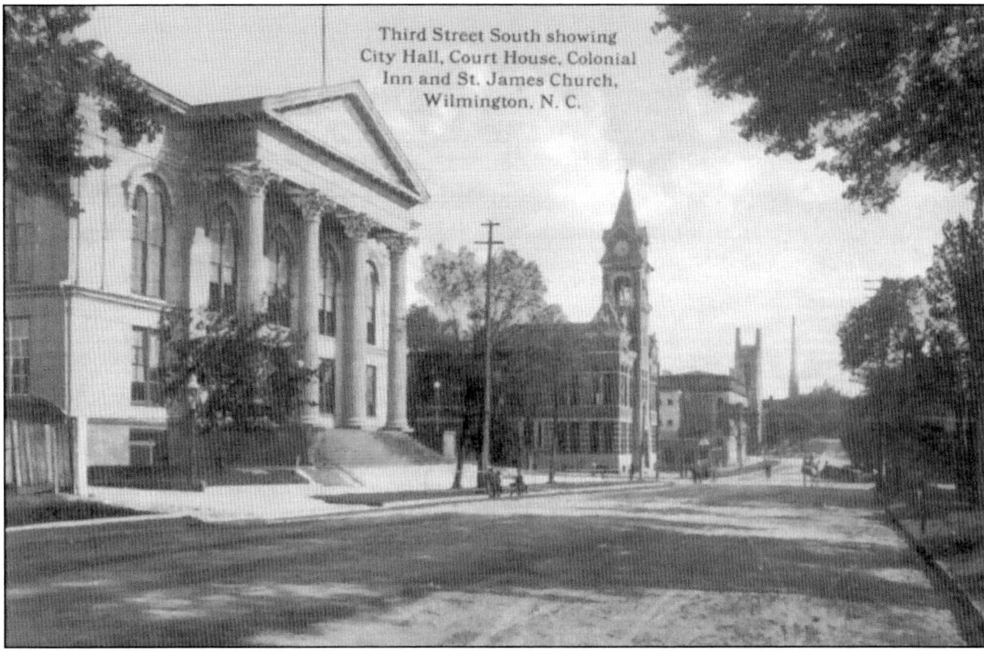

THIRD STREET, LOOKING SOUTH, *c.* 1910. One of the most attractive vistas in Wilmington is this scene. One can see some of the city's most impressive buildings, including City Hall, the New Hanover County Courthouse, the rear of the Colonial Inn, the tower of St. James Episcopal Church, and the spire of First Presbyterian Church. Note that this main street appears to be unpaved.

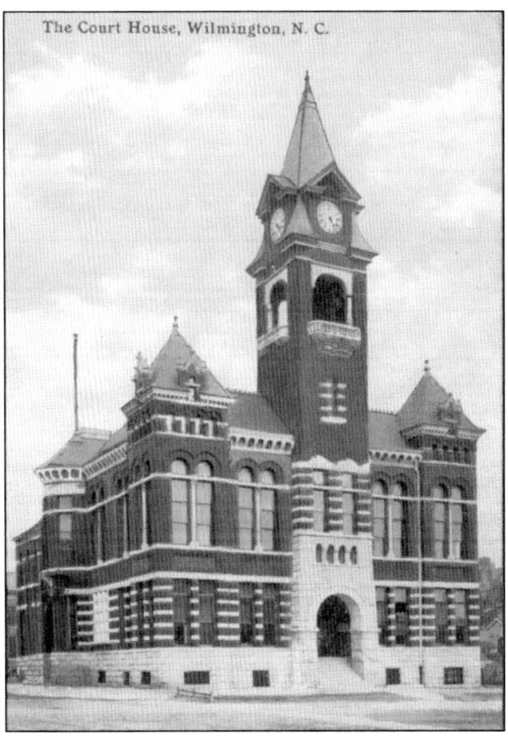

NEW HANOVER COUNTY COURTHOUSE, 1911. The building was designed by Savannah architect A.S. Eichberg. As with the City Hall, some 35 years earlier, versatile local architect James F. Post supervised the construction in 1891–1892. The center tower contains a four-sided clock and a 2,000-pound bell. Constructed of several kinds of brick and stone, the Queen Anne–style building was first occupied in April 1892, when the spring term of superior court was held. The first case was a suit for divorce, which the judge deemed, "a bad beginning."

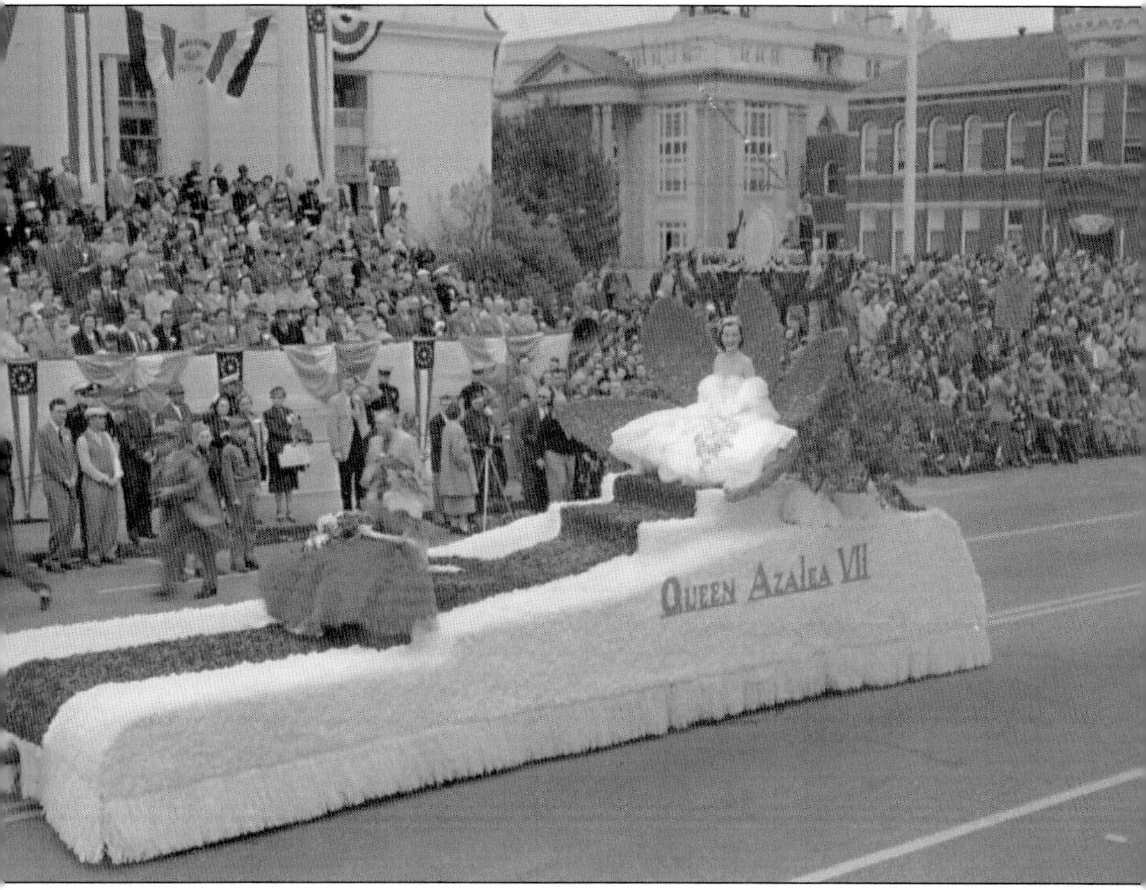

Azalea Festival Parade, 1954. In 1948, Wilmington civic leaders conceived the idea of having a festival dedicated to the azalea, which every spring turns the city into a colorful fairyland. The leaders chose the capable and energetic Hugh Morton to be the first president. From those beginnings, the festival has hosted thousands of visitors. The Azalea Queen has always been a movie or television actress. For years, the queen's identity was a closely guarded secret, only revealed the Sunday before the festival in the *Star-News*. A grand parade and entertaining events are held throughout the area. Some of the celebrities who have attended the festival as guests are as follows: former President Ronald Reagan; North Carolina native Andy Griffith; Bob Hope; and local basketball hero Michael Jordan. In the 1954 parade, Queen Azalea VII, Ella Raines, passes the reviewing stand, located on the City Hall steps. (Courtesy of Hugh Morton.)

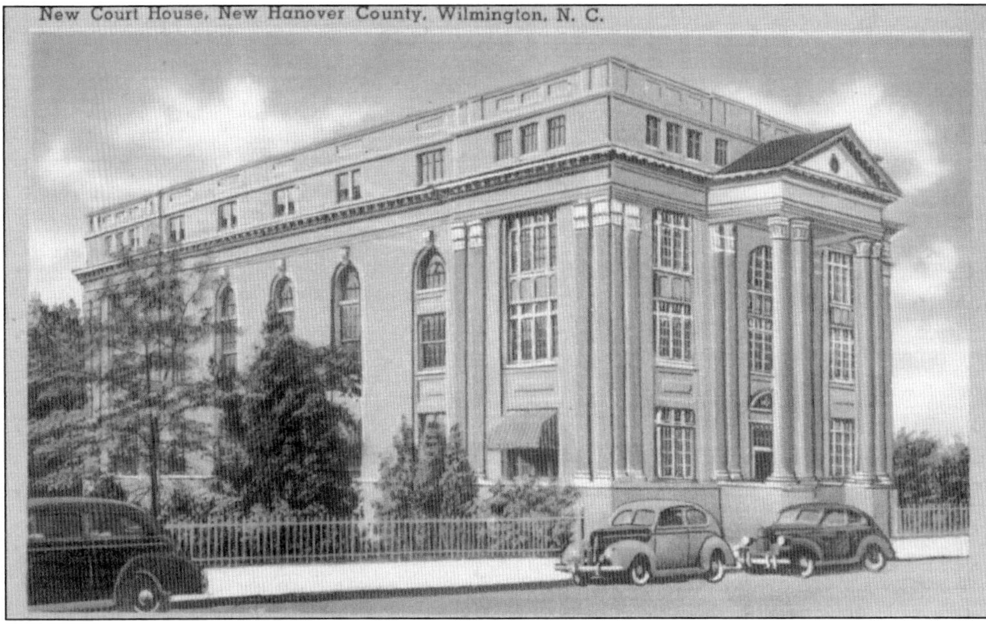

NEW HANOVER COUNTY COURTHOUSE ANNEX, 1940. The cornerstone for the courthouse annex was laid on February 6, 1925, and the structure was occupied later the same year. Leslie N. Boney designed the stone-faced Neo-Classical Revival–style building. For a number of years, the county jail was on the top floor. At one time, the New Hanover County Museum (now Cape Fear Museum) had quarters just across from the entrance to the jail.

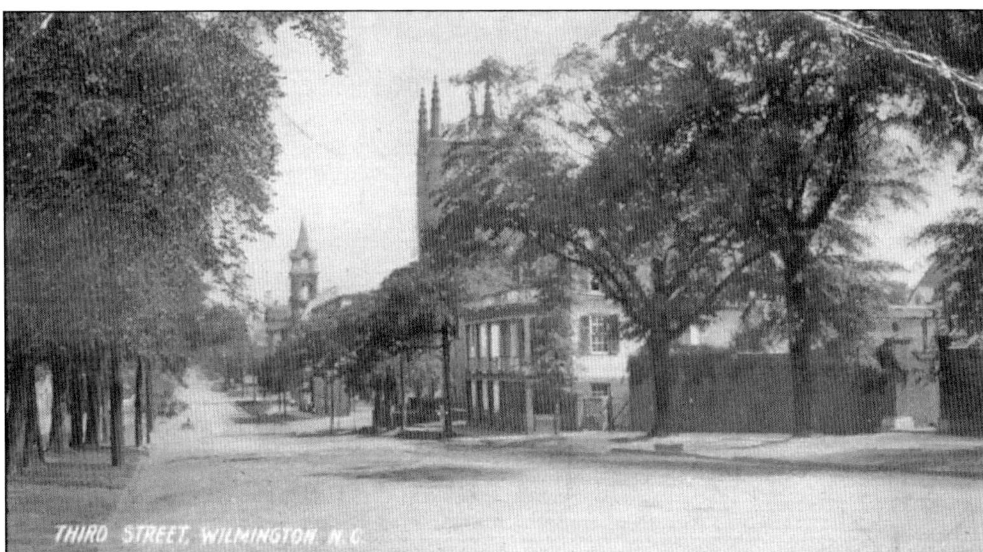

THIRD STREET, LOOKING NORTH FROM DOCK STREET, 1907. The house (at center) is the Hill-Wright-Wootten House. Built in the early 1800s by Dr. John Hill, it came into the Wright family by marriage. The Reverend Edward and Eliza Jewett Wootten purchased the house in the late 1800s. It remained in the Wootten family until it was sold to their neighbor, St. James Episcopal Church in 1952, who demolished the house in 1955. The tower of St. James is visible through the trees.

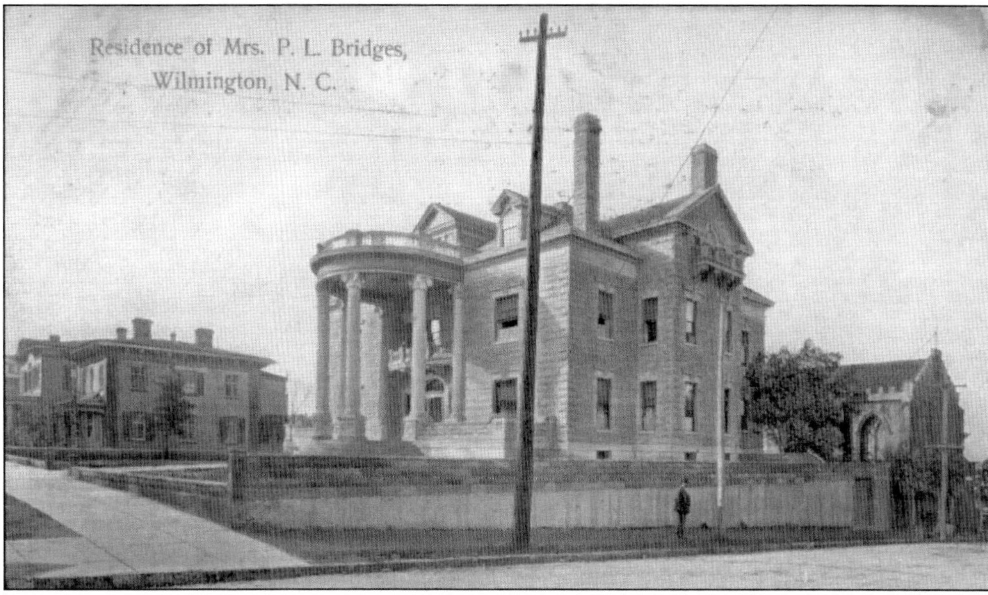

BRIDGERS HOUSE, 1909. In 1905, Mrs. Elizabeth Eagle Haywood Bridgers was the widow of Preston L. Bridgers, a well-known railroad official. Mrs. Bridgers chose architect Charles McMillen to design her residence on the southwestern corner of South Third and Dock Streets. The house is a massive Neoclassical Revival–style structure made of Indiana stone. On the extreme right is St. Thomas the Apostle Roman Catholic Church.

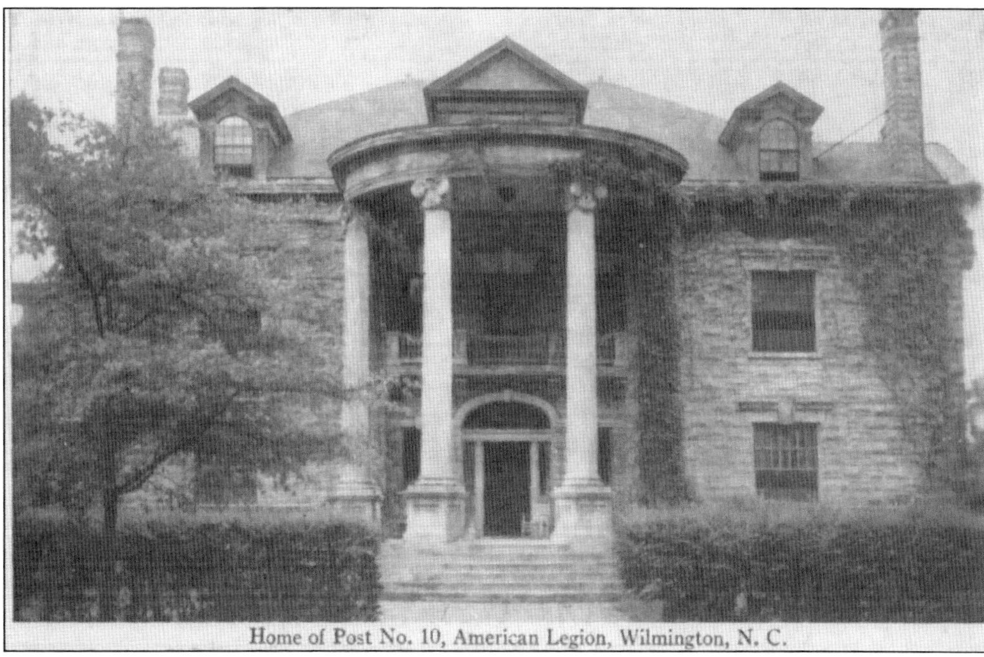

AMERICAN LEGION HOME, *c.* 1945. The most impressive feature of the Bridgers House is the grand entrance with a semi-circular portico supported by huge Ionic columns. In 1944, Post No. 10, American Legion purchased the house to use as a headquarters for veterans. In the 1990s, the house became a bed and breakfast establishment.

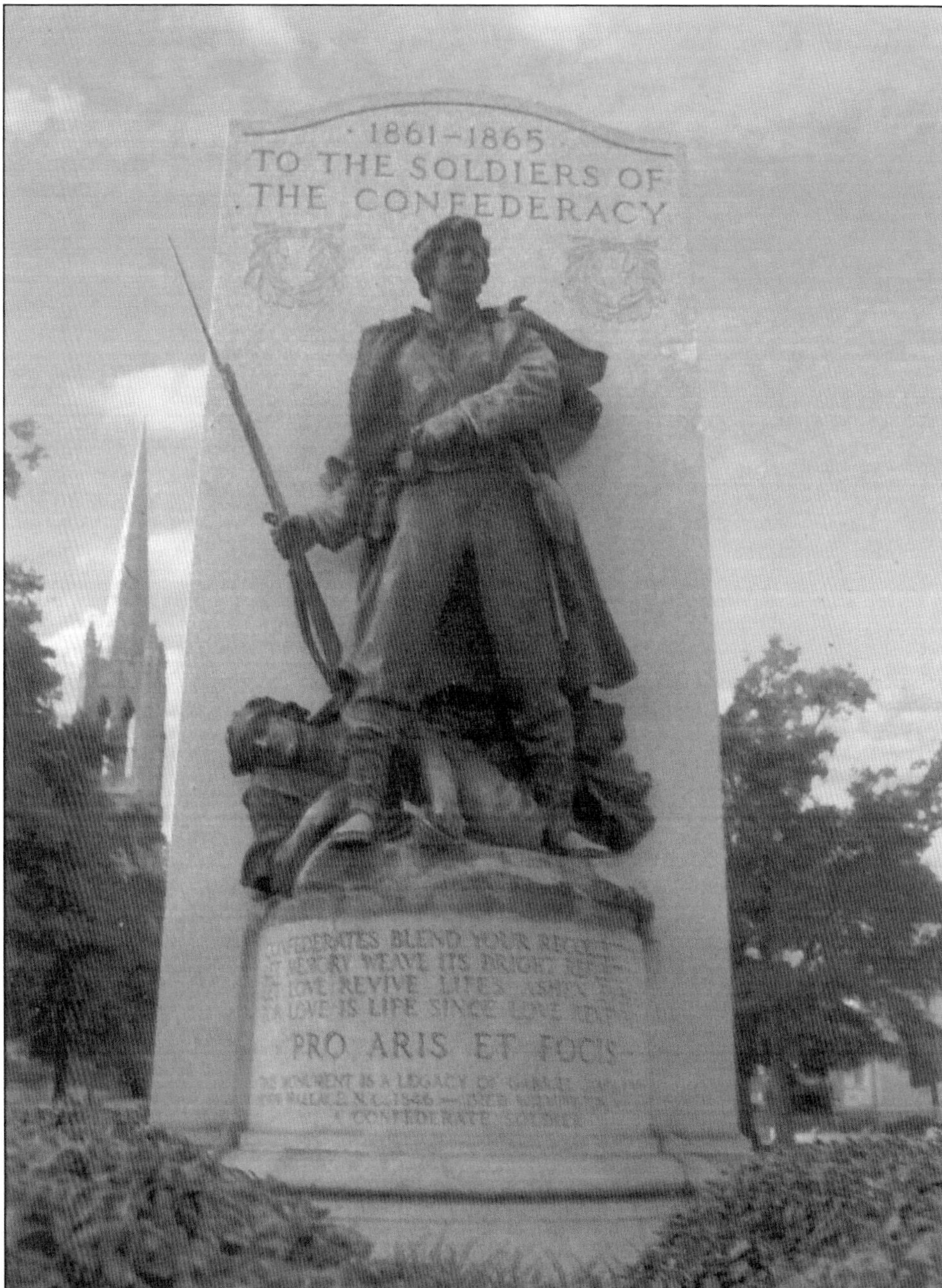

Confederate Memorial Monument, c. 1960. The monument was a gift to the City of Wilmington by Gabriel Boney in memory of the soldiers who fought for the Confederacy. Erected in 1924 on the plaza at the intersection of Third and Dock Streets, it was designed by Henry Bacon. The two bronze figures were executed by sculptor Frank H. Packer. Since the invention of the automobile, the monument has been hit several times. In 1999, the last time the monument was hit, a crane dropped the base of the monument causing even more damage. (Courtesy of Tom and Jerry's Card Co.)

Three

AROUND TOWN AND THE COUNTY

For a number of years, the Wilmington city limits stopped at Fifth Street. Once called Boundary Street, it was marked by several large oak trees, one of which survives in the Tileston School yard. The city limits have been extended frequently. The streetcar suburbs of Carolina Place and Carolina Heights were the first residential areas developed beyond Seventeenth Street.

Wilmington is the county seat of New Hanover County, which was formed in 1729 from Craven County. Named for the British Royal House of Hanover, the county is the second smallest in North Carolina. Once, it contained a number of truck farms; however, urban sprawl has claimed much of the county's undeveloped land. The estimated county population in 2000 is 155,595. In recent years, new residents have flocked into the area, taking advantage of the mild climate, bustling economy, and many recreational facilities.

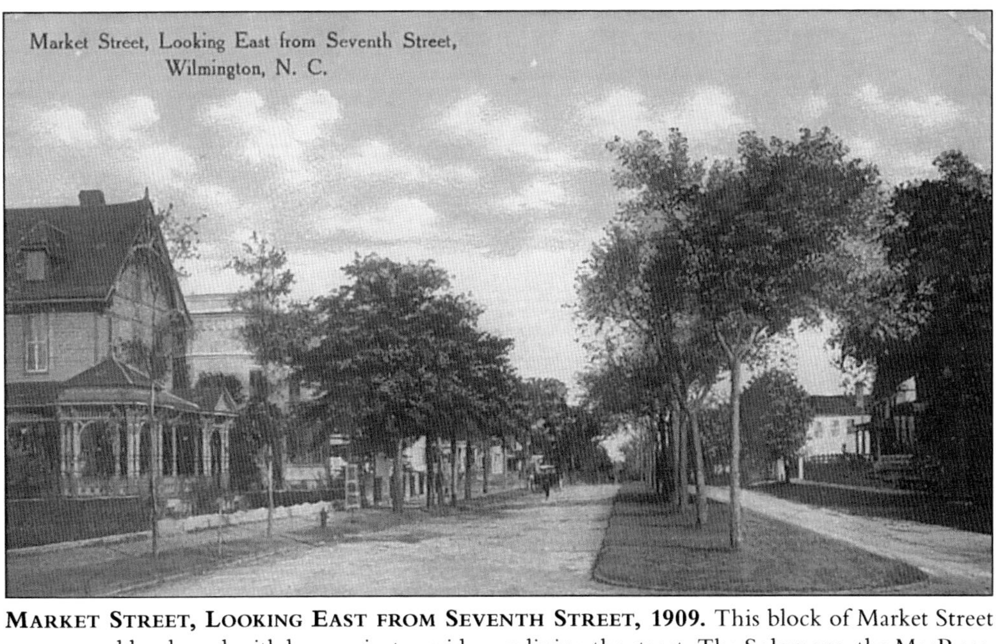

MARKET STREET, LOOKING EAST FROM SEVENTH STREET, 1909. This block of Market Street was a grand boulevard with large private residences lining the street. The Solomons, the MacRaes, the Kucks, the Gilchrists, and the Vollers had homes in this block. Sadly, with the exception of the Gilchrist House, all of these lovely houses have been torn down.

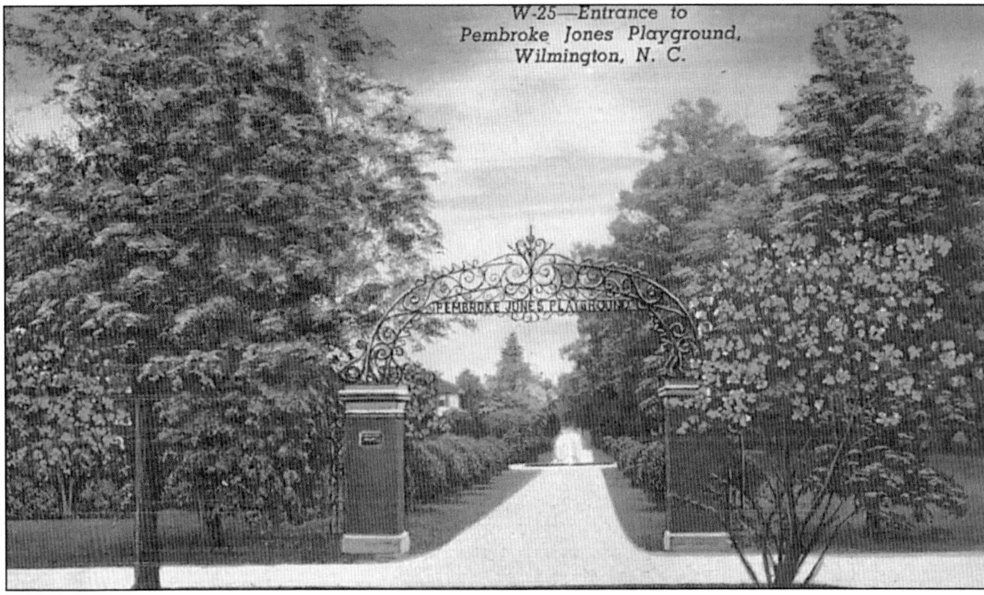

PEMBROKE JONES PARK, C. 1930. In 1919, funds from the Pembroke Jones Estate were used to finance a playground on Market Street at Fourteenth Street. Jones was a Wilmington native and the wealthy owner of Airlie-on-the-Sound. In 1925, the lovely, delicate iron arch over the entrance was cast by Wilmington Iron Works.

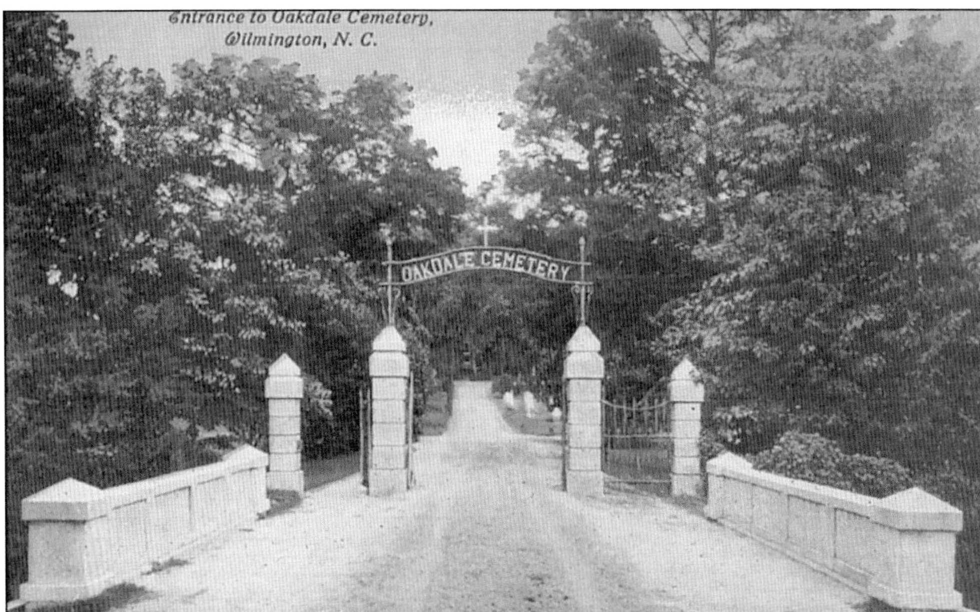

ENTRANCE TO OAKDALE CEMETERY, 1914. Originally, the entrance to Oakdale Cemetery was at the eastern end of Miller Street, which is one block north of Red Cross Street. Chartered in 1852, Oakdale was the fifth landscaped cemetery in the United States, following similar ones in Cambridge, Massachusetts; Philadelphia, Pennsylvania; Brooklyn, New York; and Richmond, Virginia. The first burial in 1855 was that of Annie deRosset, the six-year-old daughter of one of the cemetery's founding fathers, Dr. Armand deRosset.

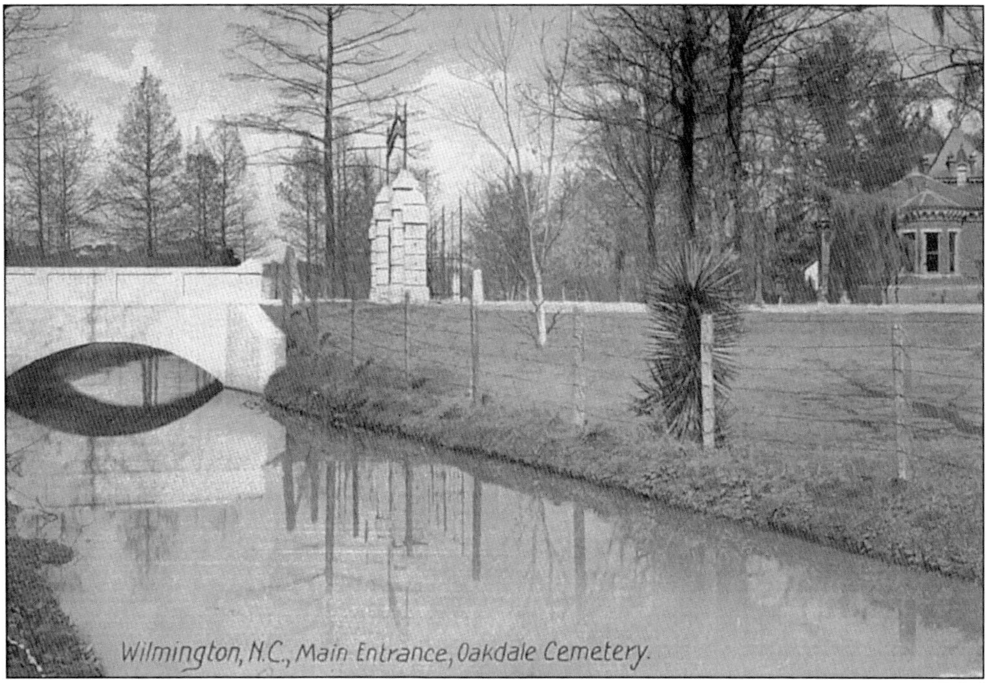

OAKDALE CEMETERY, 1912. The old entrance to Oakdale Cemetery was via a bridge over Burnt Mill Creek, which meanders along the western edge of the cemetery. The side of the lodge, which is sometimes called a chapel, is at right. In 1915, the main entrance to the cemetery was changed to the northern end of Fifteenth Street.

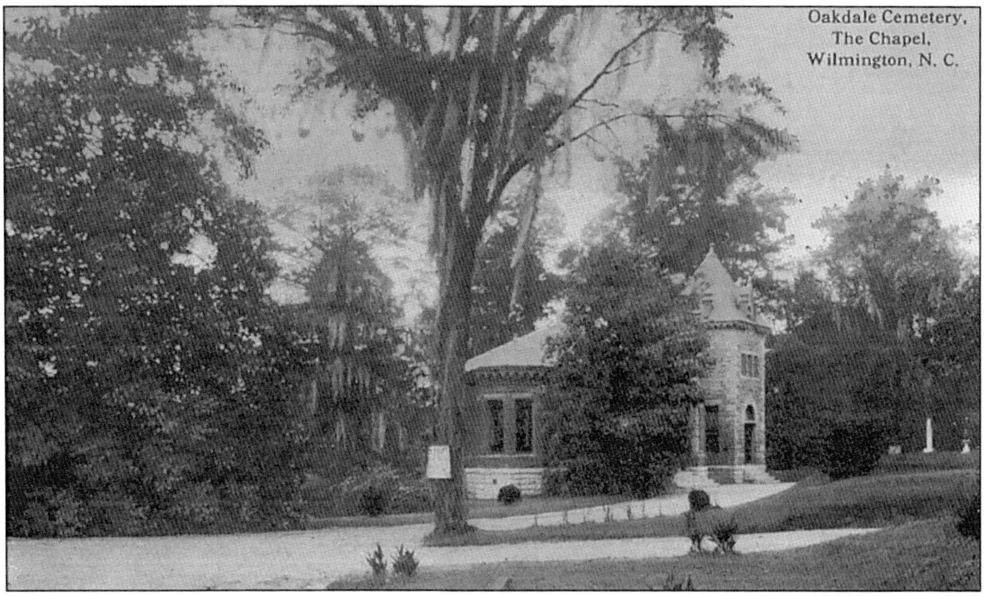

LODGE, OAKDALE CEMETERY, 1919. The stone chapel or lodge at Oakdale Cemetery replaced an earlier, less elaborate structure, which burned in 1896. James F. Post designed the lodge, which was used for funeral services and other gatherings. The lodge was torn down in the mid-1940s, and its foundation forms the outer wall of the Frederick Willetts lot.

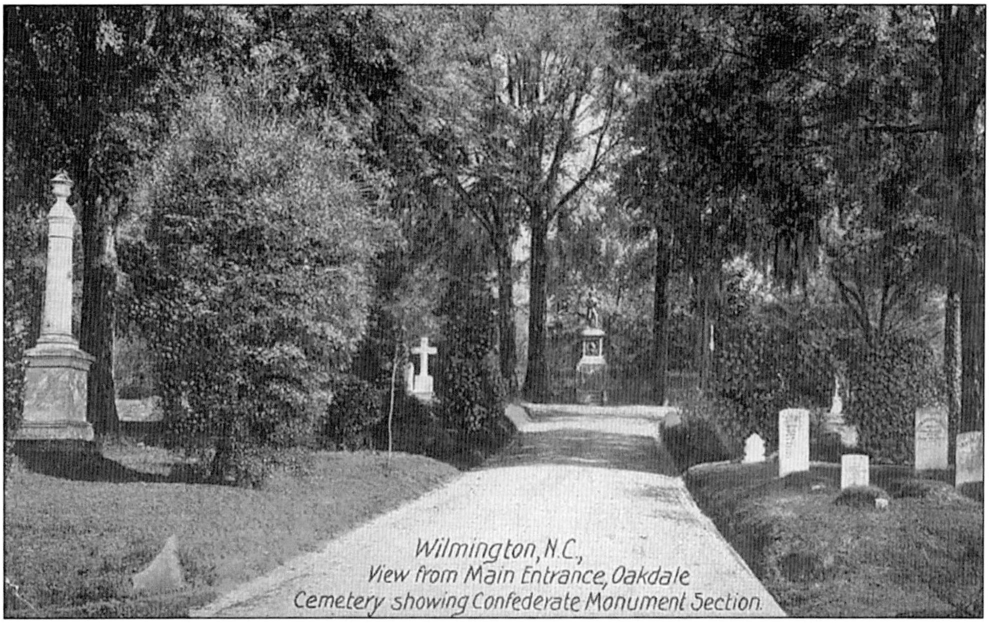

View from Main Entrance, Oakdale Cemetery, 1908. The main road inclined up the gentle hill from the old Oakdale Cemetery entrance to the Confederate Monument, seen in the background. The variety and beauty of the stones in the cemetery are astonishing, including a number with excellent examples of Victorian funerary symbols.

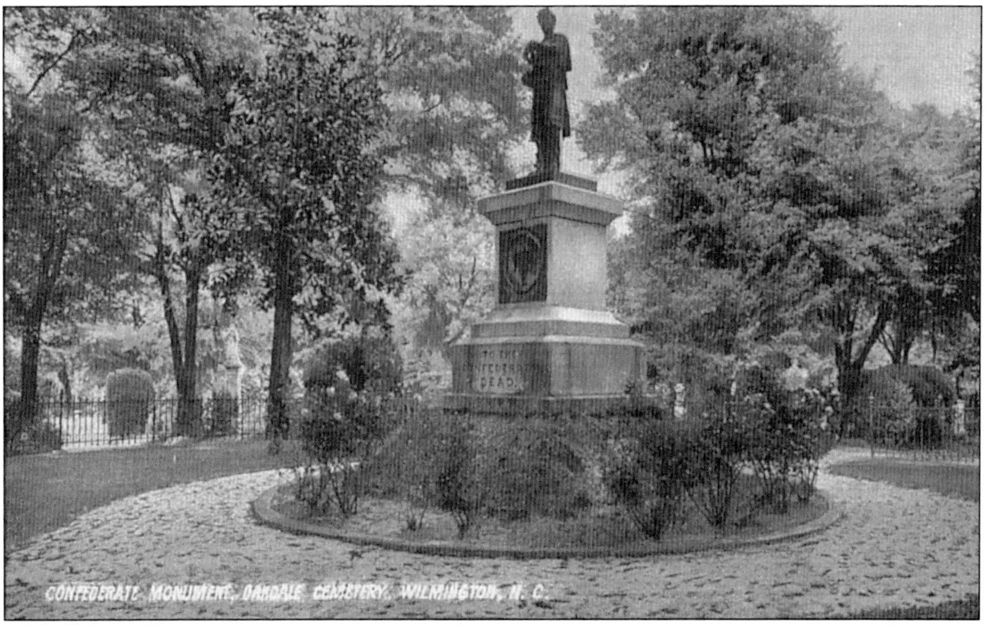

Confederate Monument, Oakdale Cemetery, 1909. On Confederate Memorial Day, May 10, 1872, this monument was unveiled by the Ladies Memorial Association. It marks the graves of over 400 unknown Confederate soldiers. The large bronze soldier on a granite pedestal was designed by William Randolph O'Donovan and executed by Maurice J. Power at the National Art Foundry in New York.

Oakdale Cemetery, c. 1912. One of the important features of Oakdale Cemetery is the abundance of lovely iron fences and gates. Most of the very early ones were cast by Hart & Bailey, a forerunner of the Wilmington Iron Works. Note the fence at left.

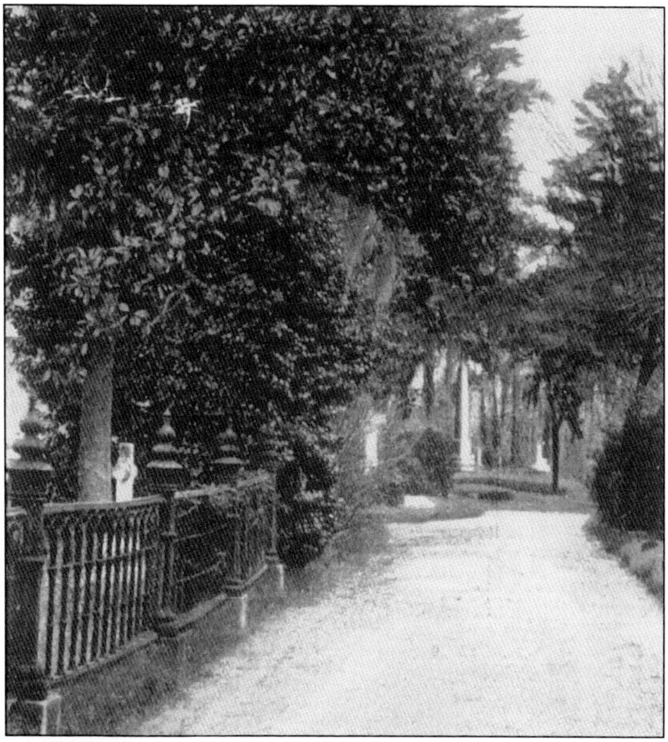

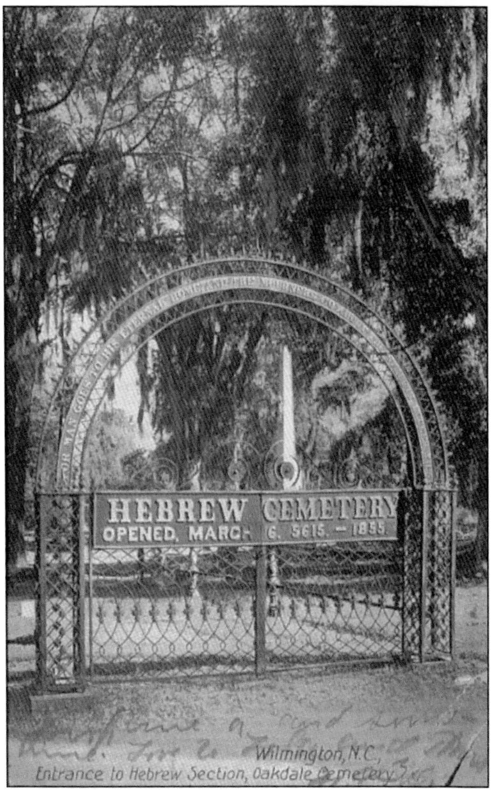

Hebrew Section, Oakdale Cemetery, 1909. Among the best and earliest examples of iron work in Oakdale Cemetery is the delicate arched gate that marks the entrance to the Hebrew Cemetery. This section was dedicated March 6, 1855 or 5615 (Jewish year). In the enclosed area is the grave of Arthur Bluethenthal, the first Wilmington native killed in World War I.

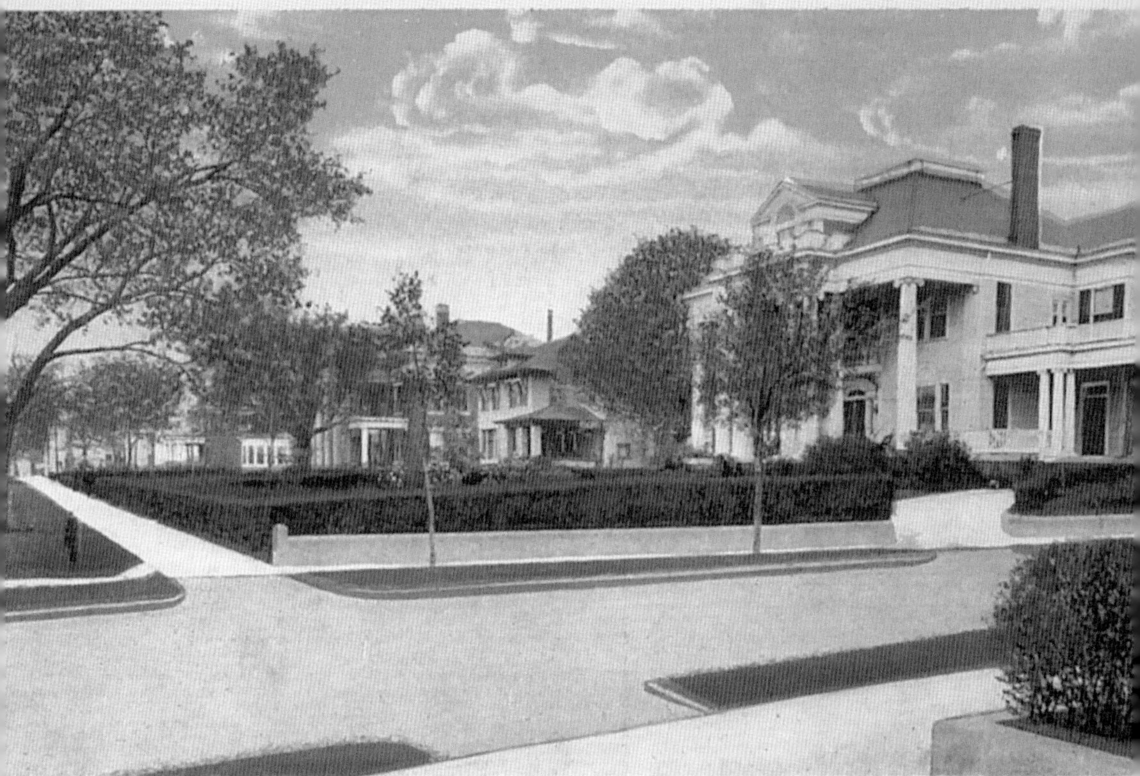

CAROLINA HEIGHTS, C. 1915. An early Wilmington streetcar suburb, Carolina Heights was developed by Miss Mary Bridgers. On the corner of Eighteenth and Market Streets, the large white house at right is the Holt-Wise House, built in 1908–1909 by Edwin C. Holt, president of Delgado Mills. Jessie Kenan Wise, an heiress to the Flagler railroad fortune, purchased the house in 1916. Mrs. Wise's sister, Sarah Kenan, owned a large red-brick house on the corner of Seventeenth and Market Streets. Between the two mansions was a smaller Prairie-style house (at center) that was built for Ella Weil in 1907. At a later date, both Mrs. Wise and Mrs. Kenan erected high brick walls around their properties, after which one local wit referred to the Weil house as "the walled-off." All three residences were designed by Burett H. Stephens. Mrs. Kenan and Mrs. Wise gave their mansions to the University of North Carolina at Wilmington for use as the Chancellor's residence and the headquarters of the University's Alumni Association. The Weil House was razed in the 1970s. (Courtesy of Bellamy Mansion Museum.)

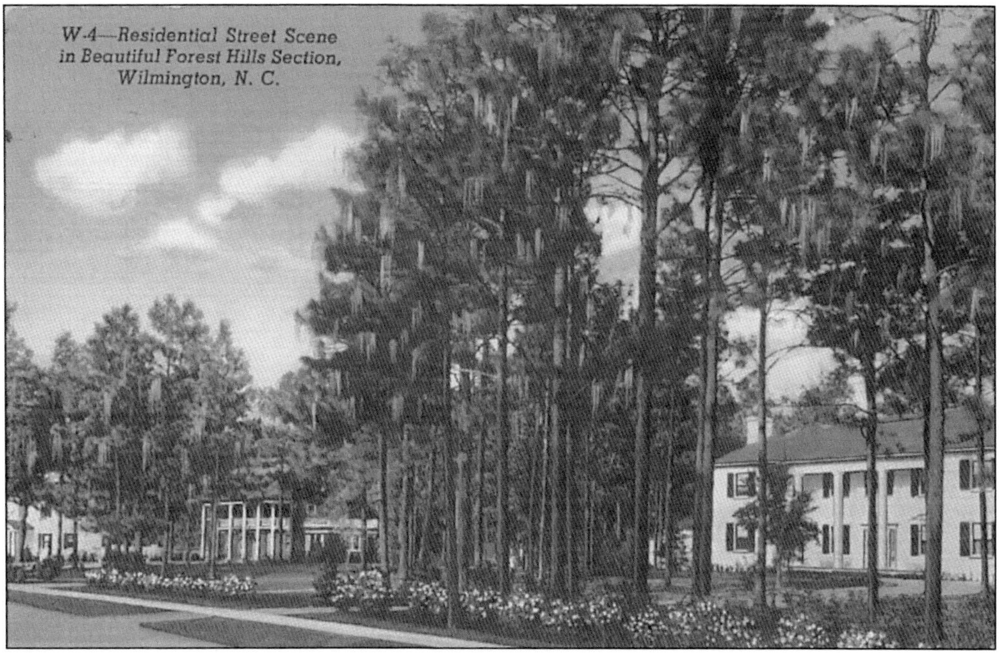

FOREST HILLS, 1944. In 1927, an advertising flyer announced lots for sale by the Forest Hills Development Company, W.A. McGirt, agent. The next year, another ad stated that it was "a charming hilly area, with lovely glens and generous building sites." The price was $1,500 upward. This residential area became one of the best addresses in the city. (Courtesy of Bellamy Mansion Museum.)

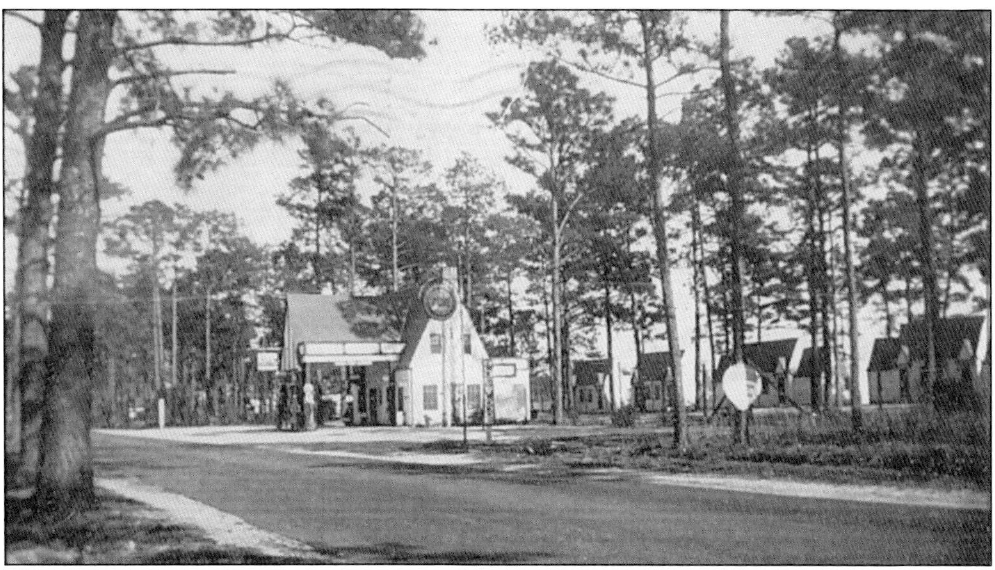

BLUE TOP LODGE, 1940. Before the advent of major national motel chains, motor lodges dotted the landscape along major highways. Catering to travelers, the Blue Top Lodge was located on the Market Street Road, designated U.S. Highway 17. The office was in a Pure Oil filling station, surrounded by tiny cottages. Each cottage had two units and the barest and most basic facilities.

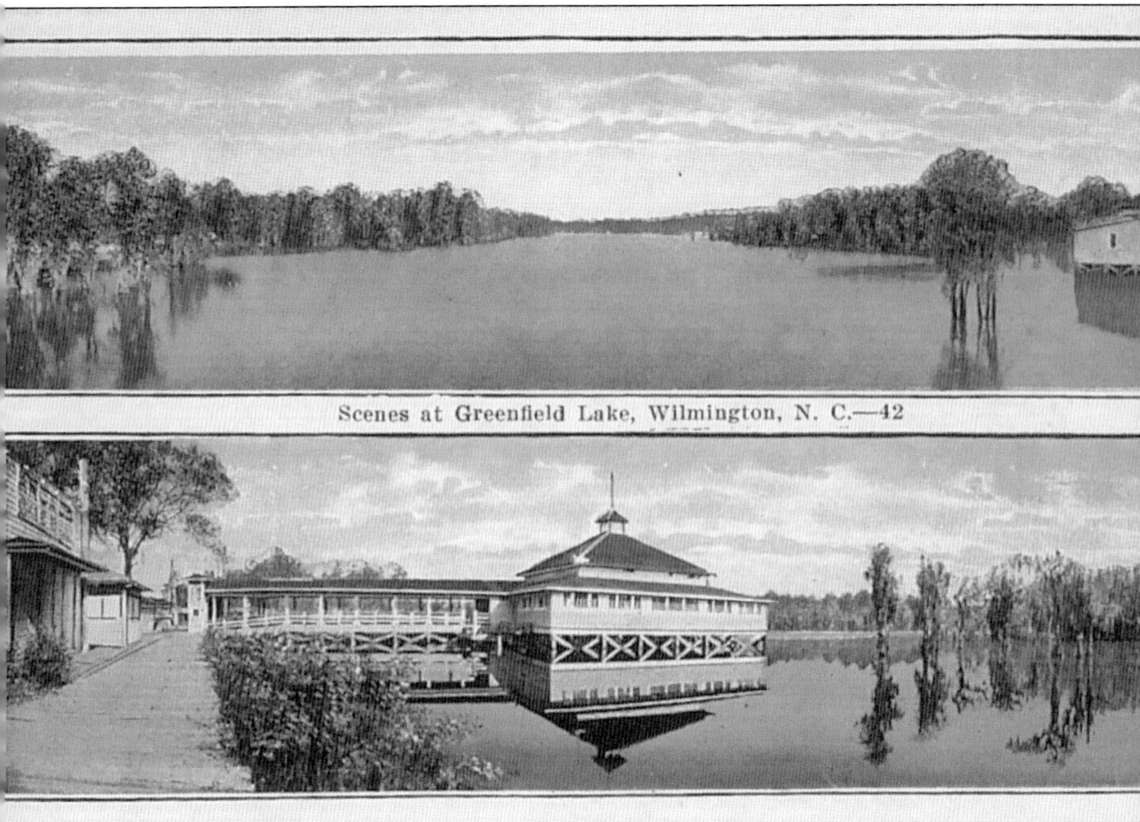

GREENFIELD LAKE, *C.* 1932. Greenfield Lake was named for Dr. Samuel Green, who owned a colonial rice plantation on the site. In 1918, a local women's club, the North Carolina Sorosis, advocated that the city purchase the property for a public park. It was finally acquired in 1925. During the Depression, construction workers for a WPA project completed a 5-mile drive around the perimeter of the lake. It was financed by locally employed workers, who donated a day's pay to help create work for some of the vast numbers of the area's unemployed. With the aid of Dr. Houston Moore and city Public Works Commissioner James E.L. Wade, thousands of azaleas and other flowering shrubs were planted in the park. Cypress trees in the freshwater lake and the Overlake Pavilion are shown in the photographs.

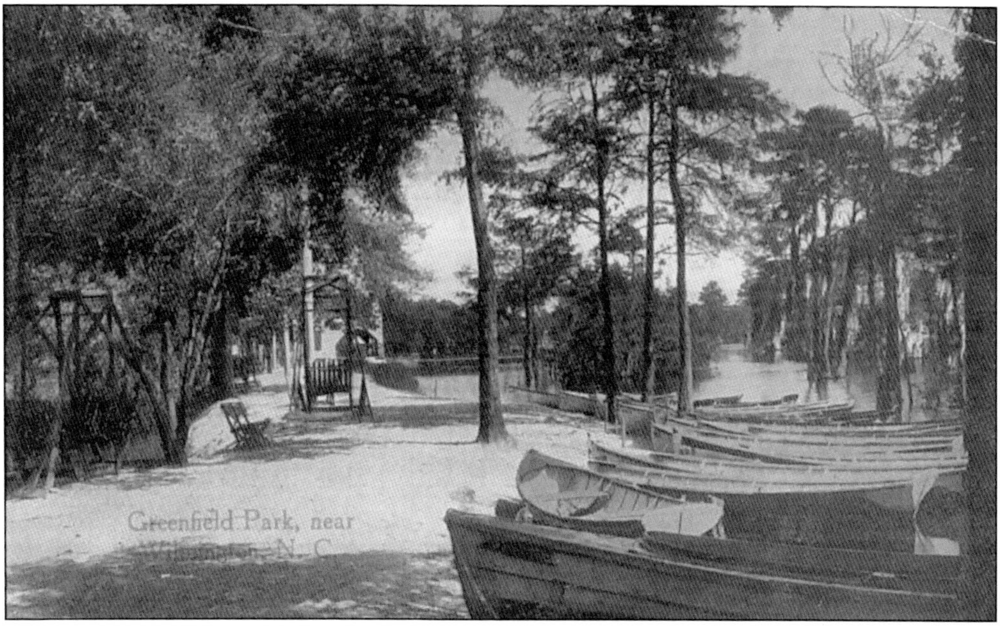

Greenfield Park, 1915. Boats could be rented by the public to leisurely row around tranquil Greenfield Lake. As late as the 1940s, a spring and pump, located near the spillway, provided local residents with drinking water. Many swore by that water's healthful benefits. On occasion, ministers from local churches would baptize their flock by immersion in the lake.

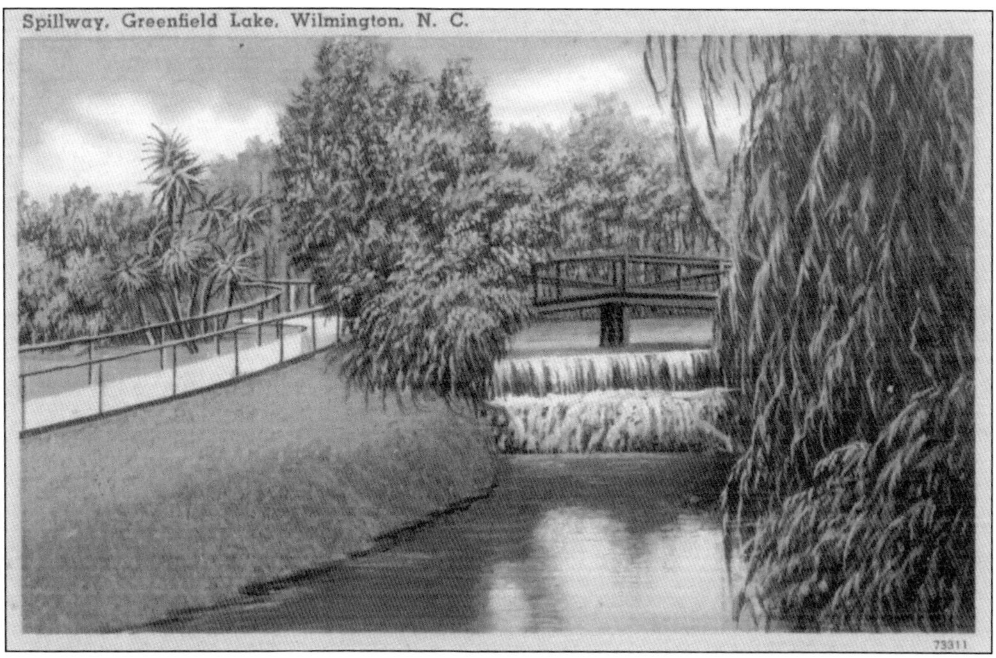

Spillway at Greenfield Lake, 1940. The spillway controls the lake's water level. The water is piped under South Third Street and into the Cape Fear River. Once in the late 1930s, the lake froze over. Since then, that winter has been the benchmark for comparing area winters.

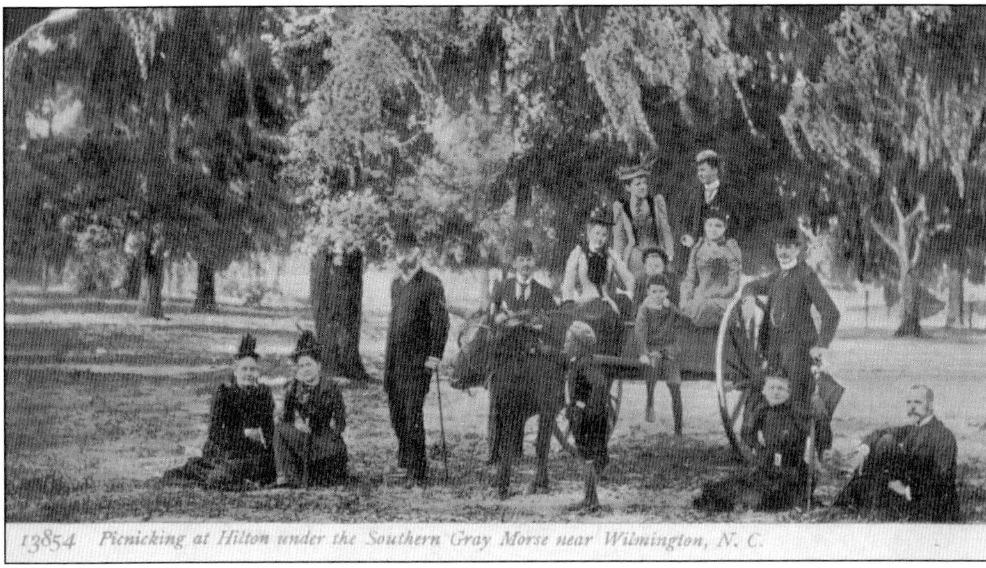

HILTON PARK, C. 1906. Located on the northern edge of Wilmington near the Cape Fear River, Hilton Park was named for the Hill family, who owned the eighteenth-century Hilton Plantation on the property. The photograph shows some local residents "picnicking under the southern gray morse." A popular gathering place, the park also provided a setting for other activities, including political rallies, church socials, golf, and baseball.

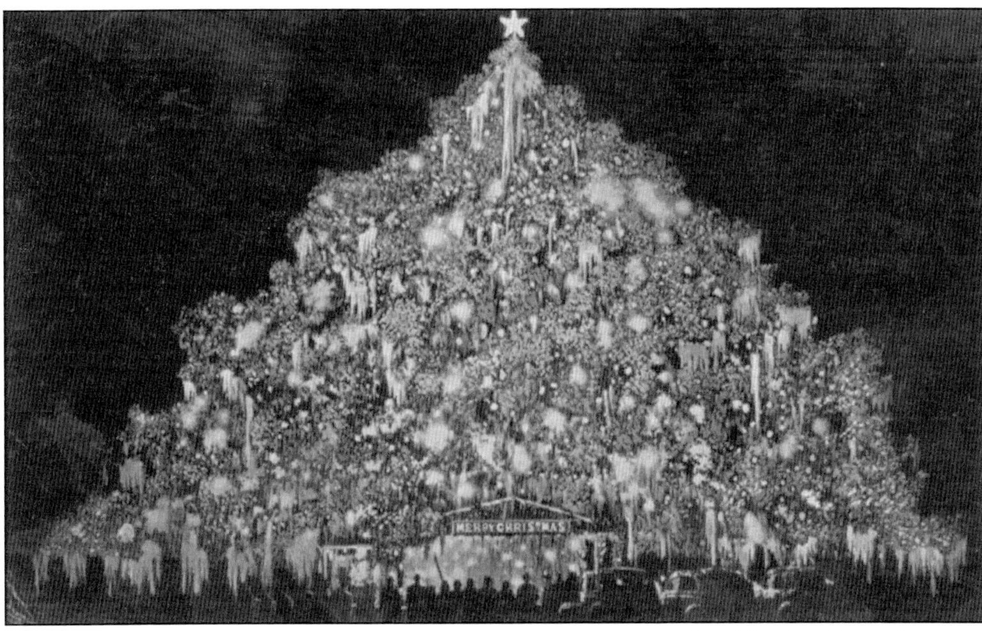

"WORLD'S LARGEST LIVING CHRISTMAS TREE," C. 1932. In the fall of 1928, Wilmington commissioner James E.L. Wade conceived the idea to have a live community Christmas tree. A contest was held to select the largest appropriate tree. A massive live oak in Hilton Park was chosen. First lighted on Christmas Eve 1928, the tree is decorated with over 500 multi-colored lights and a vast quantity of Spanish moss. Except during WW II, it has been lit annually.

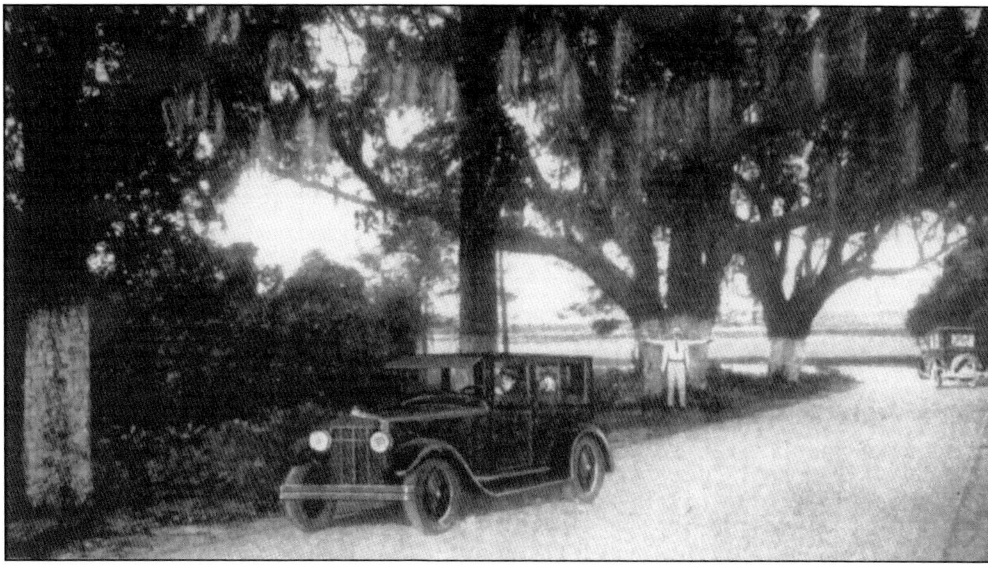

AIRLIE ROAD. One of the most beautiful drives in New Hanover County, Airlie Road begins at Oleander Drive and ends on Wrightsville Sound. The road has massive live oaks, draped with Spanish moss that form a spectacular canopy over the highway. It gets its name from the former Pembroke Jones estate that borders the southern edge of the roadway. Wrightsville Sound can be seen in the background. The whitewashed trees were a local fad during the 1920s.

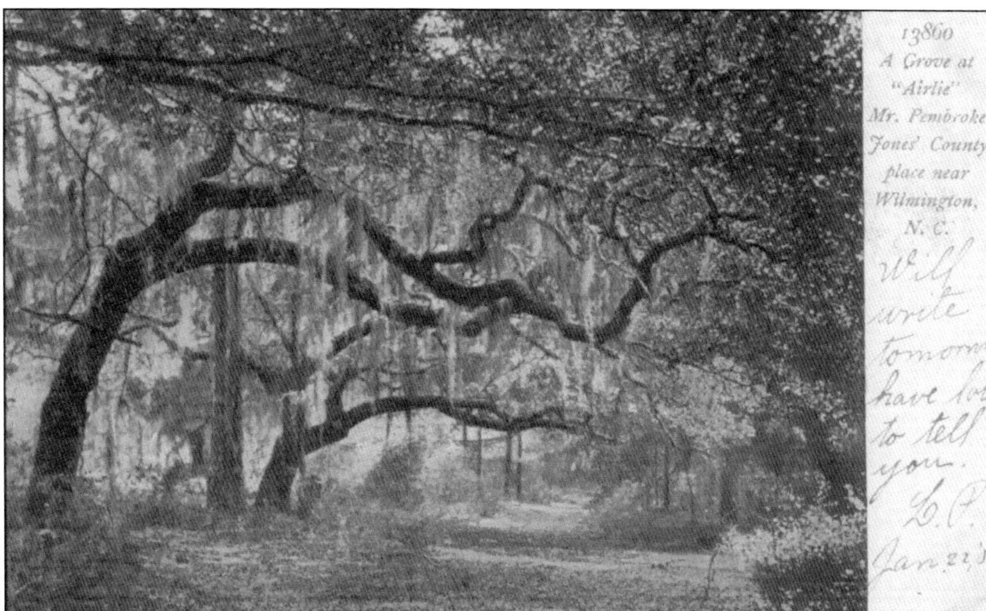

GROVE OF TREES AT AIRLIE, 1907. Between 1884 and 1891, Mr. and Mrs. Pembroke Jones acquired land that ultimately was to become the Airlie Estate on Wrightsville Sound. They used their country estate mainly in the winter and spring, spending the rest of the year in Newport, Rhode Island, or New York City. They constructed a large house on the grounds, which was habitually renovated and enlarged.

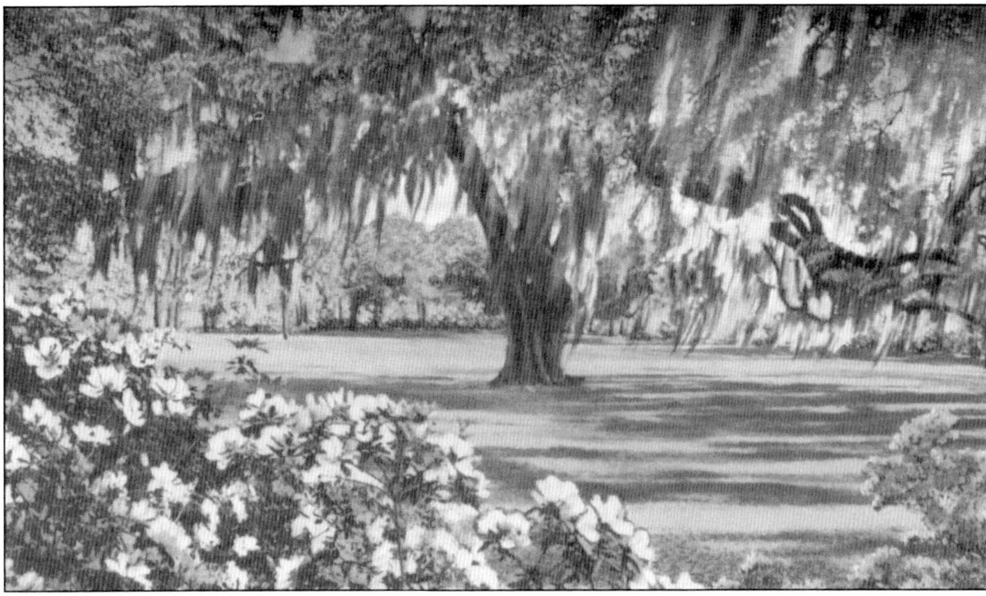

THE AIRLIE OAK, C. 1950. After Pembroke Jones's death in 1919, his widow began in earnest to improve the beautiful flower gardens at Airlie with the help of landscape gardener Rudolph A. Topel. In an interview with author E.T.H. Shaffer in 1937, she stated, "that the magnolia, the azalea, the camellia, and the wisteria were four plants that the Creator intended for Carolina Gardens by the sea," and she planted them in profusion in the gardens.

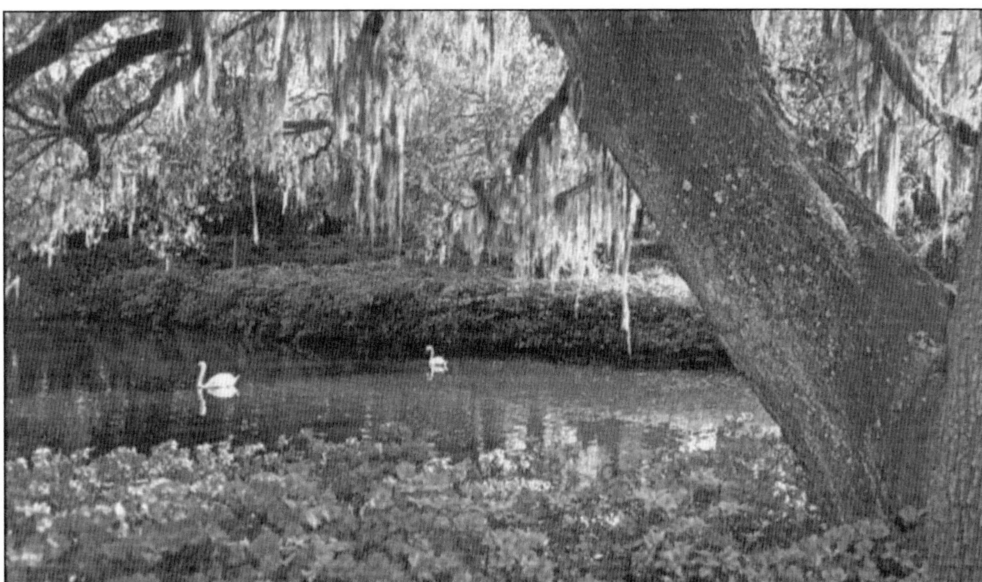

THE LAKE AT AIRLIE, C. 1960. In 1901, dams were constructed and streams were diverted to create a lake at Airlie. Graceful swans were imported to adorn the lake. The gardens were sold to Waddell A. and Bertha Barefoot Corbett in 1948, who added thousands of new plants and opened the gardens to the public each spring. The gardens were purchased by New Hanover County in 1999 for use as a public park. (Courtesy of Hugh Morton.)

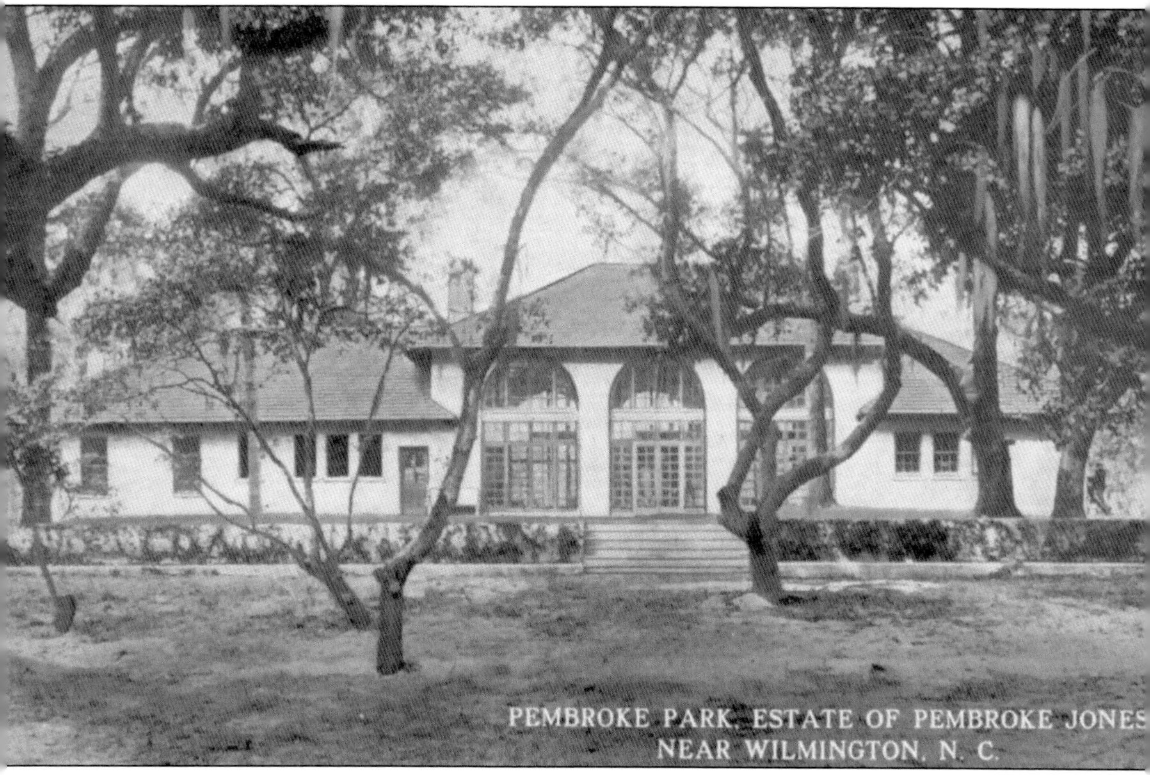

PEMBROKE PARK, WRIGHTSVILLE SOUND, *c.* 1910. A Wilmington native, the wealthy Pembroke Jones (1858–1919) made his fortune in rice milling and railroad businesses. Already the owner of Airlie, he purchased land in 1902, which bordered Wrightsville Sound near Summer's Rest. He built a shell road from his Airlie estate on Bradley Creek to the property, designated as Pembroke Park. The entrance to the park was on the Shell Road (Wrightsville Avenue) just to the west of McCumber's Station. The hunting lodge was an Italianate villa, designed by J. Stewart Barney. The house had lavish furnishings, many of which were purchased abroad. The heavily wooded park was a game preserve and a hunter's paradise. The Joneses entertained a number of New York and Newport, Rhode Island society titans, including the Vanderbilts, Drexels, and Fishes, at fabulous house parties, both at Airlie and at Pembroke Park. The only remaining structure from this "Gilded Age" era is a gazebo, designed by John Russell Pope, Jones's son-in-law. Today, the park is the gated community of Landfall.

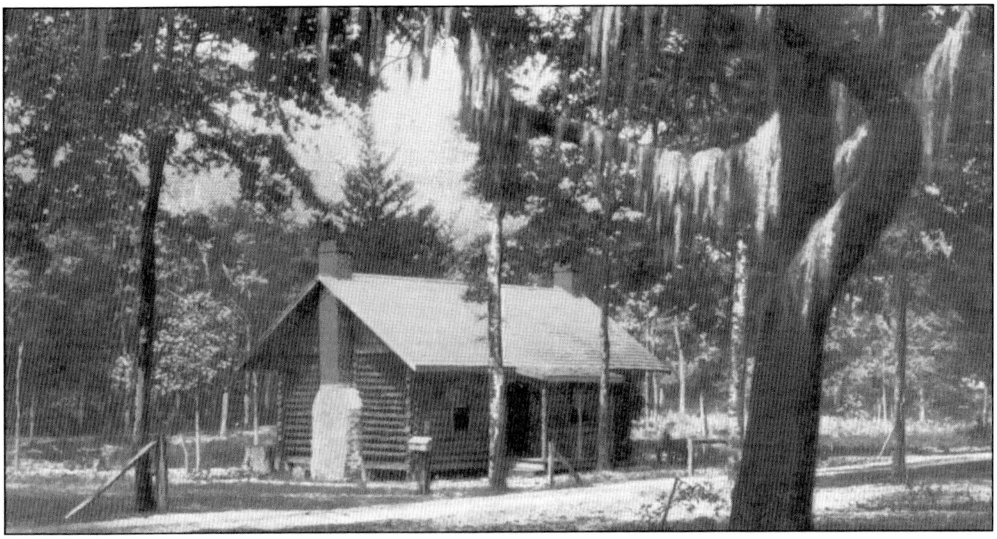

LOG CABIN, W.L. PARSLEY ESTATE, MASONBORO SOUND, 1915. Walter Linton Parsley (1856–1941) built his handsome residence, "Live Oaks," on Masonboro Sound in 1912–1913. A log cabin on the Parsley property was located across the road from this house. It appears to be servants' quarters and the date of its construction is unknown. Bill Hurst, a longtime Sound resident, recalls, "Across a private concrete road from the log cabin was a barn and for years, an old mule stood in the field. I never saw the old mule worked. He must have served his time."

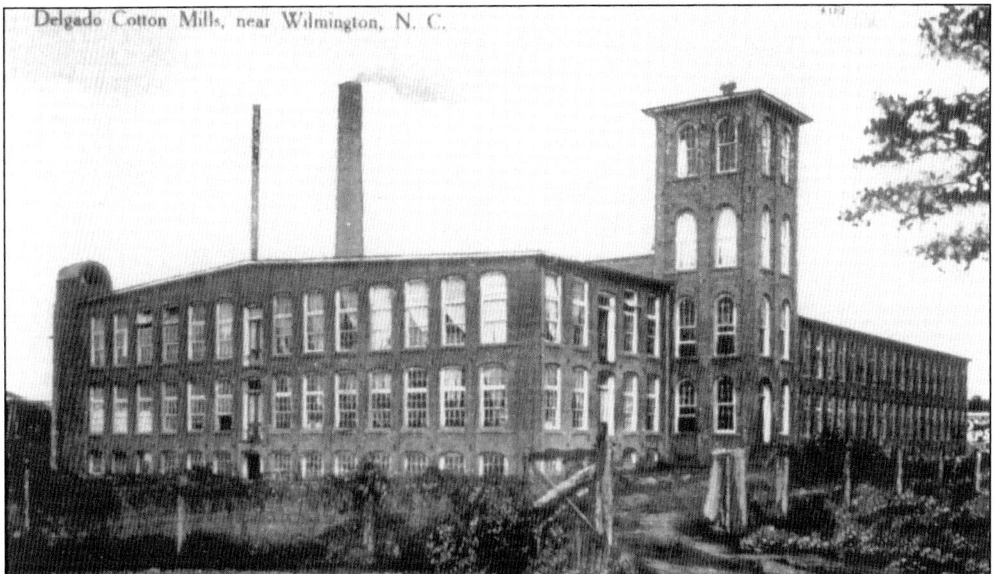

DELGADO MILLS, C. 1910. In 1899–1900, Delgado Cotton Mills and its surrounding village was constructed on the Shell Road (Wrightsville Avenue) about 2 miles east of downtown. Raleigh architects Zachery and Zachery designed the huge building that by 1920 had over 400 employees. The mill produced cotton broadcloth, madras, seersucker and gingham. Renamed Spofford Mills in 1930, it continued in operation until 1967. The building was razed in the 1972.

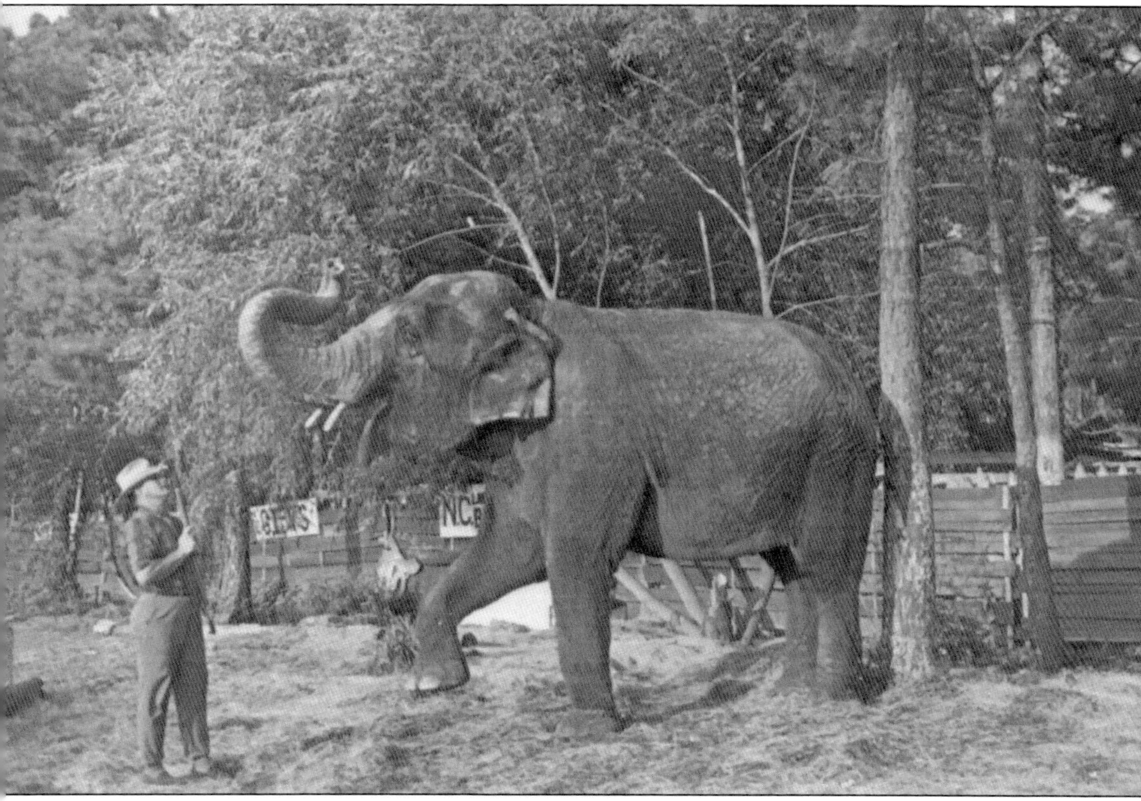

Tote-Em-In Zoo, *c.* 1960. A native of Maine, George Tregembo was stationed at Seymour Johnson Airbase near Goldsboro during WW II. Before deciding to return to the mild North Carolina climate, he operated a zoo in his home state for three years. After settling in Wilmington in January 1953, he opened the Tote-Em-In Zoo on Carolina Beach Road near Monkey Junction. This postcard announced the acquisition of Matteau, an Indian elephant, who weighed over 3.5 tons and stood 9 feet tall. Matteau died on November 22, 1991, at the age of 80. (Courtesy of George Tregembo.)

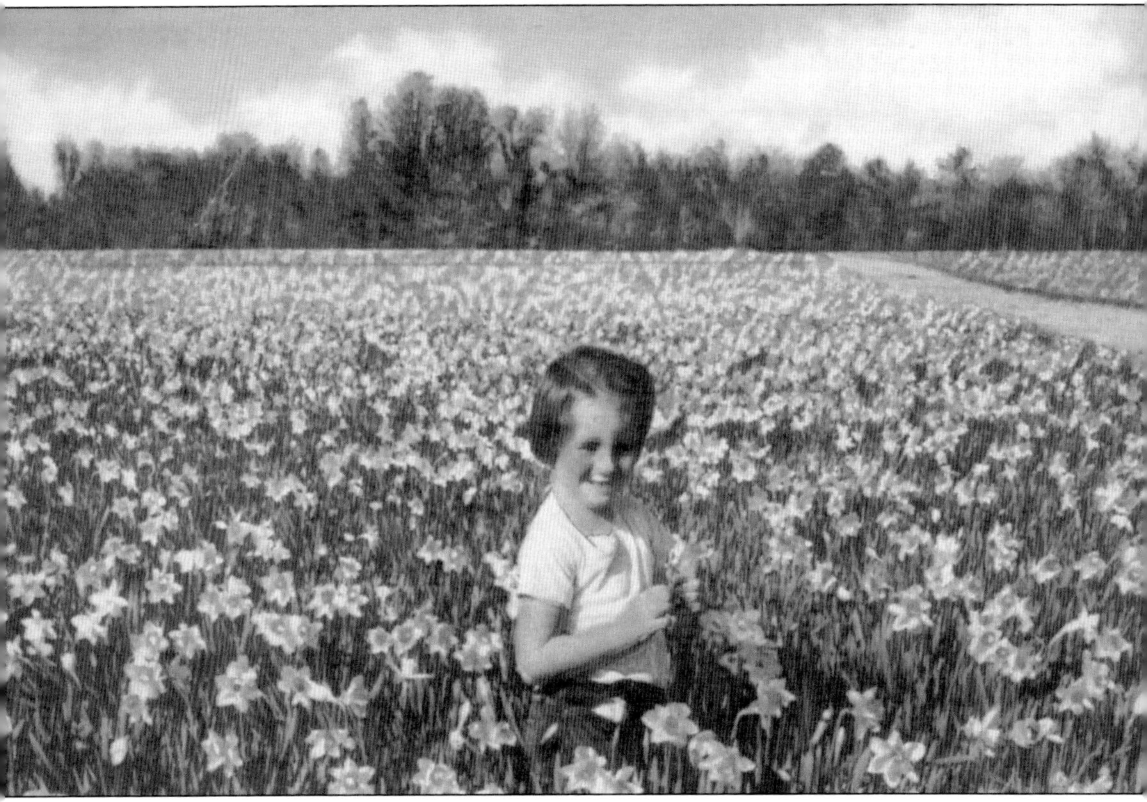

CASTLE HAYNE, *C.* 1956. Castle Hayne is an unincorporated rural community in northern New Hanover County. It was named for Colonel Roger Haynes (died before November 1739), who owned a colonial plantation in the area. During the first decades of the last century, Hugh MacRae, a Wilmington real estate developer, was instrumental in bringing a number of immigrants from the Netherlands to the county. The Dutch settlers farmed the rich soil growing tulips, daffodils, and gladioli. The cut flowers were shipped to markets all over the nation. (Courtesy of Hugh Morton.)

Four

INSTITUTIONS

Wilmington has long been known as "a city of beautiful churches." The variety of the architecture is astounding from the Moorish design of the Temple of Israel to several Gothic Revival structures and the Spanish Baroque St. Mary's Roman Catholic Church. Nationally known architects, including Thomas U. Walter, Samuel Sloan, Rafael Guastravino Sr. and Jr., and Hobart Upjohn, designed some very impressive buildings.

Elementary schools, such as Big Union, Isaac Bear, and Tileston, evoke many childhood memories of favorite teachers and fellow pupils. Who doesn't recall the high school years of attending football and basketball games or the senior prom? Today, many local residents are proud alumni of Wilmington College, which is now the University of North Carolina at Wilmington.

The hospitals have been scenes of joy and sorrow. The clubs have provided recreation and leisure activities. All of these institutions have touched our lives in one way or another.

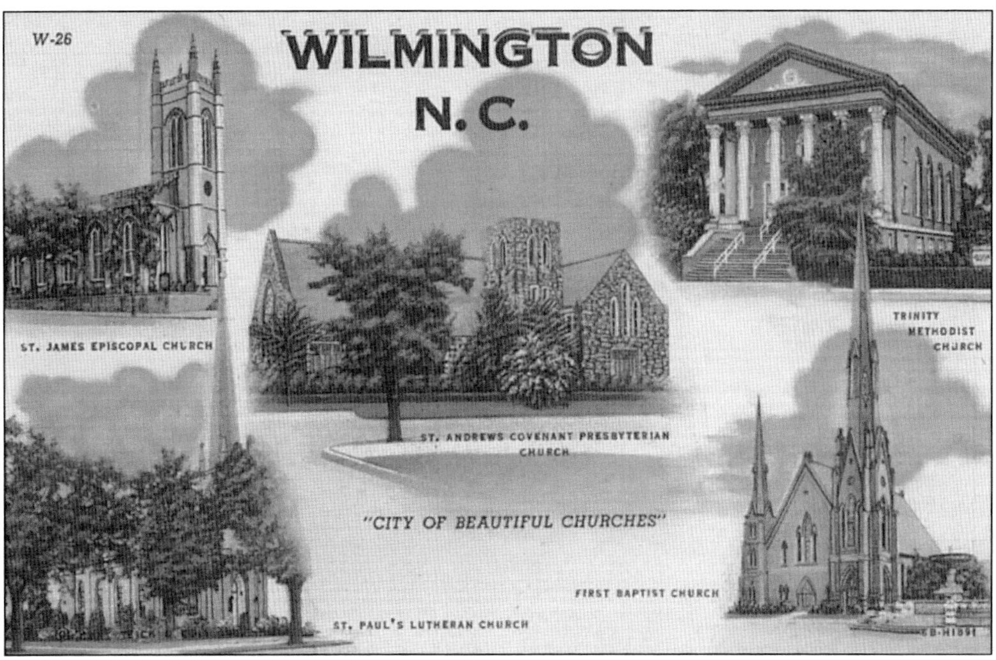

"CITY OF BEAUTIFUL CHURCHES," 1940S. Five churches are shown in this montage, including Trinity United Methodist Church in the top right-hand corner. Designed by architect Leslie N. Boney for W.J. Wilkins & Co. of Wilmington, the Neo-Classical Revival–style building is located at Fourteenth and Market Streets.

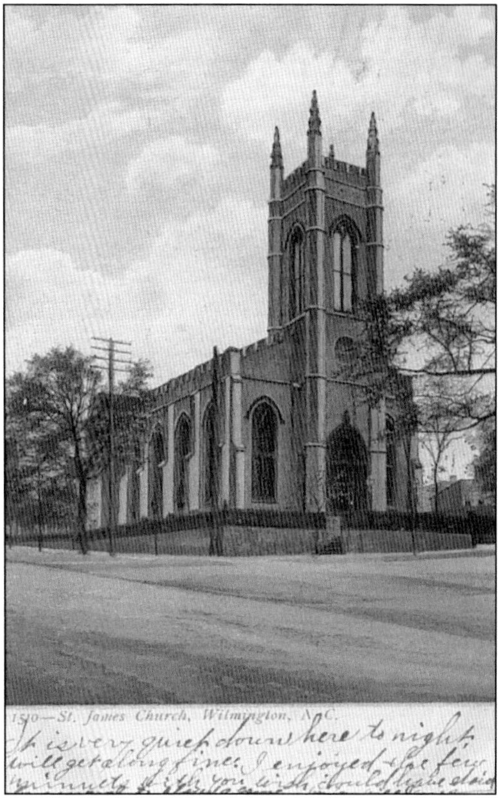

ST. JAMES EPISCOPAL CHURCH, 1910. St. James Parish was established by the General Assembly of the Colony of Carolina in 1729. The original church (built between 1751 and 1770) was in the middle of what is now Market Street, between Third and Fourth Streets. Thomas U. Walter of New York designed this second Gothic Revival–style building, which was consecrated on March 29, 1840.

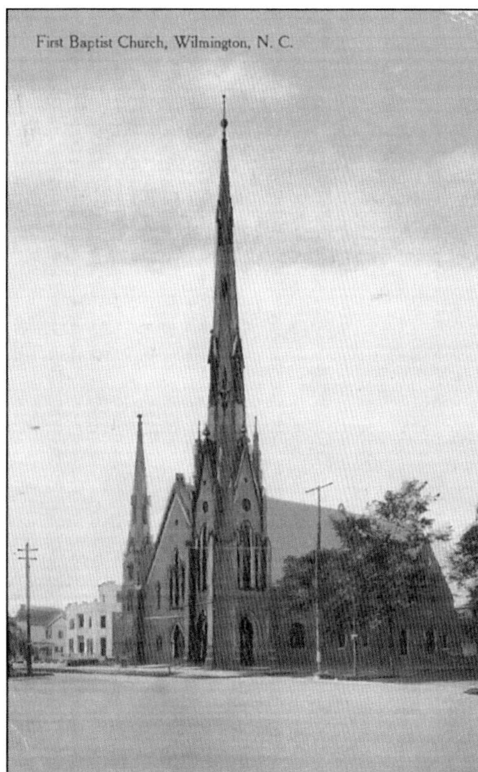

FIRST BAPTIST CHURCH, 1913. In 1808, Baptists began worshipping in a frame building on North Front Street between Ann and Nun Streets. In 1859, construction began on the First Baptist Church at the corner of Fifth and Market Streets. Designed by Samuel Sloan, this impressive building of red brick and stone has twin spires. The highest steeple rises 197 feet and was said to be the tallest in the United States when it was completed in 1870. In 1996, winds of Hurricane Fran toppled the lofty steeple and it has since been rebuilt and returned to its original style.

FIRST PRESBYTERIAN CHURCH, 1910. Fire destroyed the first two sanctuaries of First Presbyterian Church. After the last fire in 1859, the church purchased a lot on the corner of Third and Orange Streets and constructed a Gothic Revival–style building, designed by Samuel Sloan. It was completed in 1861. The manse (far right) was the home of the Reverend Joseph R. Wilson, pastor, 1874–1885, and father of U.S. President Woodrow Wilson. For the third time, a sanctuary of this church was devastated by a midnight fire on New Year's Eve 1925.

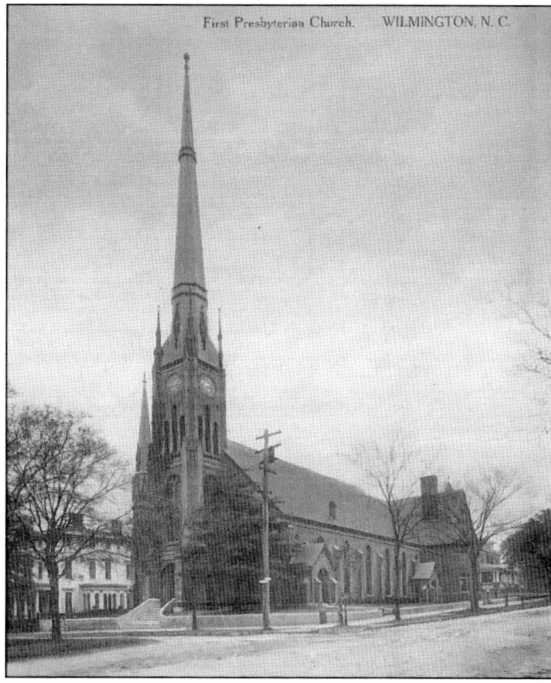

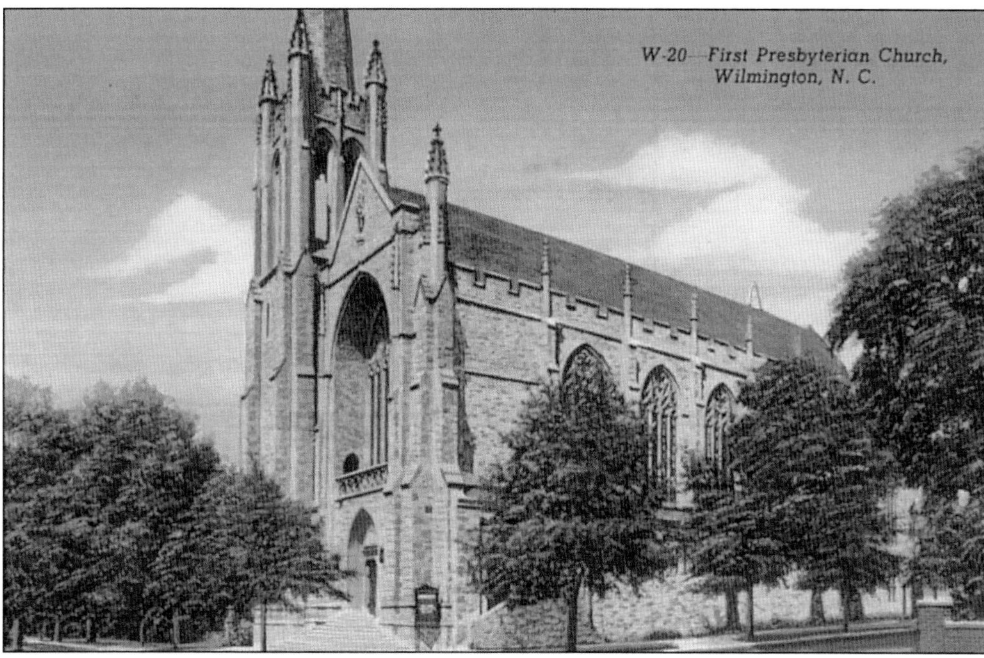

FIRST PRESBYTERIAN CHURCH, C. 1940. After the 1925 fire, plans were begun immediately to rebuild the First Presbyterian Church on the same site. Hobart Upjohn, a noted ecclesiastical architect, was chosen to design the new building. The late Gothic Revival–style structure was built of rough-edged stone and contains a small Norman chapel. A rooster weather vane cast by Wilmington Iron Works tops the spire. The church was dedicated November 18, 1928. (Courtesy of Bellamy Mansion Museum.)

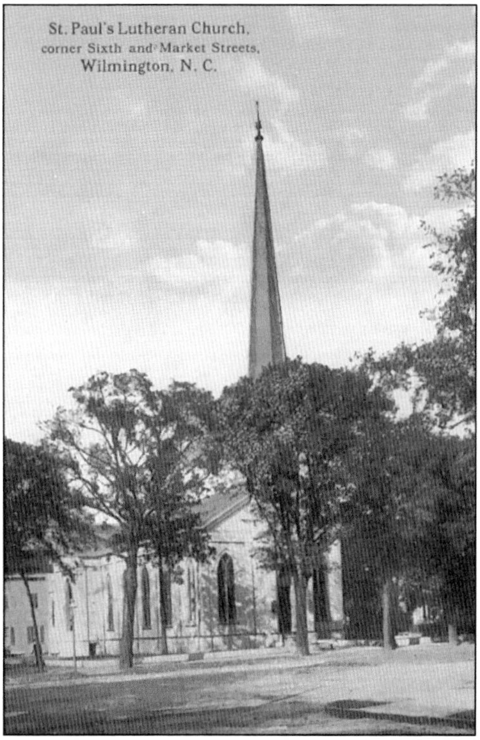

ST. PAUL'S EVANGELICAL LUTHERAN CHURCH, 1910. In May 1858, St. Paul's was organized by German immigrants, most of whom were from the Kingdom of Hannover. The Gothic Revival–style building was begun in 1859. War, the yellow fever epidemic, and the Federal occupation of Wilmington delayed the completion of the building until 1869. Fourteen memorial windows of opalescent stained glass were installed between 1908 and 1921 by the Frank Ellsworth Weeder Company of Philadelphia.

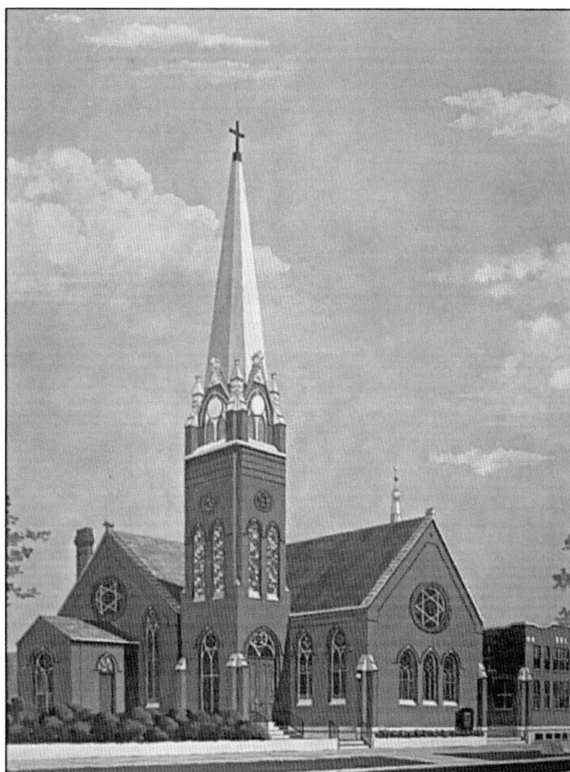

FIFTH AVENUE METHODIST CHURCH. Organized in 1847 as a mission from Front Street Methodist Church, the building was designed by architect B.D. Price. The Gothic building replaced an older frame structure, in which Charlie Soong was converted to Christianity in 1880. Soong was the father of two daughters who married Sun Yat-Sen and Chaing Kai-Shek, famous Chinese leaders. When this sanctuary was completed in 1890, reputedly, it had the largest seating capacity of any church in North Carolina at 1,500.

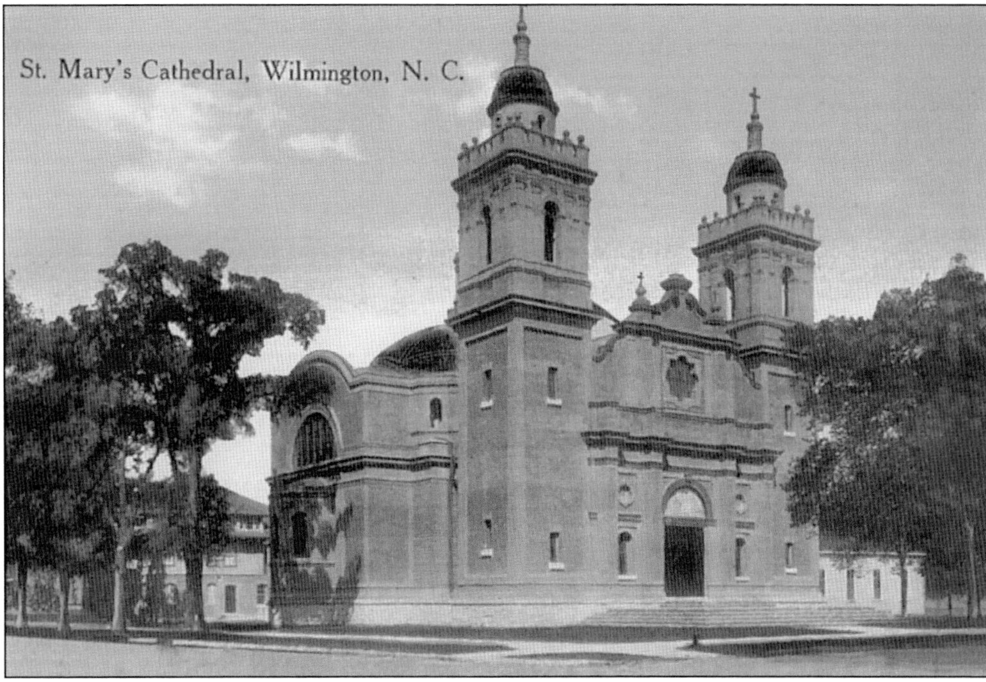

ST. MARY'S ROMAN CATHOLIC PRO-CATHEDRAL, 1918. Dedicated on April 28, 1912, the Spanish Baroque–style church was built on the northwestern corner of Fifth Avenue and Ann Street by Rafael Guastavino (father) and Rafael Guastavino (son), both natives of Spain. At the time of the construction, local residents were amazed that the structure contained no nails. Instead, the builders made extensive use of brick and tile.

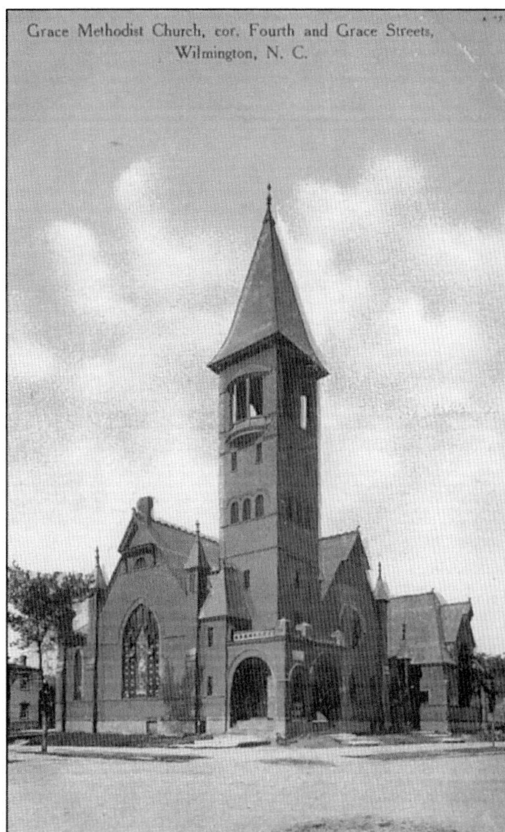

GRACE METHODIST CHURCH, *c.* 1910. Organized in 1796 as Front Street Methodist Church, the church has had four fires in its long history. After a disastrous fire in 1886, the church moved from Front Street to the northeastern corner of Fourth and Mulberry Streets and was renamed Grace Methodist Church. It was dedicated on December 7, 1890. Mulberry Street was renamed Grace Street in 1895. Unbelievably, the church burned again on March 21, 1947. Designed by Harold Wagner of Philadelphia, the present church was rebuilt on the same site.

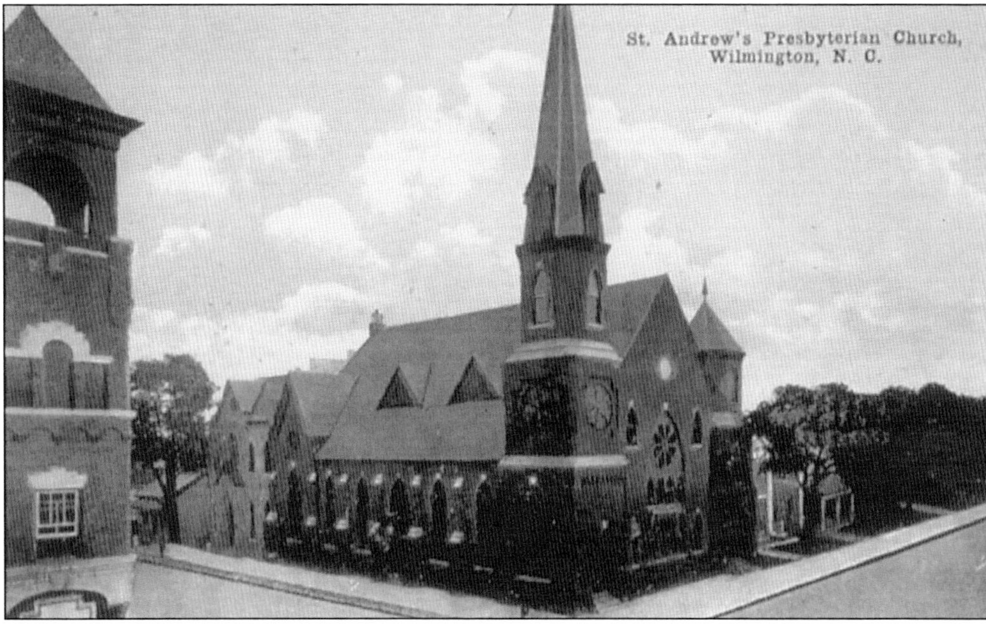

ST. ANDREWS PRESBYTERIAN CHURCH. Known as Second Presbyterian Church when it organized in 1858, St. Andrews was originally located on Chestnut Street. It was re-organized, renamed, and relocated in 1872. Designed by Adolphus Gustav Bauer, St. Andrews Presbyterian Church at 520 North Fourth Street was built in 1888–1889. In 1944, the church merged with the Church of the Covenant, occupying the latter's Fifteenth Street facilities. Through preservation efforts, this church building was saved from demolition in the 1990s.

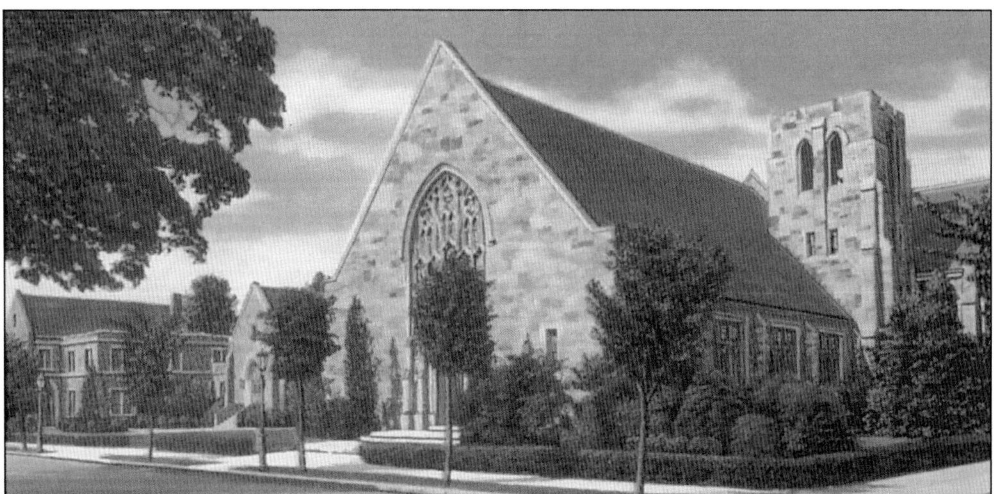

ST. ANDREWS-COVENANT PRESBYTERIAN CHURCH, 1948. Organized in 1917, the Church of the Covenant Presbyterian Church was designed in the Gothic Revival style by Kenneth M. Murchison and James Gause. When the two churches merged in 1944, both names were adopted. Each spring, Wilmingtonians traveling down Market Street marvel at the unusual ginkgo trees in bloom. The trees were brought from China to Wilmington by missionaries and planted in 1918–1919.

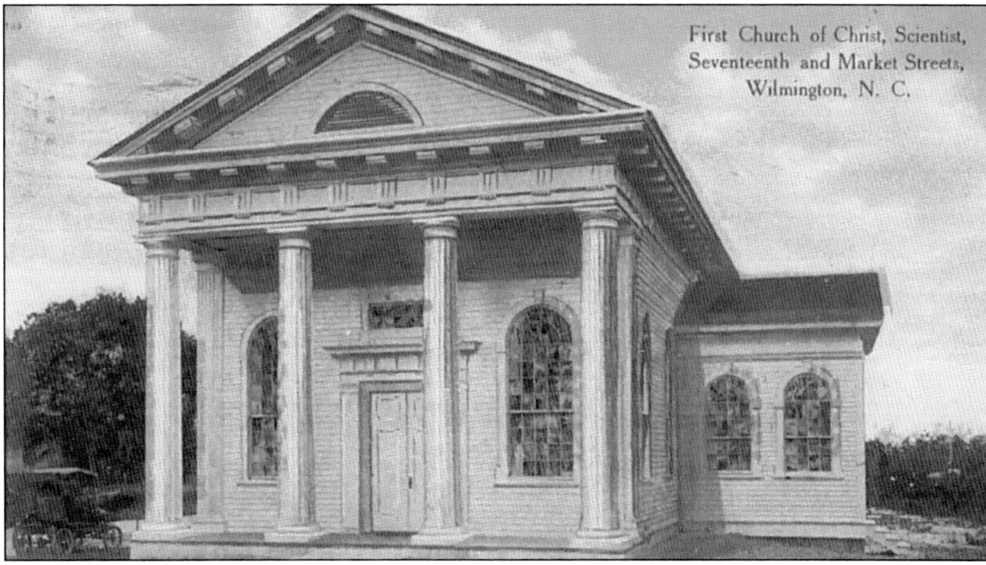

THE FIRST CHURCH OF CHRIST, SCIENTIST, 1910. Located on the southeastern corner of Seventeenth and Market Streets, the Neo-Classical Revival–style church was built on land donated by Mary Bridgers, a devout Christian Scientist and developer of Carolina Heights. Completed in 1907, the building was sold to Temple Baptist Church in 1923 after the Christian Scientists moved to their new home on the corner of Seventeenth and Chestnut Streets. This church burned in 1952.

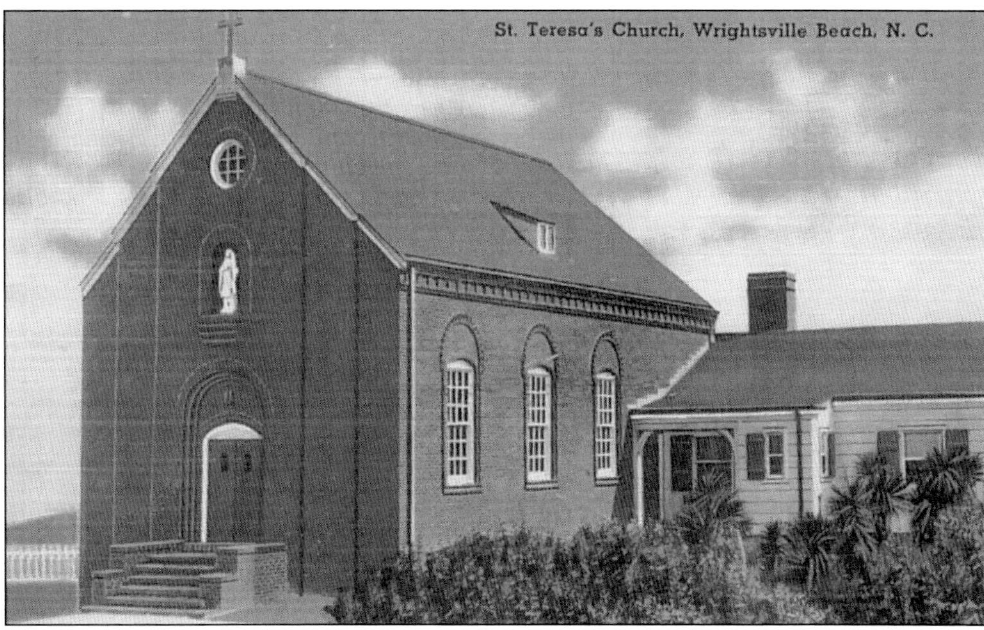

ST. THERESA'S ROMAN CATHOLIC CHURCH, *C.* 1940S. The oldest church on Wrightsville Beach, St. Theresa's was originally constructed in the late 1890s as a summer chapel for beach goers. Known first as St. Mary's-by-the Sea, the first frame building was constructed on land donated by Michael Corbett, a prominent Catholic layman. The name was changed in 1944 when the new brick structure, shown above, was erected.

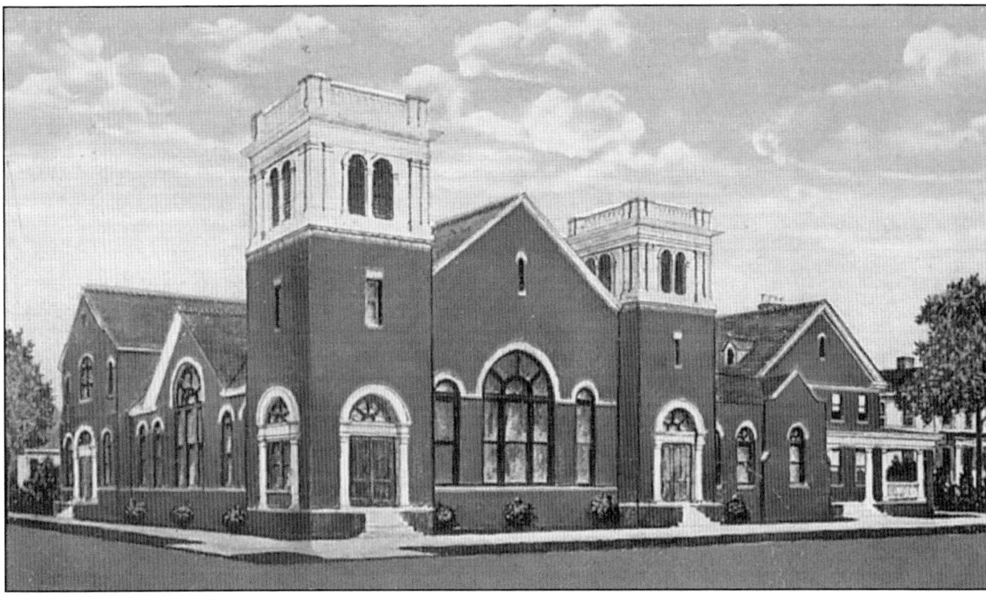

CALVARY BAPTIST CHURCH, 1922. Organized as a mission of First Baptist Church in 1886, Calvary Baptist Church served the city's growing northside population. In 1906, the church erected a large frame building on the corner of Fourth and Brunswick Streets. The outside of this building was brick veneered in 1919. In 1955, Calvary moved to the suburbs on North Twenty-Third Street.

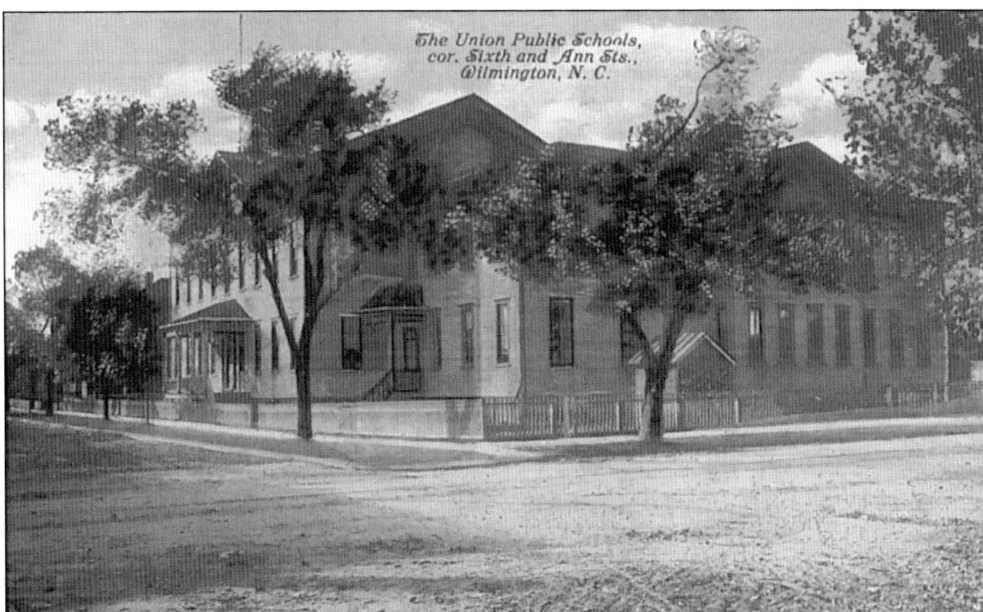

UNION SCHOOL, 1910. Known to pupils as "Big Union School," this large wooden structure was built on the northwestern corner of Sixth and Ann Streets in 1891. It replaced a former school that had burned in the spring of that year. The dedicated staff included Miss Mary C. "Nellie" Cook, principal, and teachers including Maude Kingsbury, Hester Struthers, and Miriam McEachern. The strictest one was Miss Addie Meares, a legend in her own time.

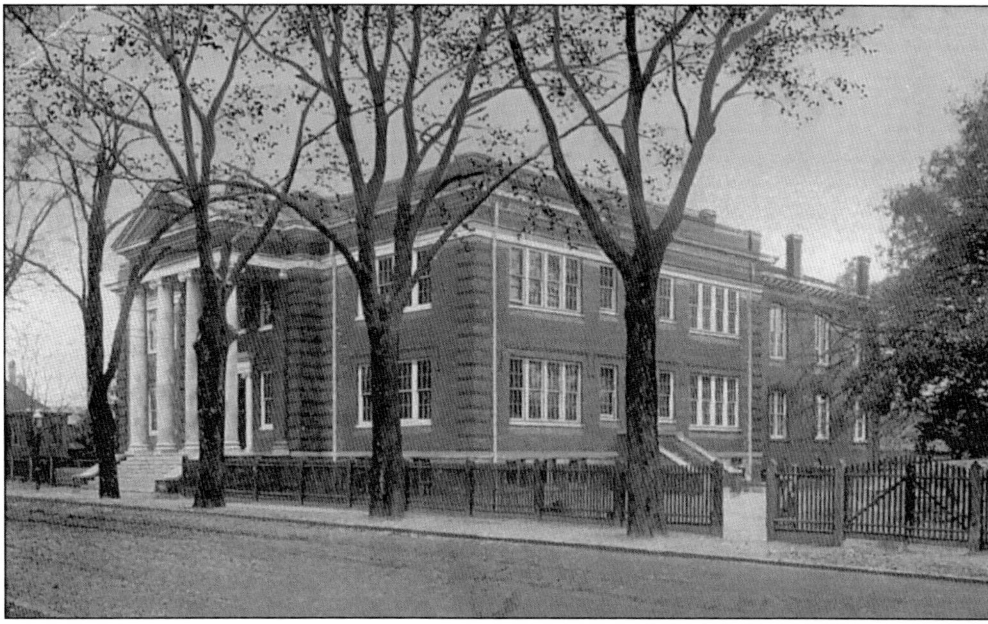

Wilmington High School, c. 1910. The area's oldest surviving school building, Wilmington High School was funded by wealthy Boston philanthropist Mary Tileston Hemingway, who named the school after her father. Opened in 1872 as Tileston Normal School, the Italianate-style building was designed by John A. Fox of Boston. In the early 1900s, the structure became Wilmington High School, serving in that capacity until New Hanover High School was opened in the early 1920s. Since then, at various times, it has been an elementary or junior high school and now is owned by St. Mary's Roman Catholic Church.

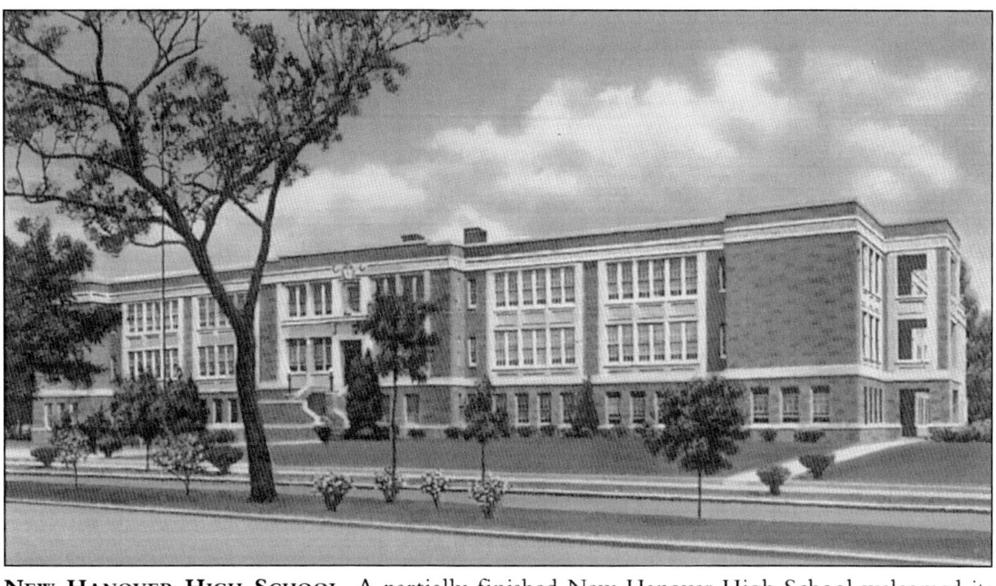

New Hanover High School. A partially finished New Hanover High School welcomed its first students in 1920. By 1922, the school was the largest high school in North Carolina with 840 students. Located on Market Street between Thirteenth and Fourteenth Streets, the huge yellow-brick building was designed by W.J. Wilkins & Co., Architects.

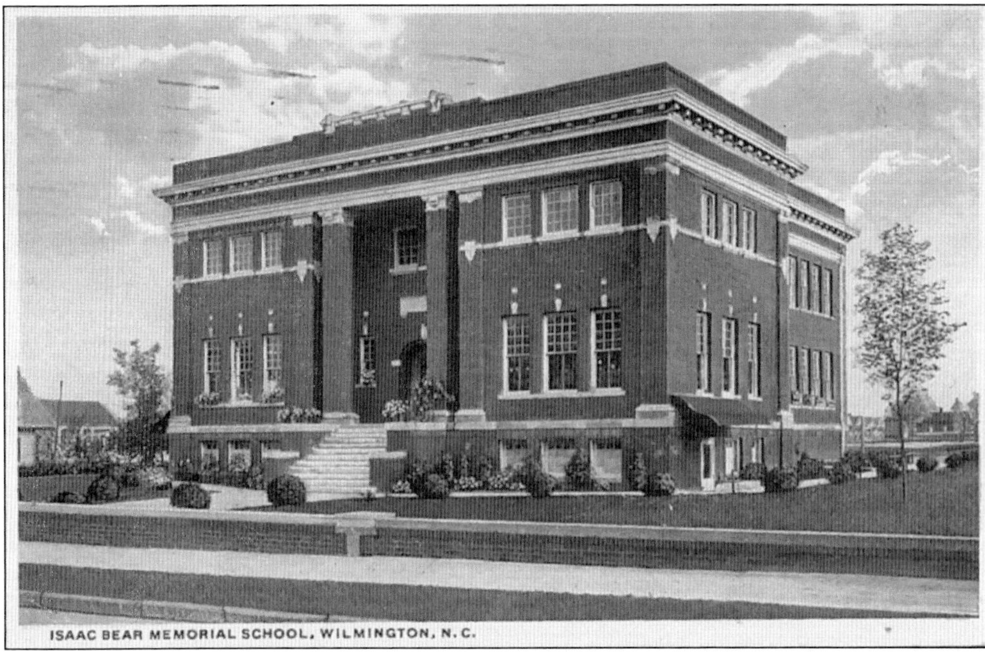

ISAAC BEAR SCHOOL, *C.* 1918. Built in 1912, Isaac Bear School was funded by Samuel Bear (*c.* 1854–1916) as a memorial to his brother, Isaac Bear (1852–1911). The handsome building was an elementary school until the mid-1940s, serving students residing in the eastern part of the city. It was the first home of Wilmington College (UNC-W). The main building was razed in the 1960s.

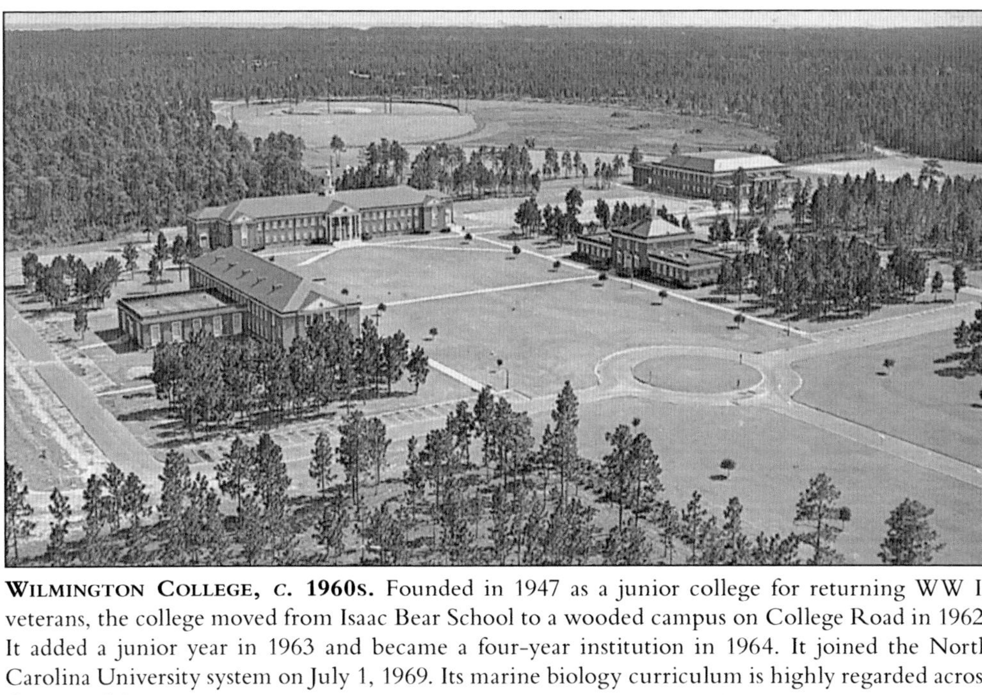

WILMINGTON COLLEGE, *C.* 1960S. Founded in 1947 as a junior college for returning WW II veterans, the college moved from Isaac Bear School to a wooded campus on College Road in 1962. It added a junior year in 1963 and became a four-year institution in 1964. It joined the North Carolina University system on July 1, 1969. Its marine biology curriculum is highly regarded across the United States.

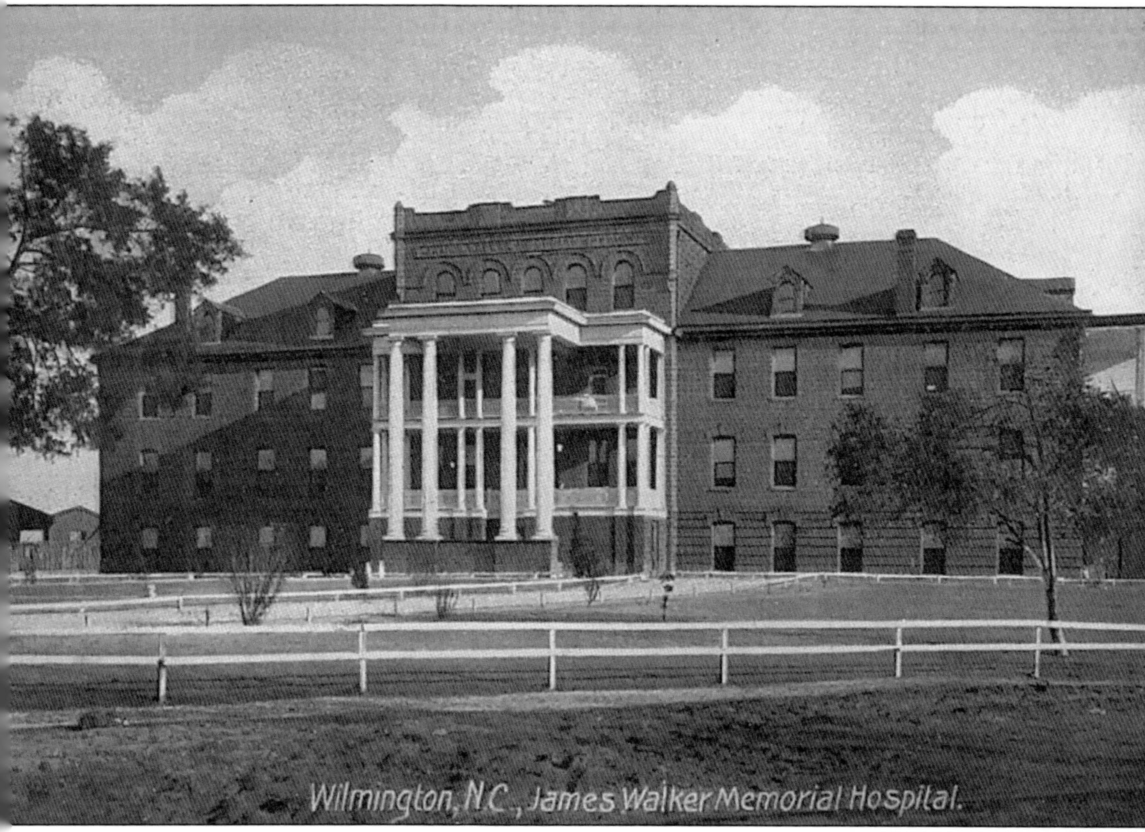

JAMES WALKER MEMORIAL HOSPITAL, 1907. A contractor, James Walker was a native of Douglas, Lanarkshire, Scotland, who first came to Wilmington in 1857 to supervise the construction of the U.S. Marine Hospital. After the completion of his initial project, he decided to make Wilmington his permanent home, living for a number of years in a modest home on the southeastern corner of Sixteenth and Market Streets. A bachelor, he amassed considerable wealth and decided to donate to his adopted home funds for a modern hospital. With this money, property was secured on the southeastern corner of Tenth and Rankin Streets, where the first ceremonial brick was laid on May 22, 1900. Unfortunately, Mr. Walker did not live to see the project completed. He died on March 15, 1901, just months before the building was completed on June 1, 1901. Designed by Kenneth M. Murchison, this hospital had space for 50 beds, a self-contained laundry, and separate wards for men and women. Over the years, other generous residents gave funds for the expansion of the hospital, including W.H. Sprunt, Samuel Bear, and Dr. and Mrs. James Sprunt.

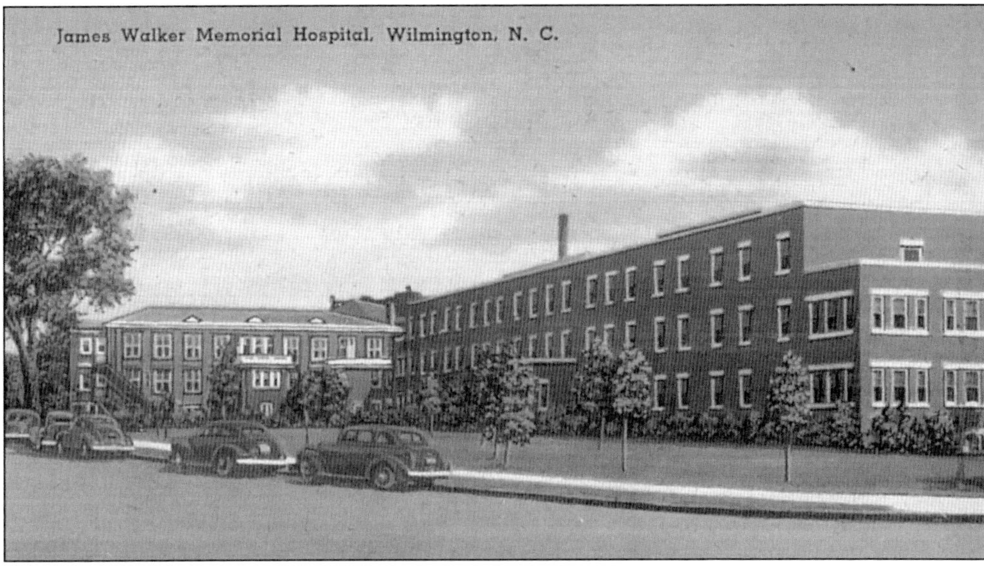

JAMES WALKER MEMORIAL HOSPITAL, *c.* 1940S. During WW II, the population of Wilmington doubled almost overnight, and an addition to James Walker Memorial Hospital became a critical need. The U.S. government funded part of the new three-story building, which contained rooms for women. Men were housed in the older buildings. All of the James Walker structures, except the Nurses' Home, were demolished in the early 1970s after the hospital moved across town.

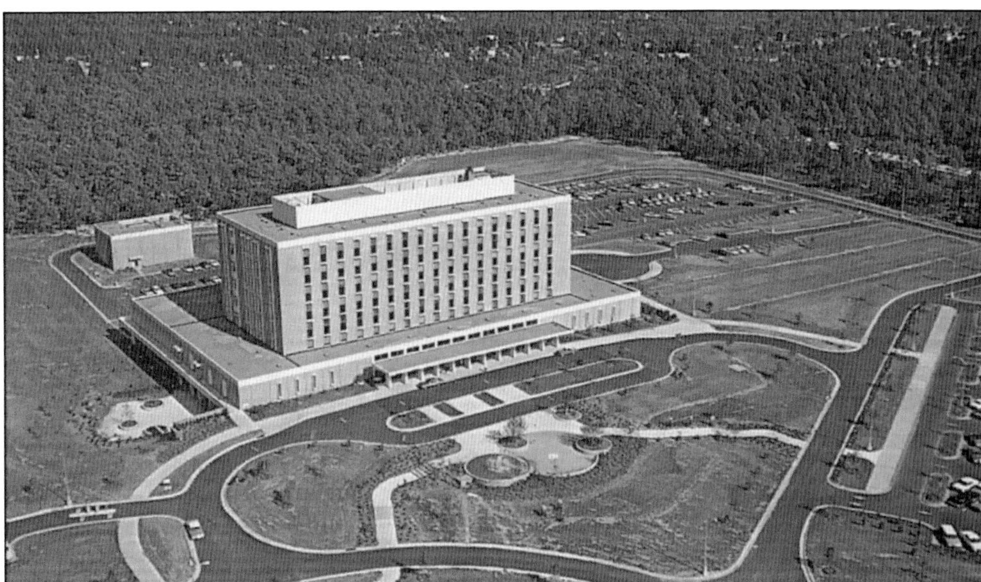

NEW HANOVER MEMORIAL HOSPITAL, 1967. In November 1961, New Hanover County residents passed a hospital bond issue by only a few hundred votes, enabling a new hospital to be built. The 404-bed facility on South Seventeenth Street was completed by June 1967 and named New Hanover Memorial Hospital. Community Hospital, which had served African-American residents since the 1920s, was closed and the new hospital was desegregated. (Courtesy of Hugh Morton.)

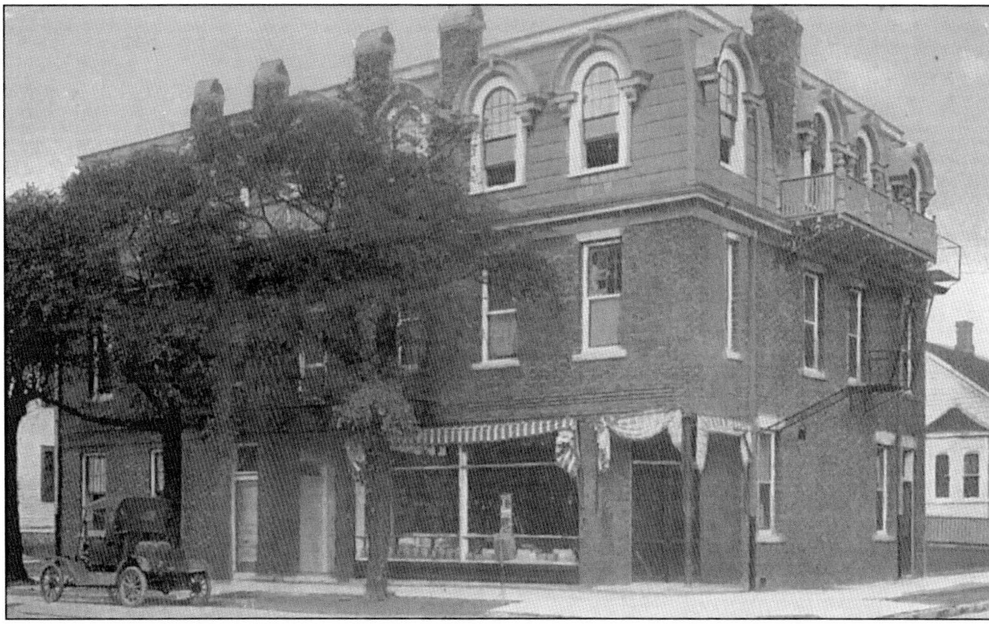

HARPER'S SANATORIUM, 1913. Dr. Charles Harper built his private hospital in 1910 on the northeastern corner of Front and Castle Streets. The hospital was in operation on the top floors of the building until shortly after Dr. Harper's death in 1915, from complications following an appendectomy. The richly detailed red-brick structure had a handsome mansard roof. In later years, a pharmacy occupied the ground floor of the building. Regrettably, the building was razed in the 1960s.

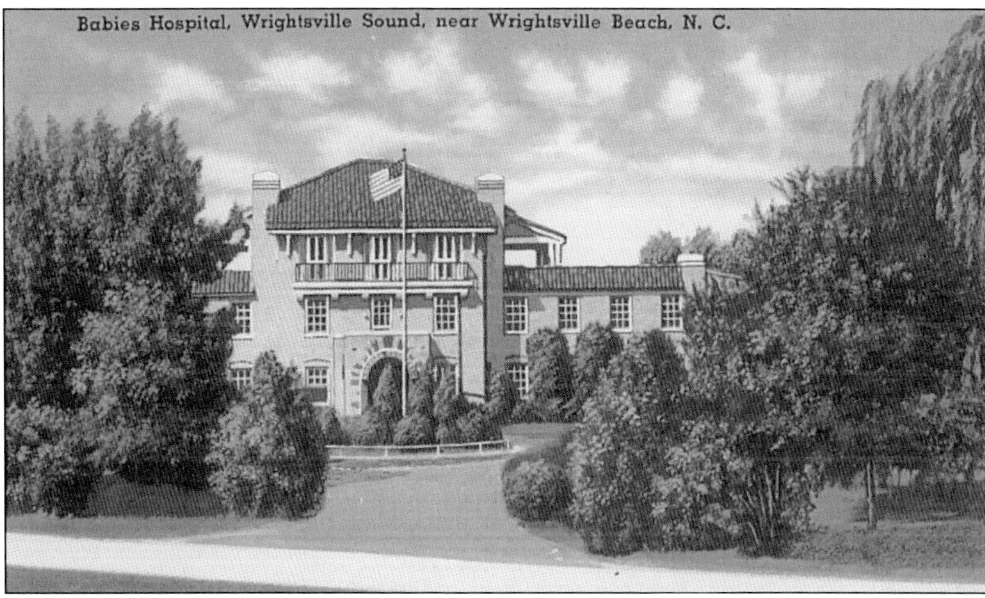

BABIES HOSPITAL, C. 1940S. Dr. James Buren Sidbury (1864–1967) founded Babies Hospital on June 6, 1920. Located on Wrightsville Sound, the original frame building burned in 1927. It was replaced by a Mediterranean-style structure. The pediatric hospital provided advanced care for local children as well as for summer visitors.

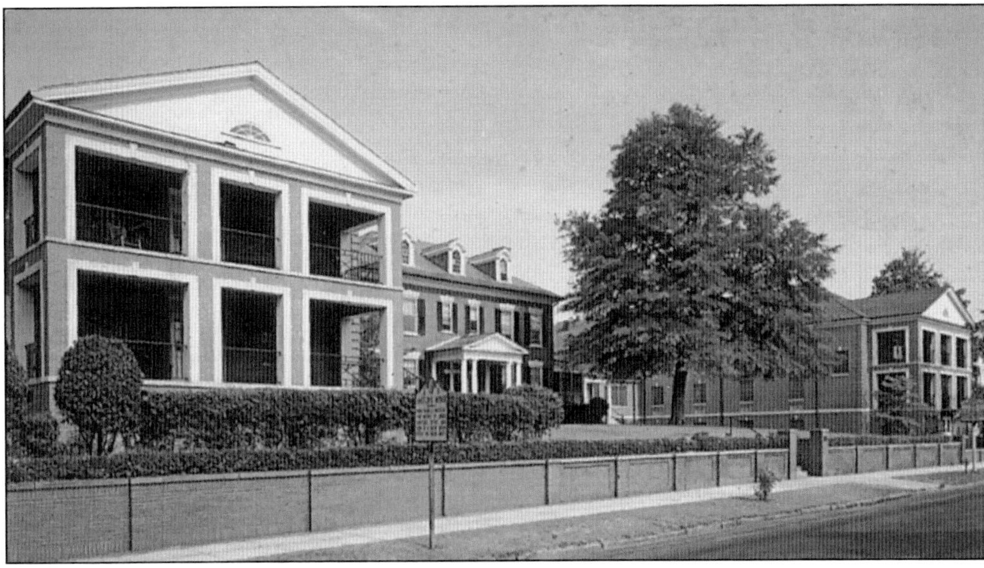

Catherine Kennedy Home, *c.* 1965. In 1845, Catherine deRosset Kennedy organized the Ladies Benevolent Society to aid elderly indigent women. In 1895, the "Old Ladies Rest Home" was located at Ninth and Princess Streets. At the time of Mrs. Kennedy's death, the name of the home was changed to honor her. In 1950, the Elliott House at 207 South Third Street was purchased. During the next 14 years, two wings were added to the facility. Sadly, the Catherine Kennedy Home was closed on July 1, 2000. (Courtesy of Hugh Morton.)

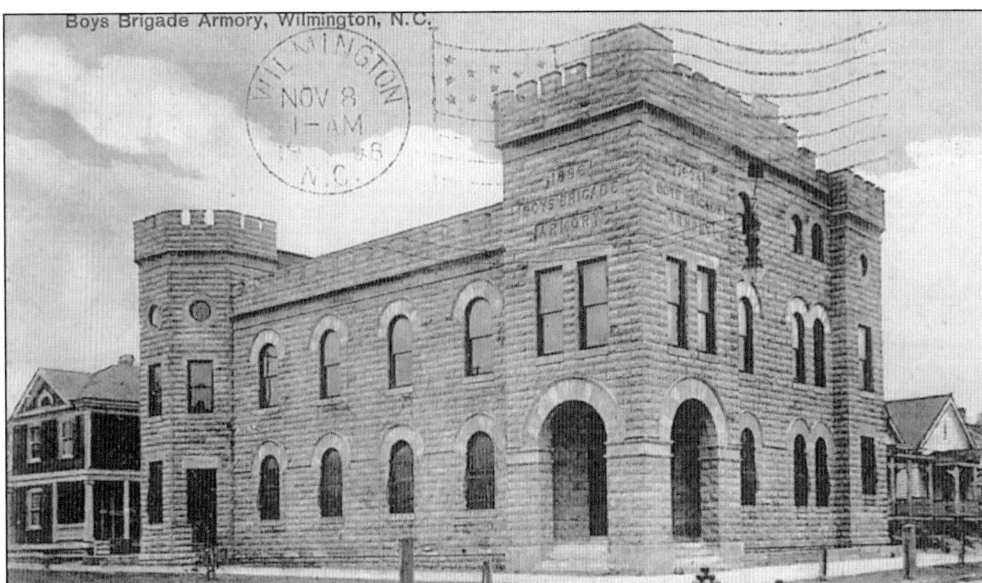

Boys Brigade Armory, 1908. Author Susan Taylor Block aptly named her history of the Boys Brigade Club, *The Character Factory.* Founded in 1896 by Colonel Walker Taylor, the club provided activities and support to underprivileged boys. Located on the corner of Second and Church Streets, the armory was given by Mary Lily Kenan Flagler as a memorial to her father, William Rand Kenan. Charles McMillen was the architect for the stone building, which was dedicated June 22, 1905. It was razed *c.* 1960.

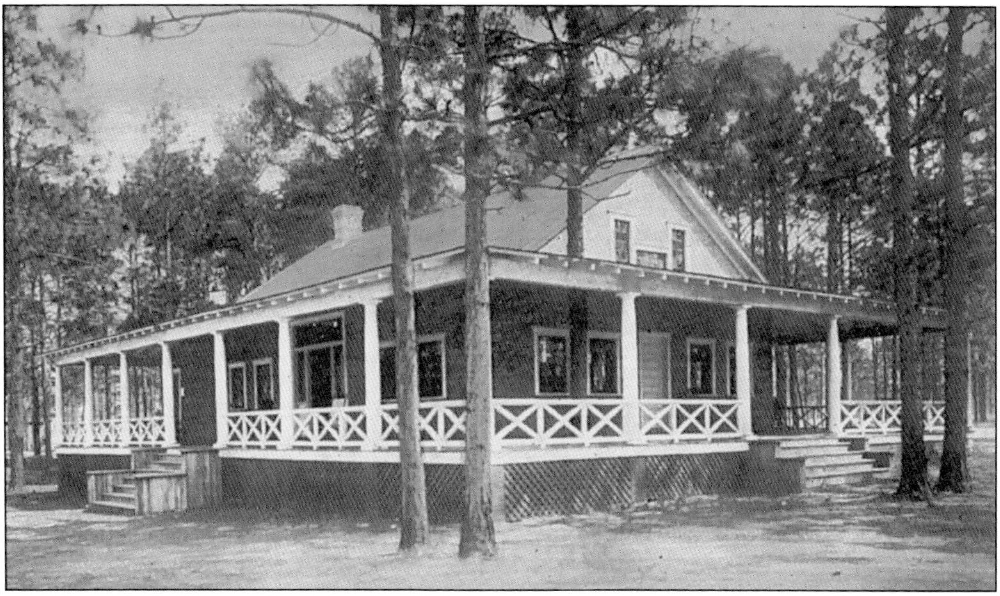

CAPE FEAR COUNTRY CLUB, 1917. Organized on March 21, 1896, members of Cape Fear Country Club first played golf at Hilton Park. In 1898, the club moved to a new location beside the railroad tracks near the North Fourth Street Bridge. The club purchased 200 acres east of the city from Thomas H. Wright in 1901, where this clubhouse was built in 1908. It was destroyed by fire in 1919.

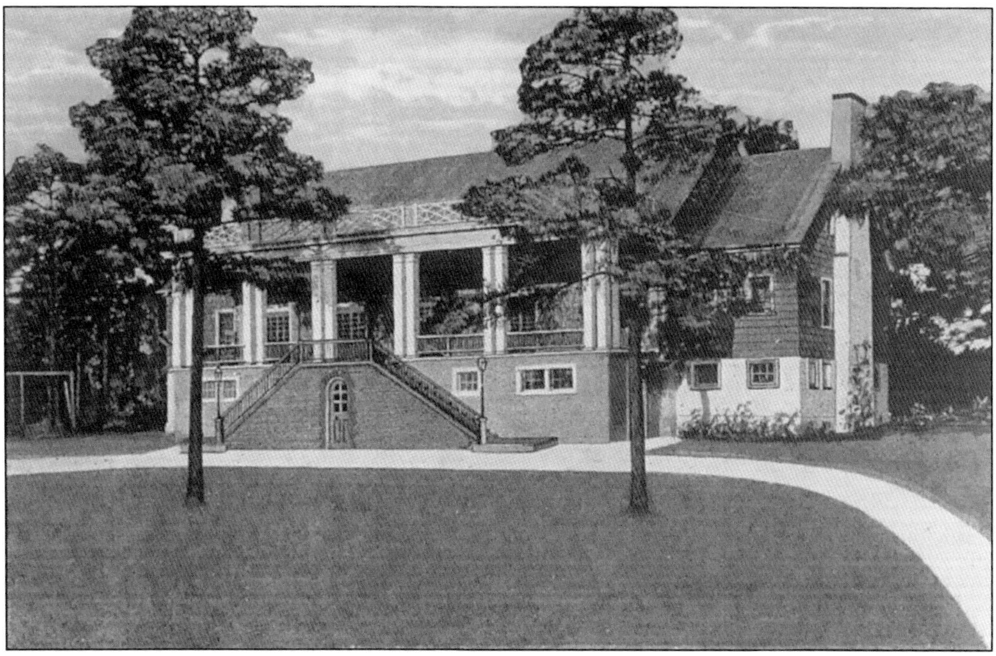

CAPE FEAR COUNTRY CLUB. Built in 1921–1922, the Cape Fear Country Club was designed by Leslie N. Boney. From 1949 to 1971, the club played host to the Azalea Open Golf Tournament, which was a regular stop on the PGA tour. The first Azalea Champion was Henry Ransome, who earned $2,000 for his win.

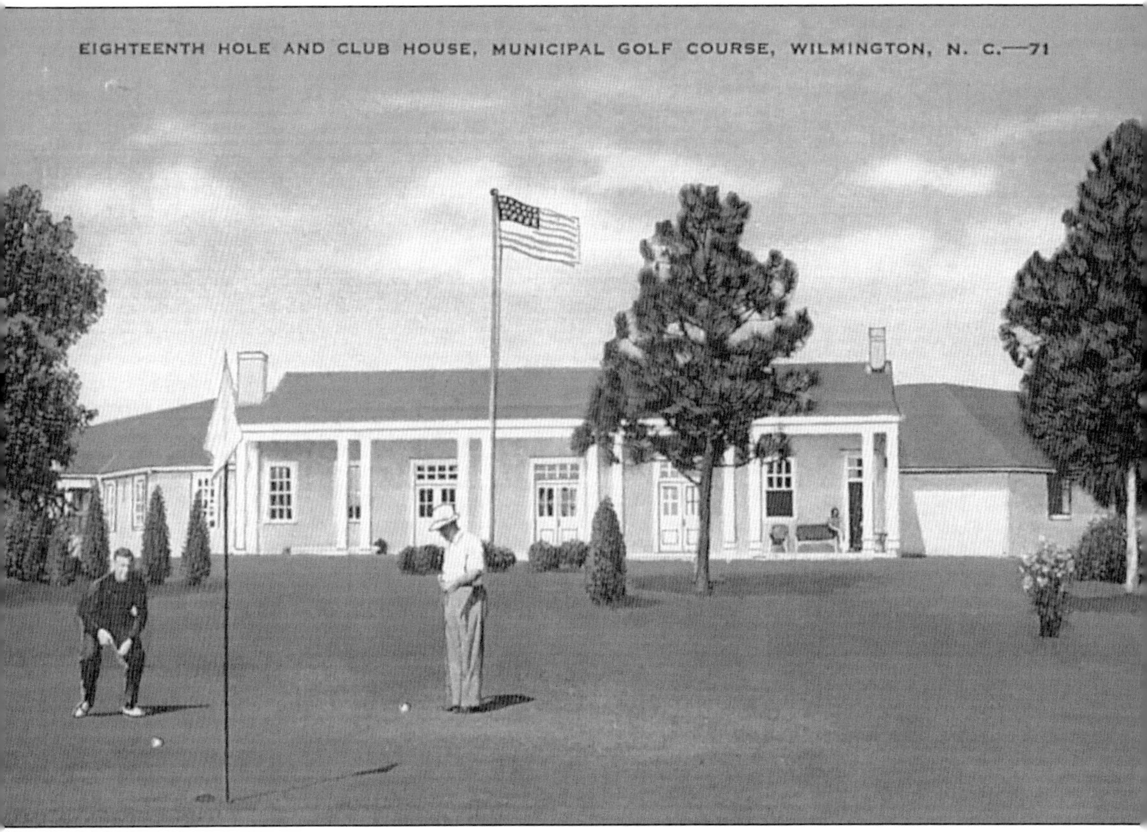

MUNICIPAL GOLF COURSE, 1945. In 1925, the Wilmington City Council acknowledged the growing popularity of golf and the need for public links in the area. They purchased land at Winter Park, formerly owned by Hugh MacRae, and hired distinguished golf course architect Donald Ross to design the 18-hole Municipal Golf Course. The clubhouse has played host to several generations of Wilmington golfers.

Five

Coastal Communities

Development of the coastal or beach communities did not begin until the last half of the nineteenth century, because roads to the coast were very poor or non-existent. In 1874–1875, the privately built Shell Road, or Wrightsville Turnpike, began at Sixteenth and Dock Streets and roughly followed the route of the present-day Wrightsville Avenue. This toll road had a surface made of rock, marl, shells, and limestone, which over the years, the sun bleached to pure white. It ended at Wrightsville Sound. In 1902, the Turnpike became a public thoroughfare when it was sold to New Hanover County for $7,500. In 1888, a beachcar line connected Wilmington to the Hammocks (Harbor Island). The same year, the railway was extended from the Hammocks to the beach. This made Wrightsville Beach and vicinity much more accessible to the general public.

Good roads to the Federal Point peninsula lagged behind. From Wilmington, the trip would take the better part of a day. The best way to get to this area was by boarding the steamer Wilmington *at the foot of Market Street and cruising down the Cape Fear River to a wharf on the river. A small train, later called the* Shoofly, *took passengers over to Carolina Beach.*

With improved transportation, the beaches became popular tourist destinations. Many local families moved to the beach every summer. Year-round beach residents were largely unknown until the middle of the twentieth century.

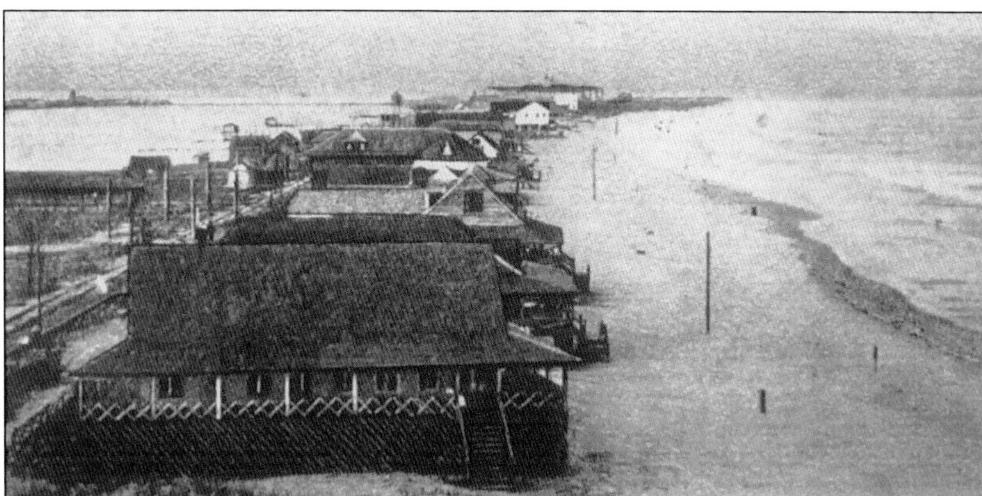

Wrightsville Beach, c. 1915. Named for Judge Joshua Grainger Wright (1758–1811), Wrightsville Beach is part of the North Carolina Banks, a chain of barrier islands that spans almost all of the North Carolina coast. This "bird's-eye view" of the beach, looking north, was taken from Lumina's water tower.

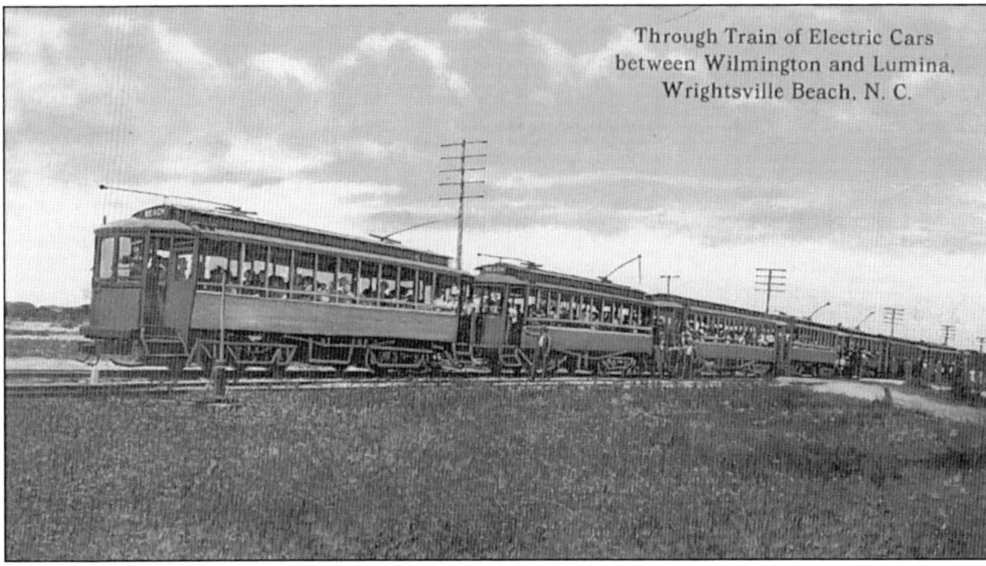

BEACHCAR LINE, C. 1910. The first steam railway was constructed from downtown Wilmington to the Hammocks (Harbor Island) in 1888. The same year, the Sea View Railroad was built from the Hammocks to Wrightsville Beach, opening up the southern extension of the beach for development. The railroad was sold to the Consolidated Railways, Light and Power Company in 1901. Shortly afterwards, it was converted from steam to an electric line.

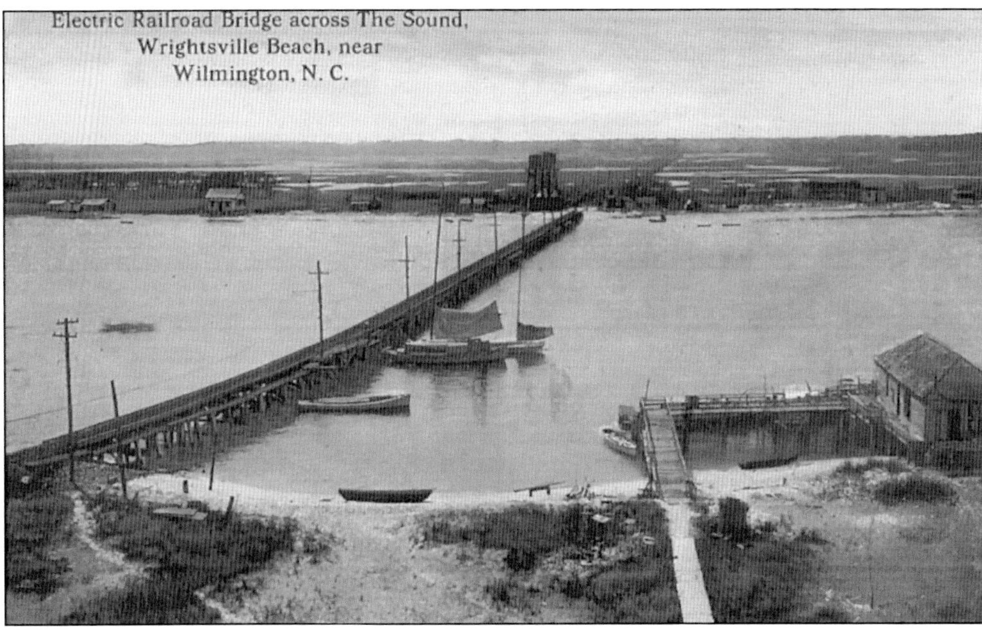

BANKS CHANNEL RAILWAY TRESTLE, C. 1910. Initially built in 1888, the railway trestle over Banks Channel was destroyed by the hurricane of 1906. Rebuilt before the 1907 summer season, it was a very narrow track and had no guardrails, making some passengers very uneasy while crossing the trestle. The Hammocks (Harbor Island) is seen in the background.

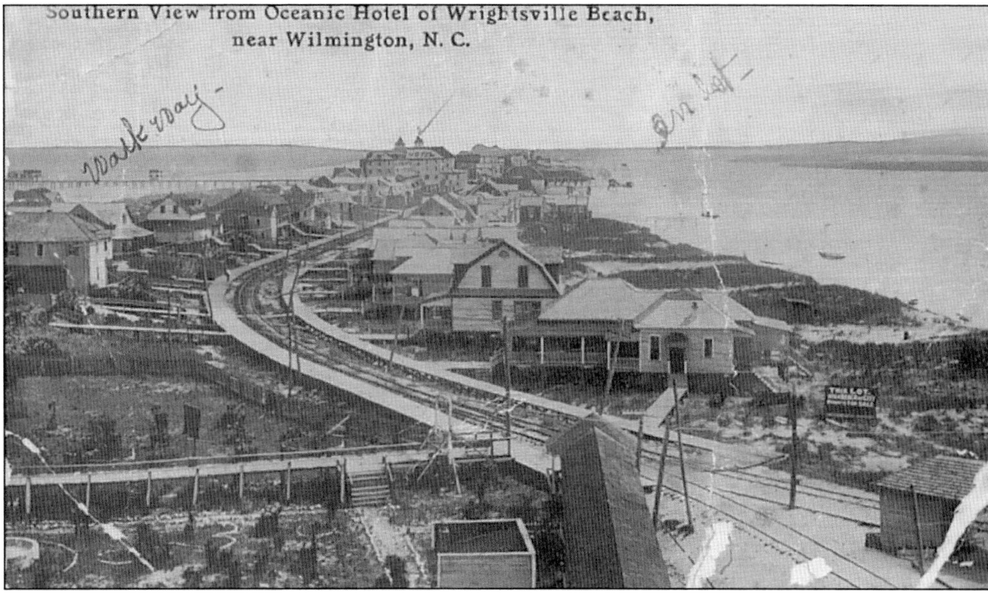

WRIGHTSVILLE BEACH, SOUTHERN VIEW, *c.* 1915. There were seven railway stations on the beach. The beachcars made their first stop just after crossing the trestle at Station One. This photograph was taken from the Oceanic Hotel, which was just north of Station One. Cottages lined both sides of the railway tracks, with those on the right, having the marsh of Banks Channel in their backyards. Wooden boardwalks flanked both sides of the tracks.

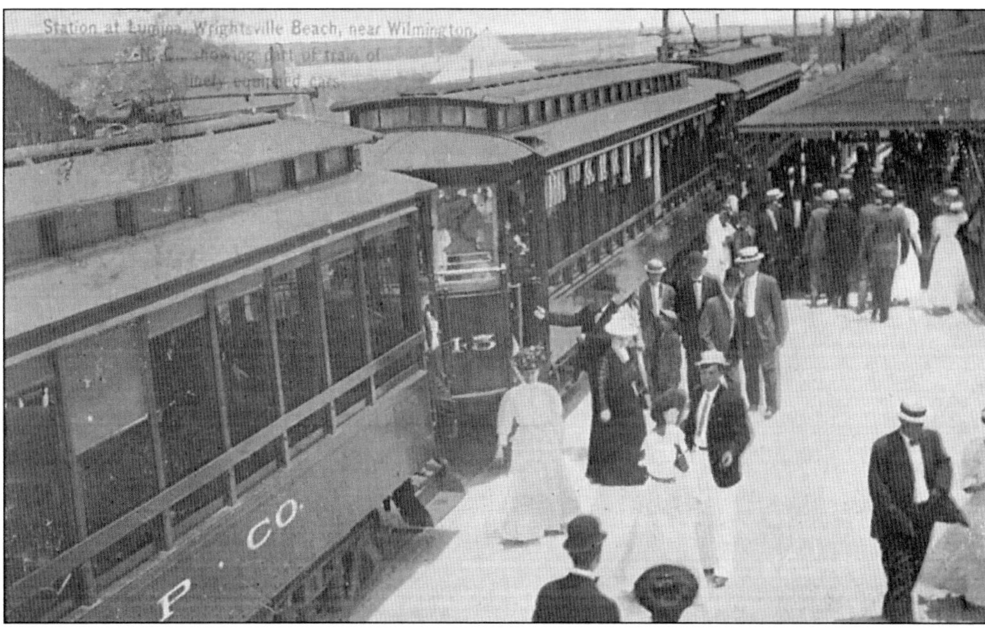

STATION SEVEN AT LUMINA, *c.* 1910. The beachcar line ended at Lumina. Since there was no turn around, the backs of the beachcar seats were flipped over to allow passengers to face forward on the trip back to Wilmington. Note the dress of the passengers disembarking the train. Today, coats, ties, and hats for the men, and hats and long dresses for the women hardly seem appropriate attire for the beach.

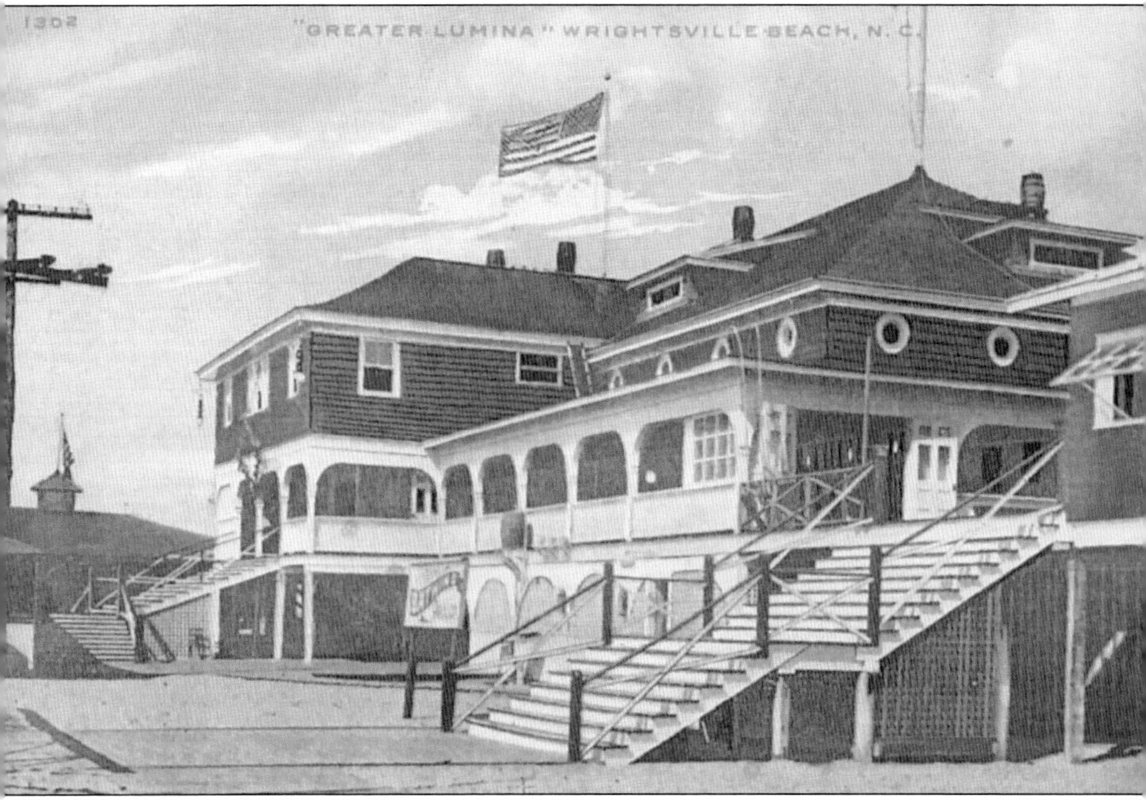

LUMINA, C. 1910. After purchasing the beachcar line in 1901, the Tidewater Power Company constructed a dance and amusement pavilion at the railway's southern terminus. Designed by Wilmington architect Henry E. Bonitz, Lumina opened June 3, 1905, and quickly became "the fun spot of the South." The name was a manufactured one, derived from the Latin word for light. The exterior of the building was illuminated with over 600 incandescent lights. The two-story pavilion was 300 feet long. On the second floor was the famous dance floor, which was 50 by 70 feet and encircled by a promenade. Bathhouses, concession stands, and an amusement area occupied the ground floor. Lumina became so popular that it was expanded in 1909, doubling the size of the dance floor and adding an orchestra shell on its western side.

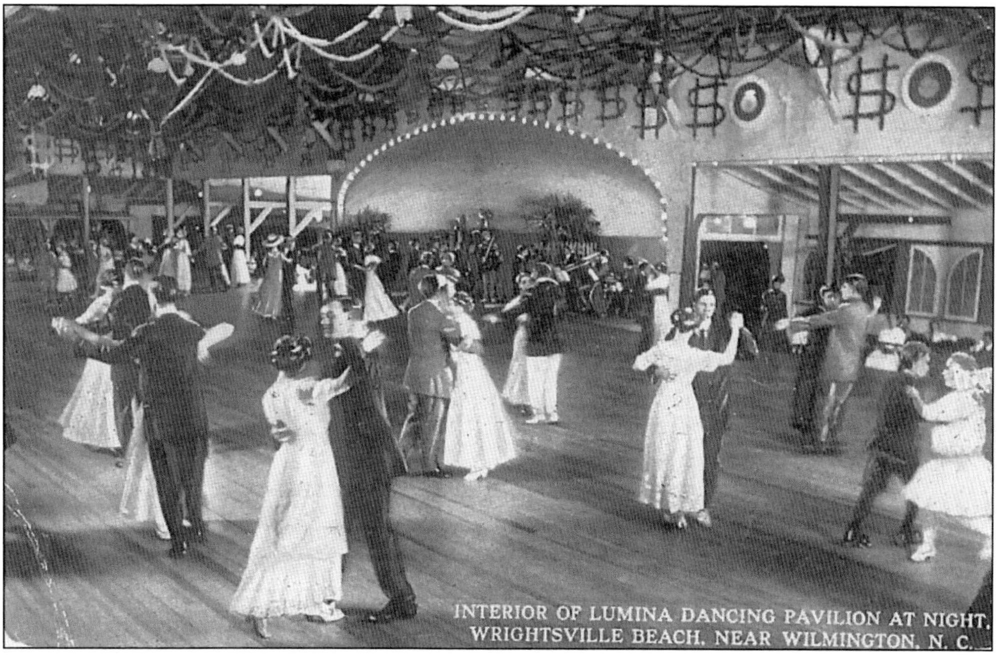

LUMINA DANCE FLOOR, 1912. Lumina hosted about every nationally known band at one time or another. The dancing etiquette was very strict and was enforced by a designated chaperone, Mrs. Culbreth Martin. In the center of the western wall, an orchestra shell (center) was capable of seating 20 musicians. The acoustics of the building were said to be the finest on the South Atlantic coast.

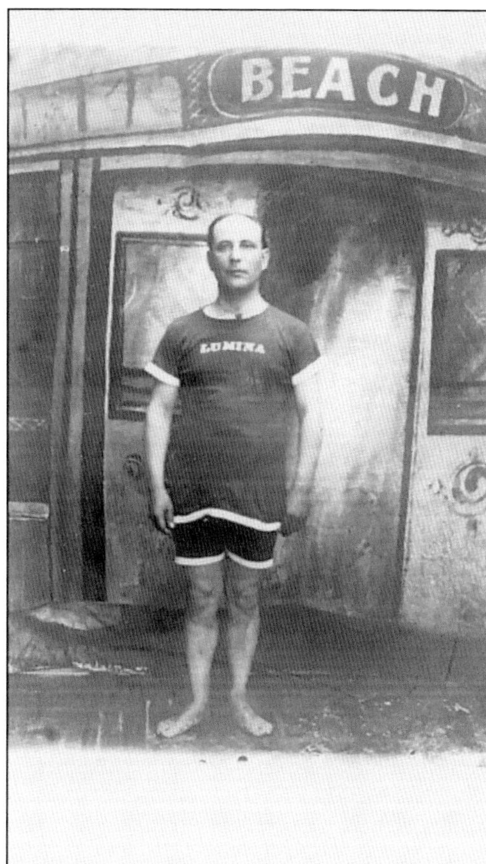

BATHING SUITS, LUMINA, *c.* 1910. An unknown and rather portly bather models a Lumina bathing suit. The suits could be rented for the day for 10¢ from bathhouses on the ground floor. Showers cost a quarter. Even today, there are certain people who shudder when they think of the icy cold water of those showers. In the beginning, ladies rarely, if ever, went in swimming because female bathing attire was almost unknown. Occasionally, they lifted their skirts to wade in the ocean.

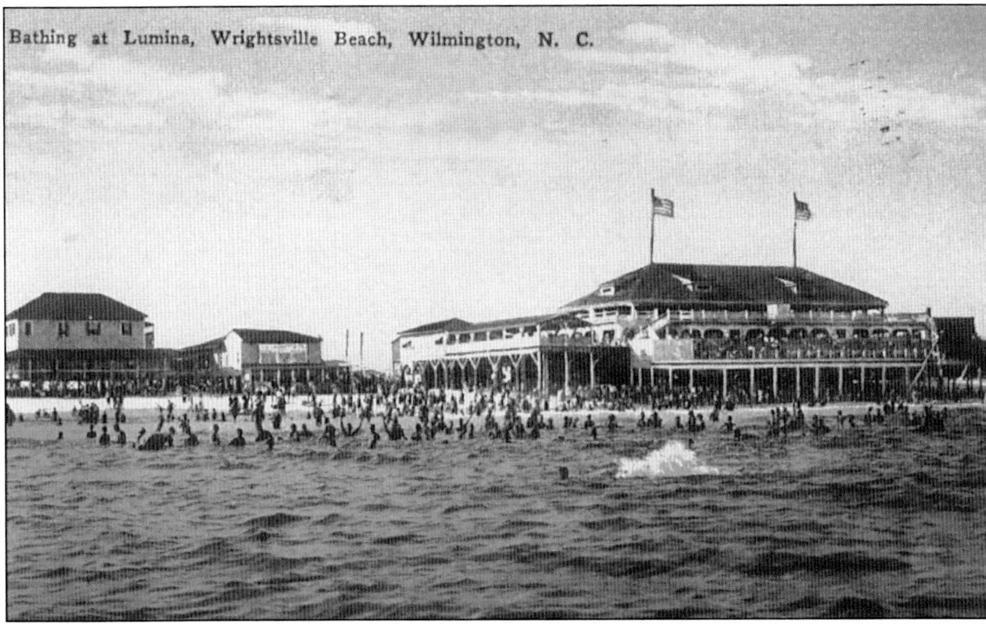

Bathing at Lumina, c. 1920. In nice weather, Lumina was very crowded on summer weekends. In 1910, it was said that over 3,000 people visited the pavilion on the Fourth of July. Extra beachcars had to be put into service to accommodate the beach go-ers. Lumina lost much of its glamour when the railway was discontinued in 1940. After years of deterioration, the building was razed in 1973.

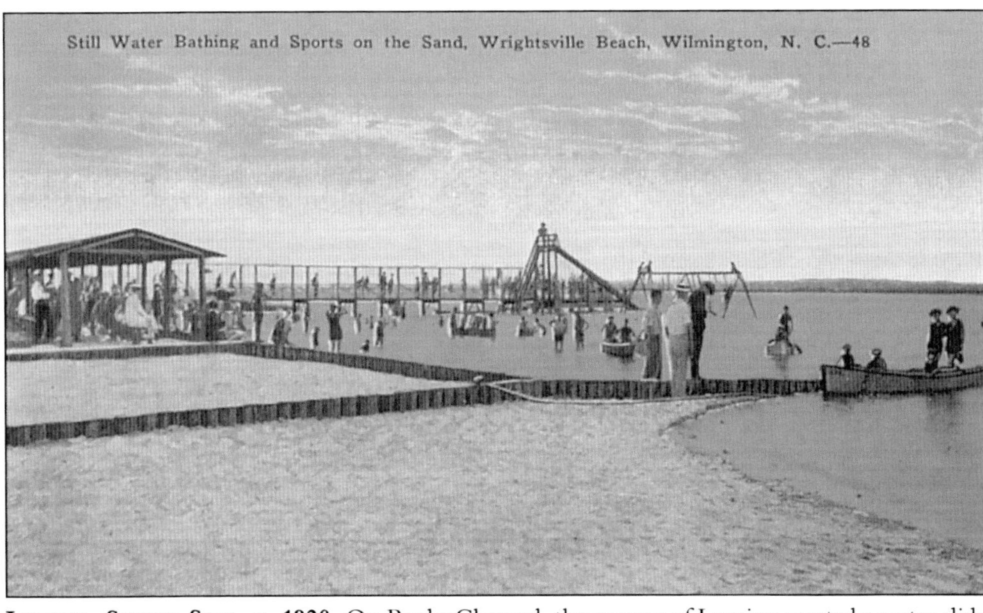

Lumina, Sound Side, c. 1920. On Banks Channel, the owners of Lumina erected a water slide, which particularly delighted children. The still waters provided more opportunity to swim than in the tempestuous surf of the ocean. Written on the back of this postcard is an advertising inscription that reads, ". . . the beach is unique, being free from mosquitoes and flies . . ."

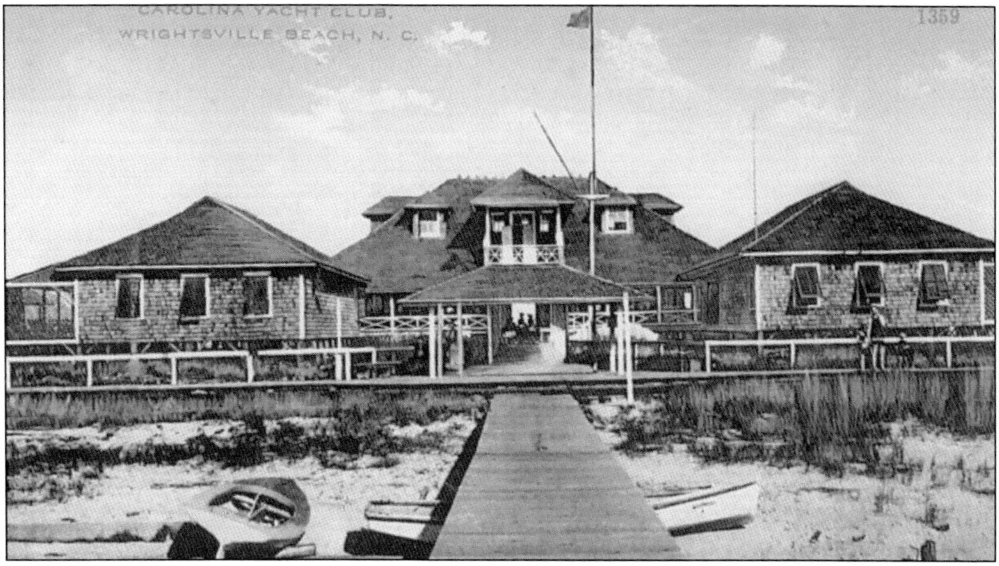

Carolina Yacht Club, 1911. The earliest structure on the beach was that of the Carolina Yacht Club, which dates from April 14, 1853. Located at Station Four, this clubhouse replaced an older one, which was destroyed in the Great Storm of 1899. Pembroke Jones was once commodore of the club and donated a trophy to be presented annually to champion sailors.

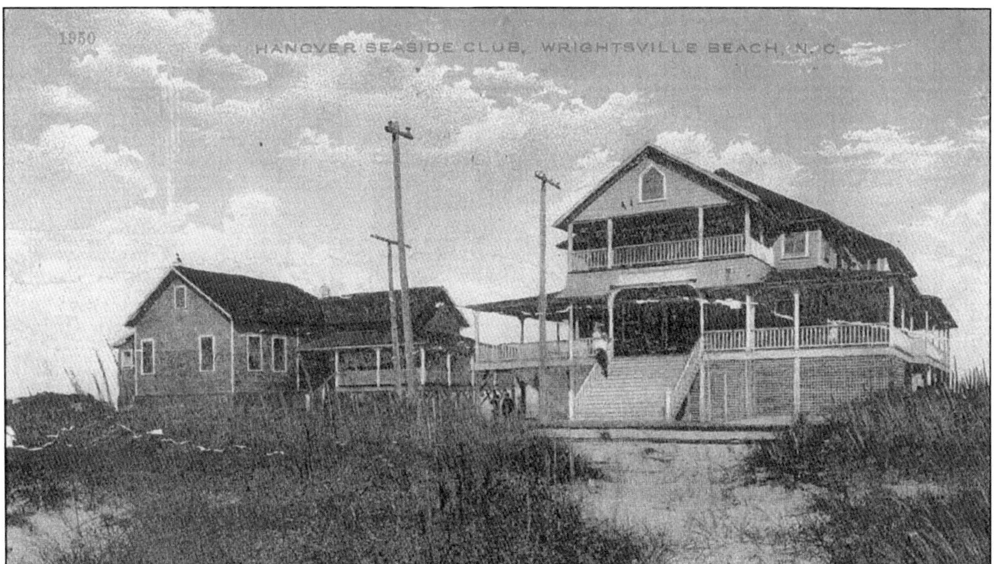

Hanover Seaside Club, 1911. The first clubhouse of the Hanover Seaside Club was built on Carolina Beach in 1898. Organized largely by German immigrants from the Province of Hannover, the club later bought property on Wrightsville Beach. Designed by club member Henry E. Bonitz, the building was opened on September 6, 1906. The structure at left is the Paris Cottage. A tragic fire on December 7, 1981, consumed the clubhouse, which was then the oldest structure on Wrightsville Beach. A new clubhouse was built and dedicated in 1983. (Courtesy of Hanover Seaside Club Archives.)

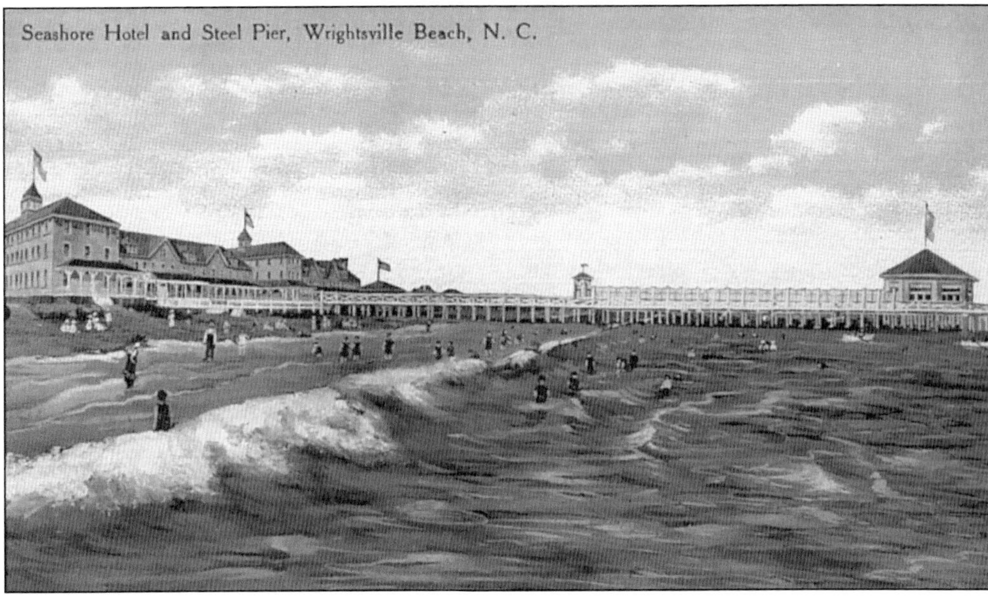

SEASHORE HOTEL AND STEEL PIER, 1918. Architect Henry E. Bonitz designed the Seashore Hotel, which was one of the first large hotels built on the beach. The cream and white building opened for guests on June 15, 1897. The Seashore Orchestra was famous for providing excellent music in the grand ballroom. The steel pier projected out into the ocean in front of the hotel.

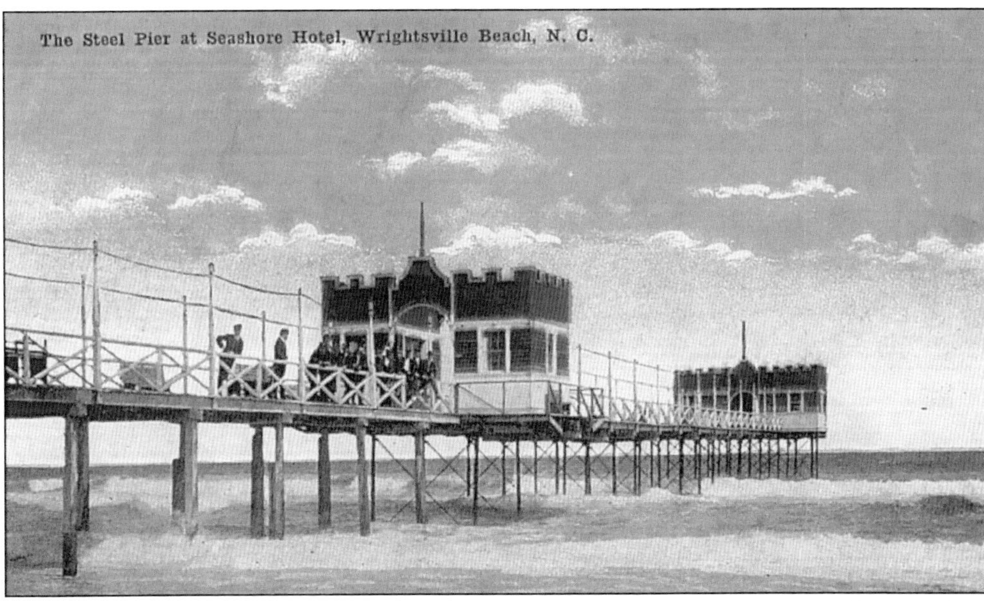

STEEL PIER AT THE SEASHORE HOTEL, 1918. In 1910, a steel pier was erected on the oceanfront of the Seashore Hotel. It extended into the ocean 700 feet and was connected to the hotel's veranda by a boardwalk. At the ocean end of the pier was a two-story pavilion and observation deck. When the pier opened, fish were caught with hand lines, since the rod and reel had not yet become popular at Wrightsville. What was left of the pier after a fire in 1919 was swept away by a violent northeaster in 1921.

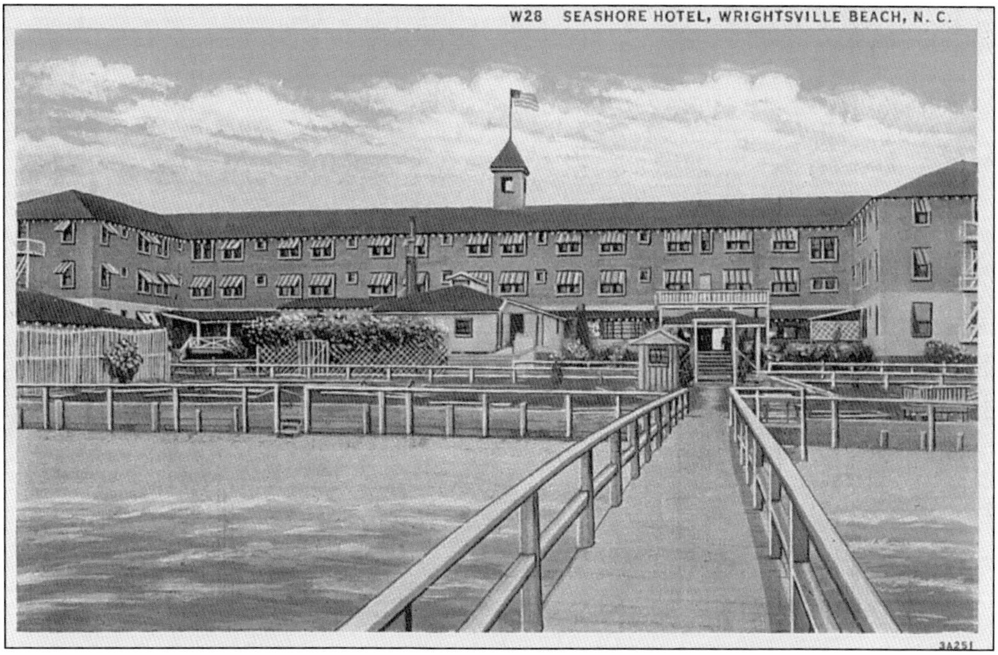

SEASHORE HOTEL, C. 1925. On June 26, 1919, the famed Seashore Hotel went up in flames. A new three-story hotel was constructed on the site in 1922 and used the same name. There was a large lobby, a ladies parlor, and an elegant dining room on the first floor. The second and third floors contained single and double rooms with baths. In 1935, Mrs. J.A. Synder leased the building and renamed it the Ocean Terrace Hotel. The structure was badly damaged by Hurricane Hazel in 1954 and burned about a year later.

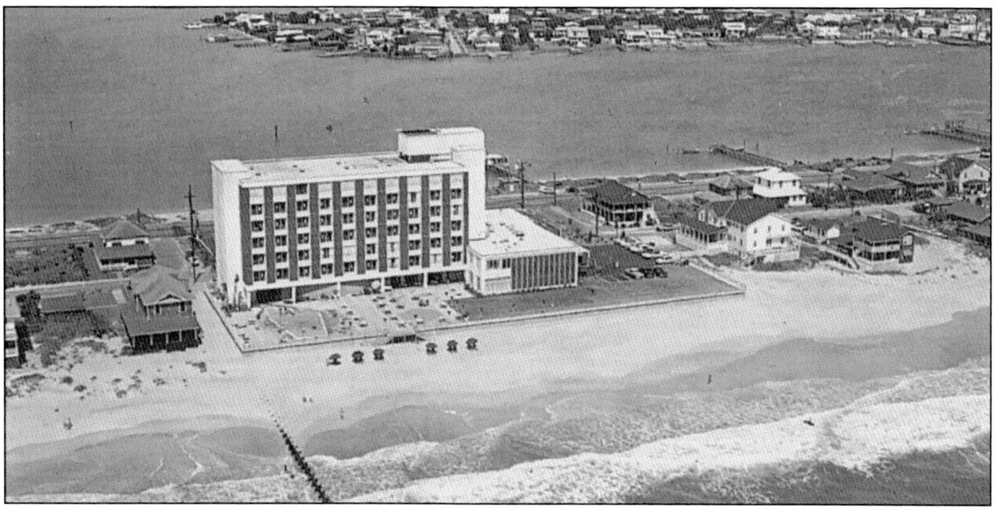

BLOCKADE RUNNER HOTEL, C. 1960. From 1954 to 1964, there was no large hotel on Wrightsville Beach. In 1962, Mr. Lawrence Lewis Jr., president of the East Coast Hotel Company of Richmond, Virginia, engaged Oliver and Smith, architects of Norfolk, Virginia, to design a seven-story building. Located on the old Seashore Hotel site, plans called for a brick structure of 120 rooms, with ample convention facilities. The Blockade Runner Hotel opened on March 22, 1964. (Courtesy of Hugh Morton.)

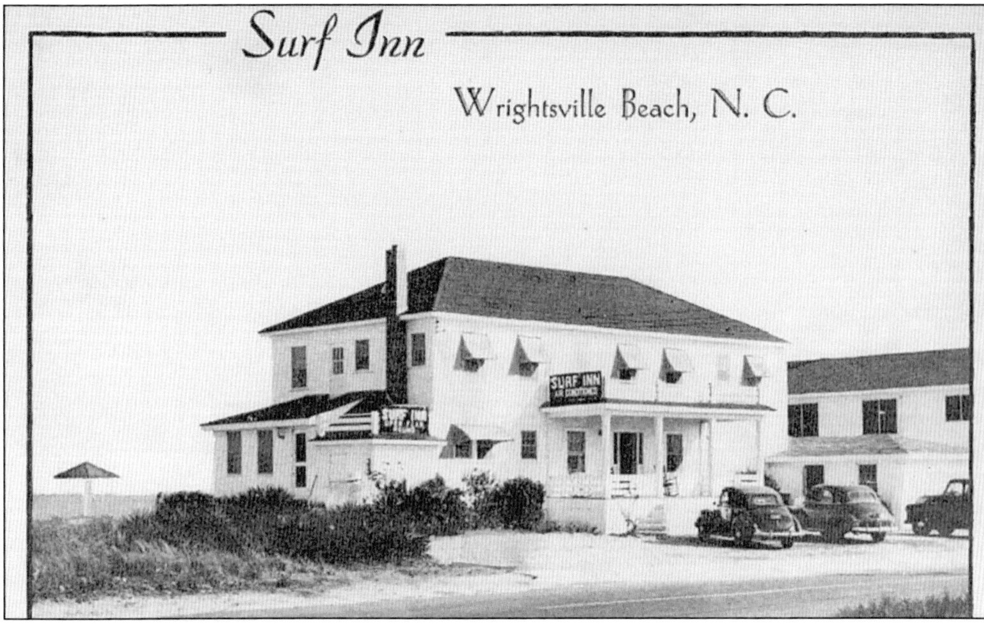

SURF INN, c. 1950. There have always been a number of large rambling cottages on the beach, which had rooms or apartments for rent. On the oceanfront near Lumina, the Surf Inn advertised that it "was open year round, air-conditioned, with hot water in every room." Mrs. Jack L. Lane was the proprietress. In 1972, a modern motel was constructed on the same site.

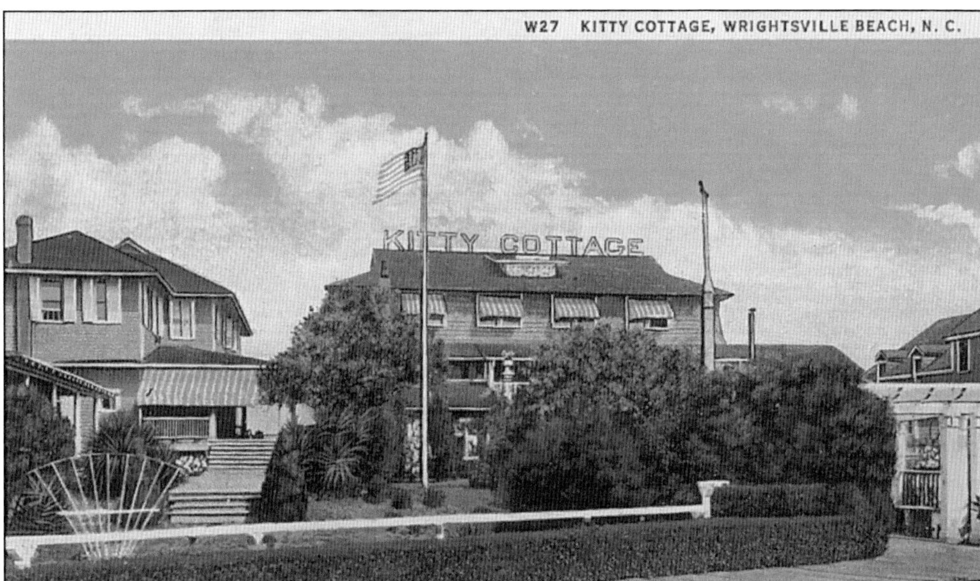

KITTY COTTAGE, 1930. A popular boarding house during the 1920s through 1940s was the Kitty Cottage. Author Greg Watkins states, "The cottage was said to have derived its name from the kitty of the poker games that were frequently held here." Located just south of the beachcar trestle, the cottage burned in 1934 and was rebuilt at a new location at Station Two.

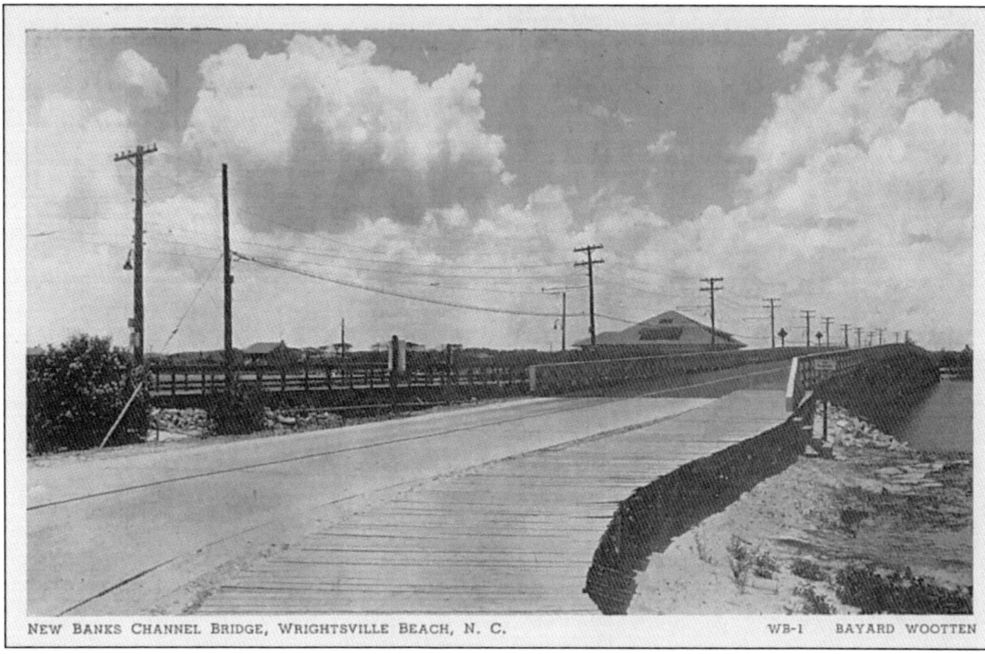

BANKS CHANNEL BRIDGE, 1930S. The Banks Channel Bridge was completed in the mid-1930s to connect with Waynick Boulevard. On the back of this postcard is written, ". . . the bridge makes it possible for motorists to drive directly to Wrightsville Beach, where ample free parking space is available." For years, pilings from the old beachcar trestle were visible south of the bridge, and the last of them were removed in 1992.

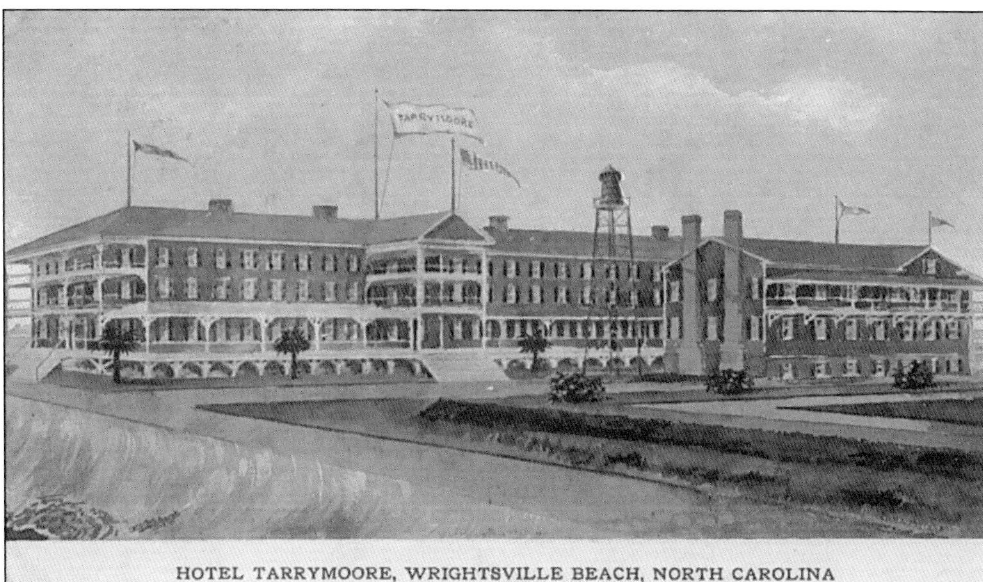

HOTEL TARRYMORE, 1908. In 1905, the Hotel Tarrymore was built just north of Station One, on property that went from Banks Channel to the ocean. It was a very large wooden structure, containing well over a hundred rooms. It had the very latest modern conveniences, such as private baths, telephones, and electric lights.

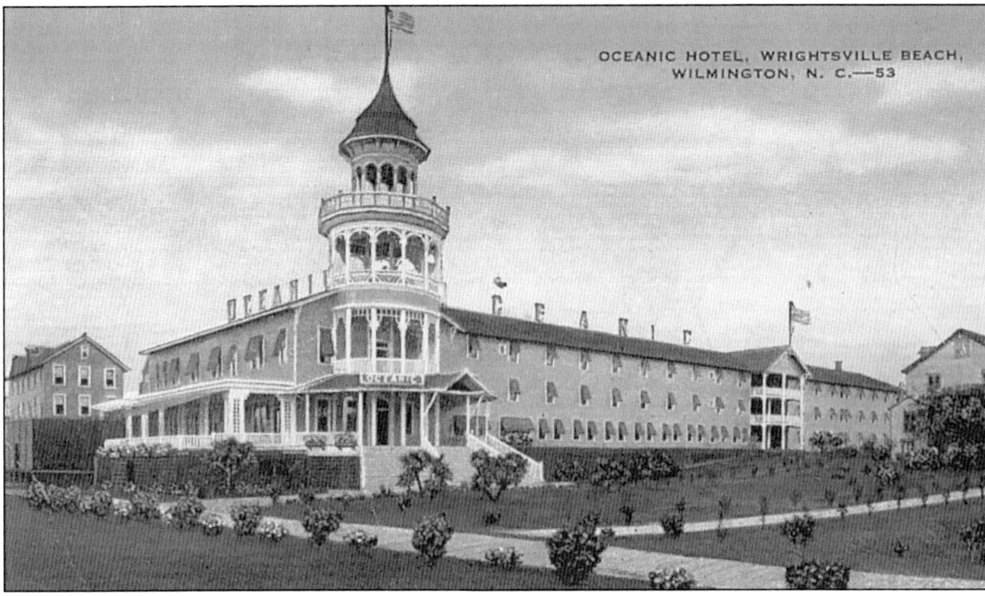

OCEANIC HOTEL, c. 1930. In about 1912, the Tarrymore Hotel was sold and renamed the Oceanic. The existing building was enlarged and the main entrance was changed to the southwestern corner. An elegant four-story tower was added, which made the hotel instantly recognizable. It became one of the social centers of the beach. Orchestras provided dinner music in the large dining room, after which the musicians would often go to Lumina to play for dances. The massive hotel was destroyed in the big fire of February 28, 1934, which left only two cottages still standing on the Northern Extension of Wrightsville Beach.

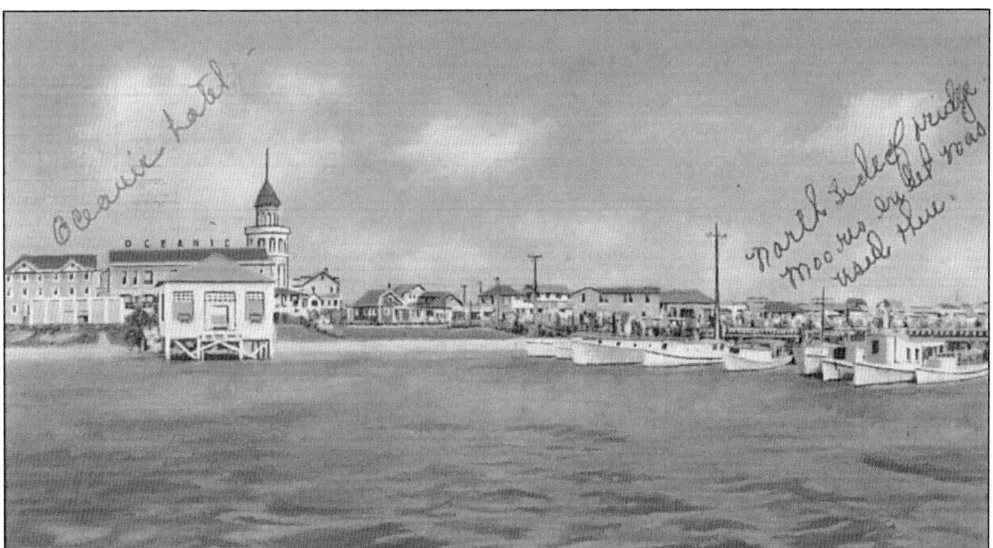

BANKS CHANNEL, c. 1930. On the sound side of the Oceanic Hotel near Station One, there was a small pavilion and dock, where boats or launches were moored. The hotel furnished these boats to take guests out into the ocean through Moore's Inlet, which was navigable at that time. Located at the northern end of the beach, the inlet separated Shell Island from Wrightsville Beach.

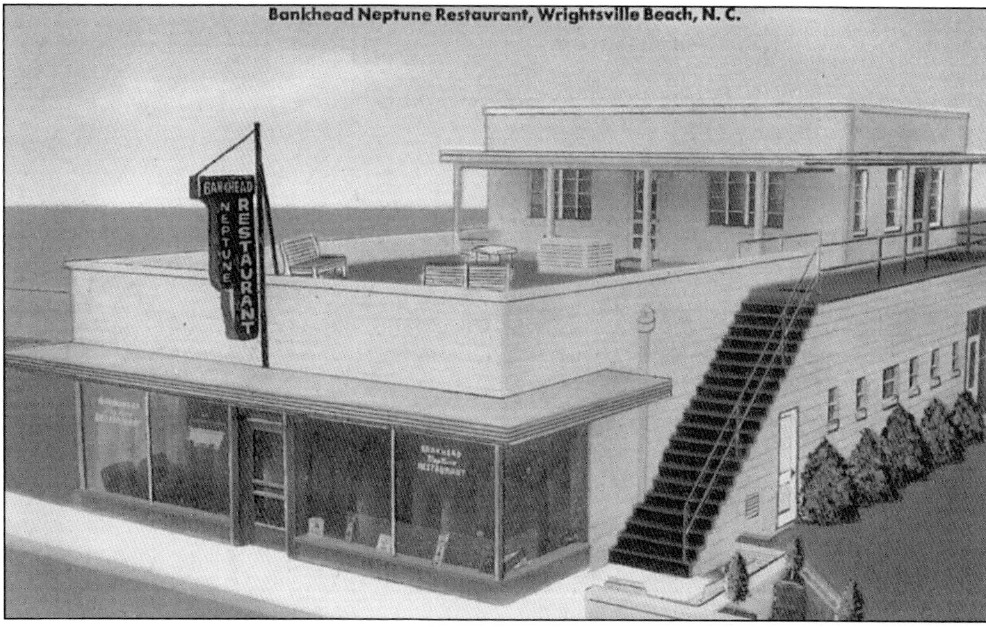

BANKHEAD NEPTUNE RESTAURANT, C. 1950. Shortly after WW II, J.L. Bankhead of Rockingham, North Carolina, opened a seafood restaurant about a block north of Station One. The Bankheads lived in an apartment on top of the building. B.C. Hedgpeth, a noted Chapel Hill restaurateur, purchased the building in 1961 and changed the name to the King Neptune Restaurant. Mr. Hedgpeth sold the restaurant in 1997.

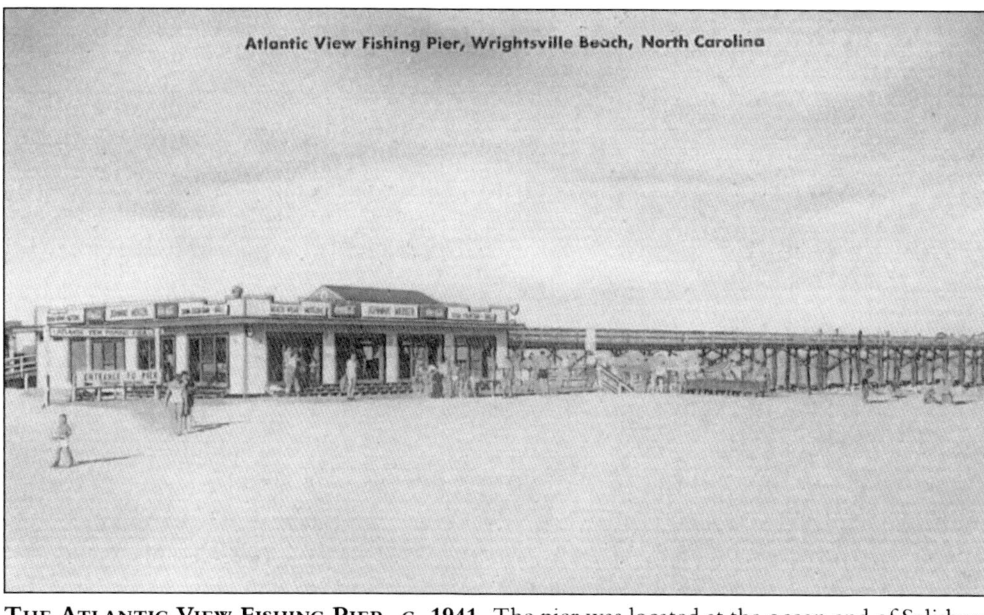

THE ATLANTIC VIEW FISHING PIER, C. 1941. The pier was located at the ocean end of Salisbury Street. Later, it was called Johnny Mercer's Pier after its owner. The store on the strand sold bait, tackle, soft drinks, pier admission tickets, beachwear, and souvenirs. After Hurricane Hazel in 1954 completely destroyed the pier, the store was relocated onto the pier at its entrance.

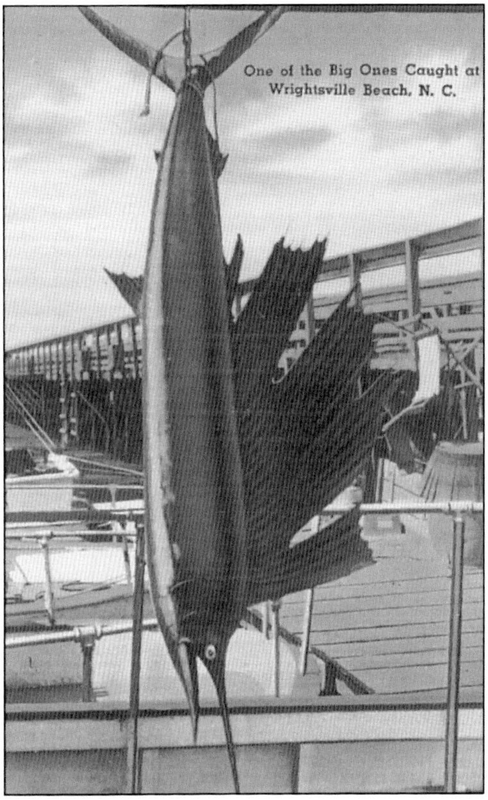

"THE BIG ONE CAUGHT AT WRIGHTSVILLE BEACH," C. 1940S. The gulf stream is 44 nautical miles off the water tank at Wrightsville Beach. Regularly, pleasure boats go there to fish for marlin, bonita mackerel, sailfish, and other large game fish. One summer in the mid-1950s, the *Wilmington Star-News* kept a daily running tally of the number of sailfish caught. There were over 100 of the coveted fish landed by season's end.

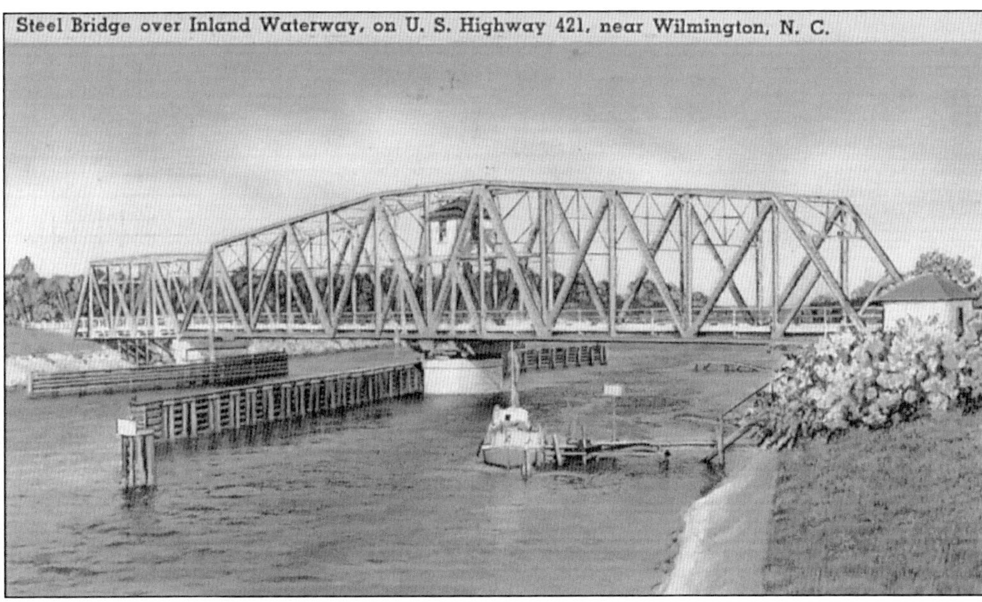

SNOW'S CUT BRIDGE, C. 1942. Completed in 1932, Snow's Cut is a section of the Intracoastal Waterway, connecting Myrtle Grove Sound with the Cape Fear River. The cut follows part of the path of Telfair Mill Creek and was named for Major W.A. Snow, one of the engineers on the project. The steel bridge rotated to allow boating traffic to pass through.

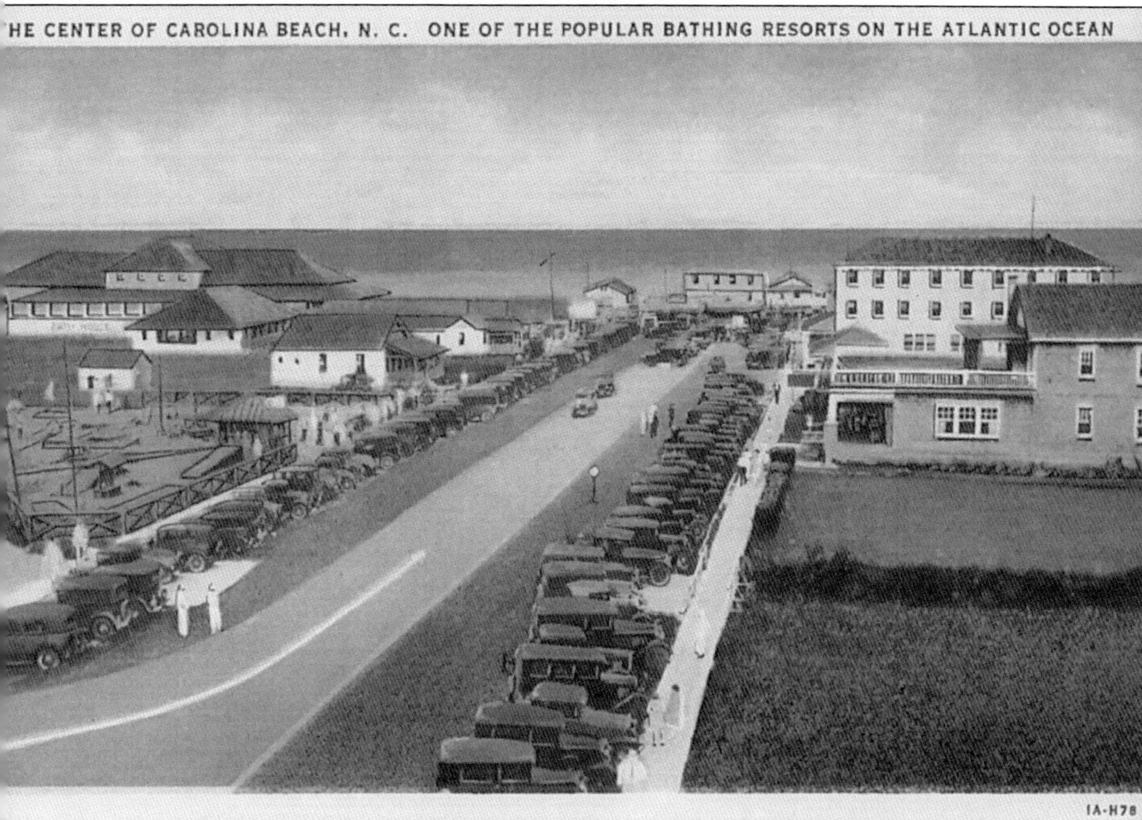

CAPE FEAR BOULEVARD, CAROLINA BEACH, *c.* 1932. In the early twentieth century, roads to the Federal Point peninsula were little more than two sandy and muddy ruts. Later, an improved road from Wilmington was designated State Highway #40. As the highway neared Carolina Beach, it followed the route of the present Dow Road and Cape Fear Boulevard to the ocean. The first structure on the right is the Greystone Inn, built in 1916, by Alexander W. Pate, an early beach developer. The building was constructed of beach sand and cement. Initially used by Pate's salesmen to entertain customers, the inn was opened to the public in 1920. In 1933, a roof garden was added on the front first-floor roof. The large building behind the inn was the Bame Hotel. The beach pavilion, constructed in 1911, is at left.

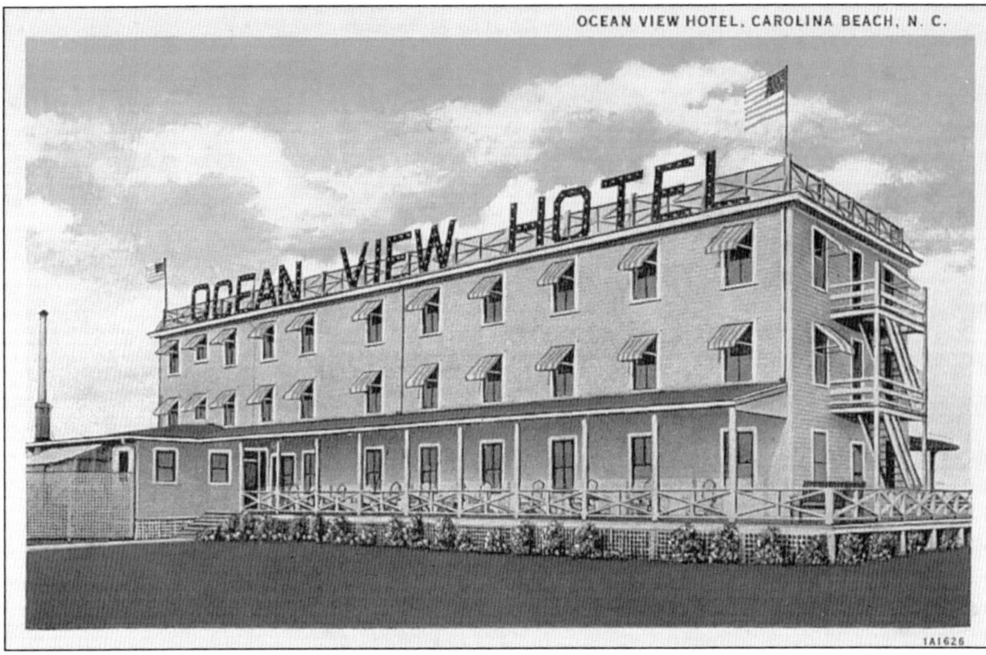

OCEAN VIEW HOTEL, c. 1932. A new highway from Wilmington to Carolina Beach was completed in the spring of 1929. The next year, Ocean View Hotel opened for guests on the oceanfront between Harper Avenue and Carolina Avenue, North. It was managed by G.L. Edwards and B.D. Bunn.

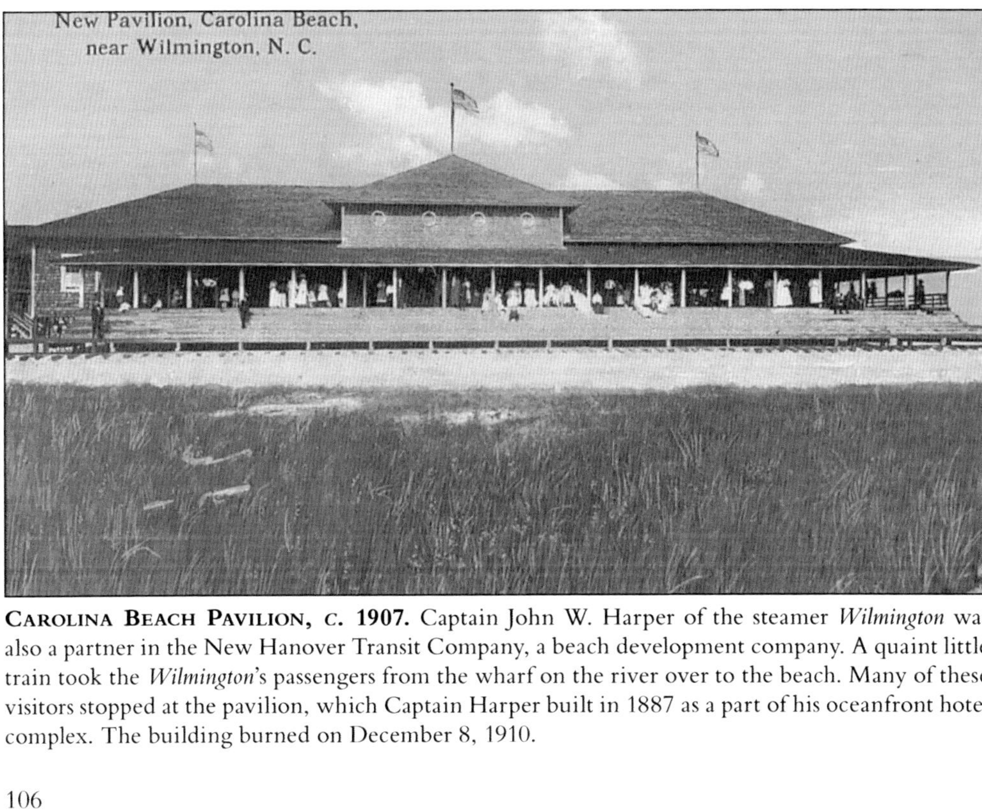

CAROLINA BEACH PAVILION, c. 1907. Captain John W. Harper of the steamer *Wilmington* was also a partner in the New Hanover Transit Company, a beach development company. A quaint little train took the *Wilmington*'s passengers from the wharf on the river over to the beach. Many of these visitors stopped at the pavilion, which Captain Harper built in 1887 as a part of his oceanfront hotel complex. The building burned on December 8, 1910.

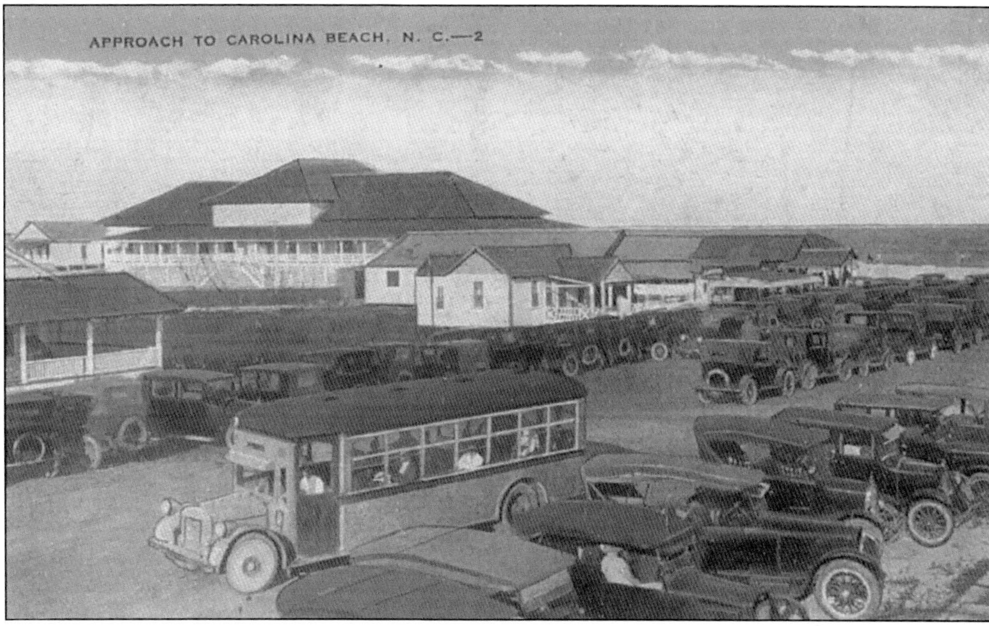

Carolina Moon Pavilion, c. 1932. Shortly after a fire destroyed the first pavilion, a new one was constructed on the same site. It contained bathhouses, a bowling alley, and a large central room, where on summer nights, a dance band played the latest popular music. Teenage boys were paid 10¢ per game to set up the bowling pins. A huge fire destroyed the pavilion on September 19, 1940, along with 24 other businesses in the immediate area.

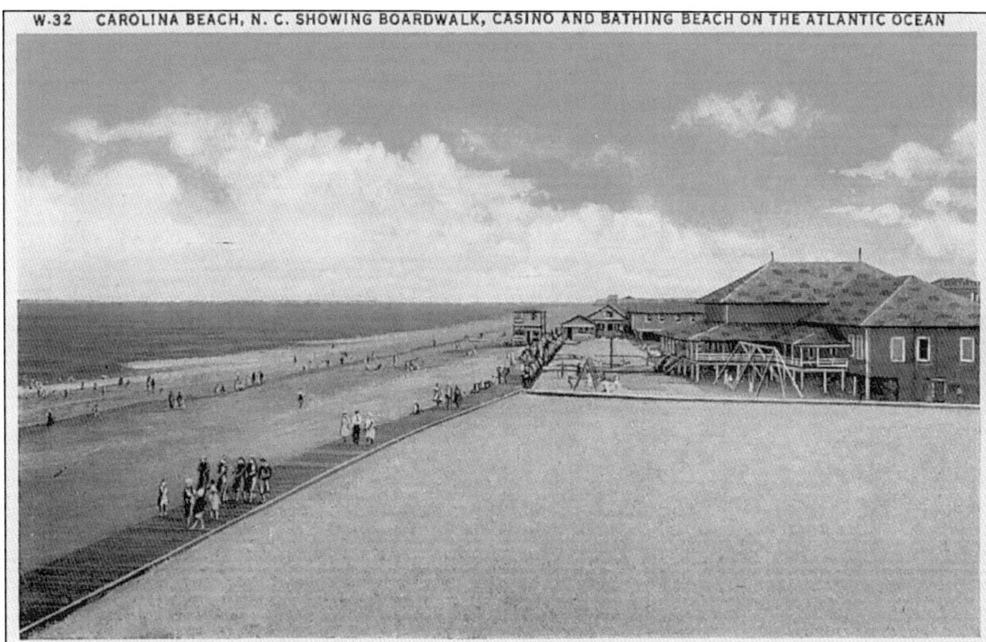

Carolina Beach Boardwalk, c. 1932. The boardwalk ran along the ocean, the length of the town's business district. The pavilion, constructed in 1911, was also called the casino. A children's playground was located on the north side.

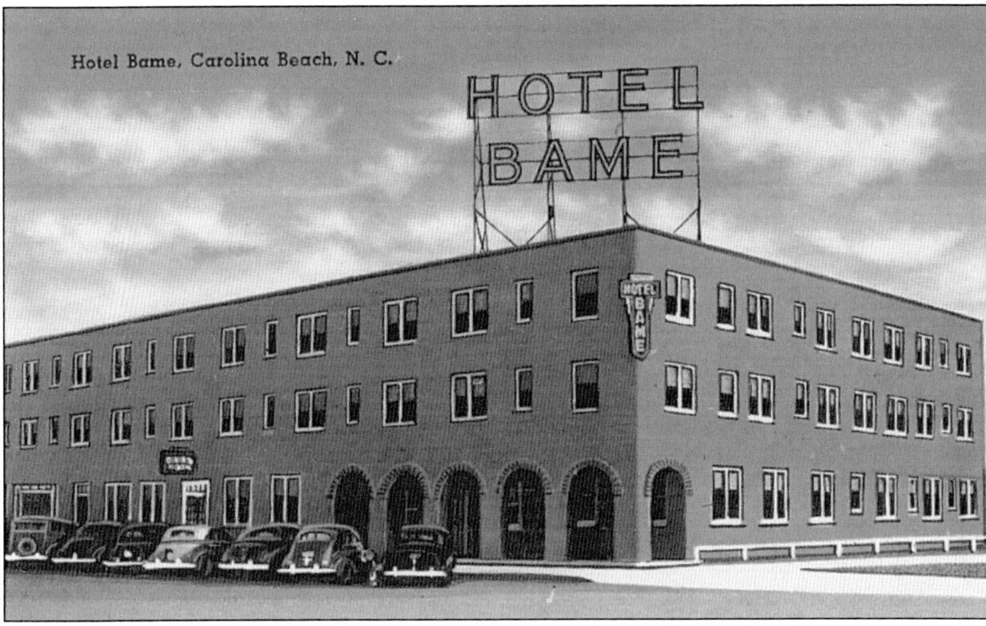

HOTEL BAME, C. 1942. In 1930, James R. and Florence Ludwig Bame built the Bame Hotel, located on Cape Fear Boulevard. It burned in the great fire of 1940. The hotel was rebuilt on the same site and reopened in the summer of 1941. This building was torn down in 1976.

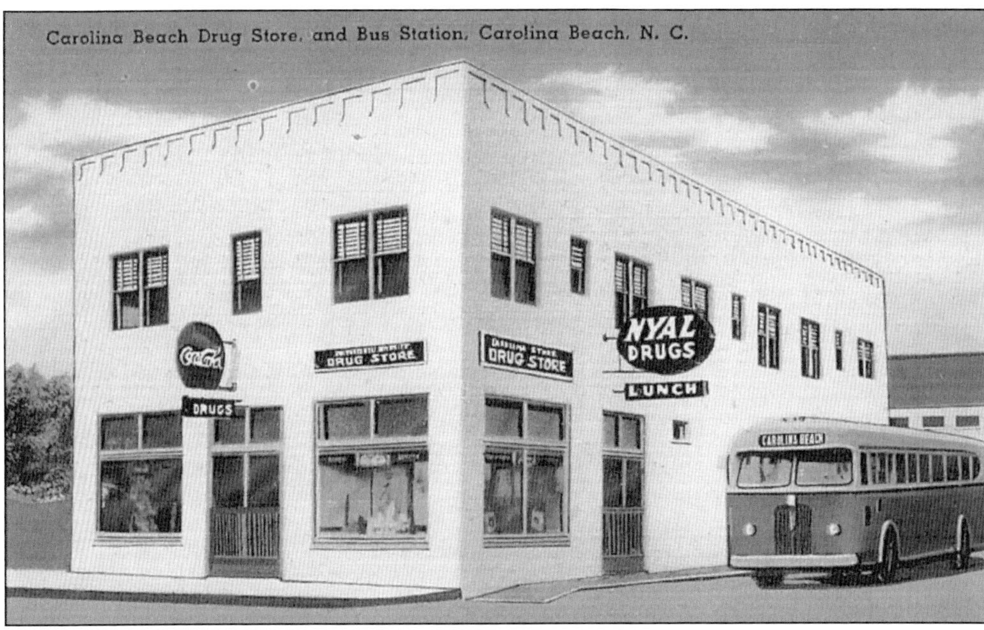

CAROLINA BEACH DRUG STORE, C. 1940S. In 1941, Mike Hall, son of Dr. Jim Hall, pharmacist and owner of Hall's Drug Store in Wilmington, opened the Carolina Beach Drug Store. Only there for a brief time, he went on active military duty shortly before Pearl Harbor. Located on the southeastern corner of Harper Avenue and Highway #421, the drugstore continued to operate under different management. The bus station, Western Union, and a small office where local residents could pay their light and water bills were located in the building.

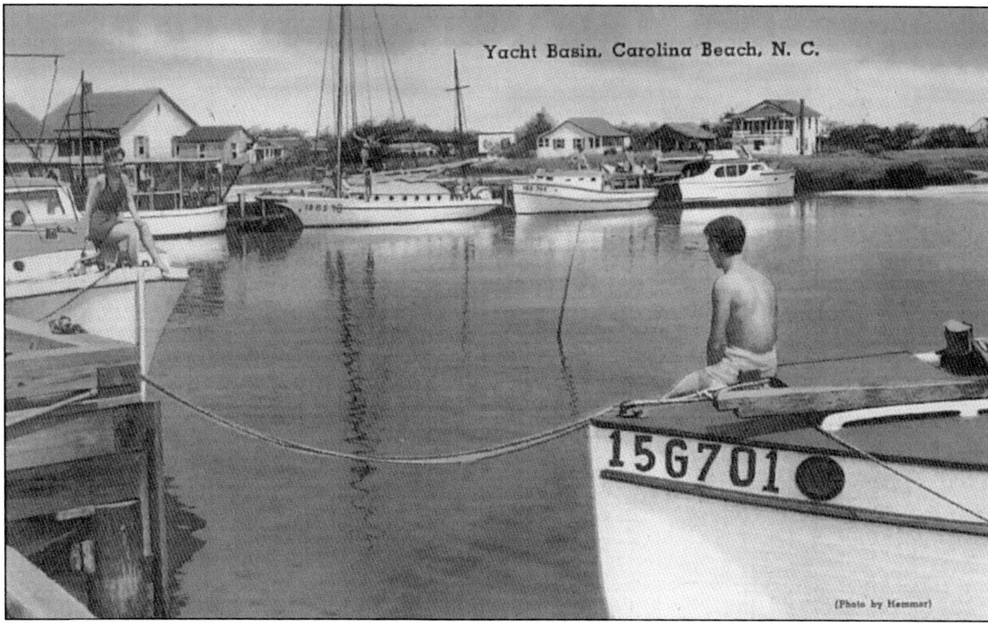

Yacht Basin, *c.* 1942. In 1939, Charles B. Parmele, Wilmington businessman, was responsible for suggesting the project of dredging Myrtle Grove Sound to make a town yacht basin. Currently, the "Skeets" Winner fleet of excursion boats ties up at this municipal dock. Winner is a descendant of Joseph L. Winner, who made the first attempt to develop Carolina Beach in the early 1880s.

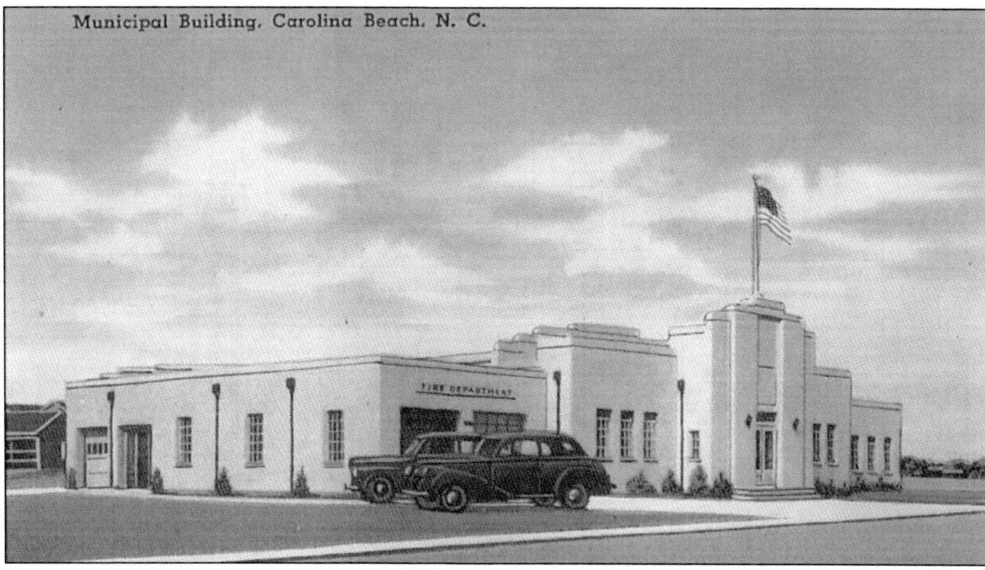

Municipal Building (Town Hall), *c.* 1942. Previously, the location of the Carolina Beach Town Hall on Canal Drive was a low marshy area, with enough water to sail a small boat. When the yacht basin was dredged, about 200 feet of land was added to the shoreline. The municipal building was started as a WPA project during the late 1930s and was completed *c.* 1942. Later, the town offices were moved to the former Blockade Runner Museum on Highway 421, and this structure was torn down in 2000.

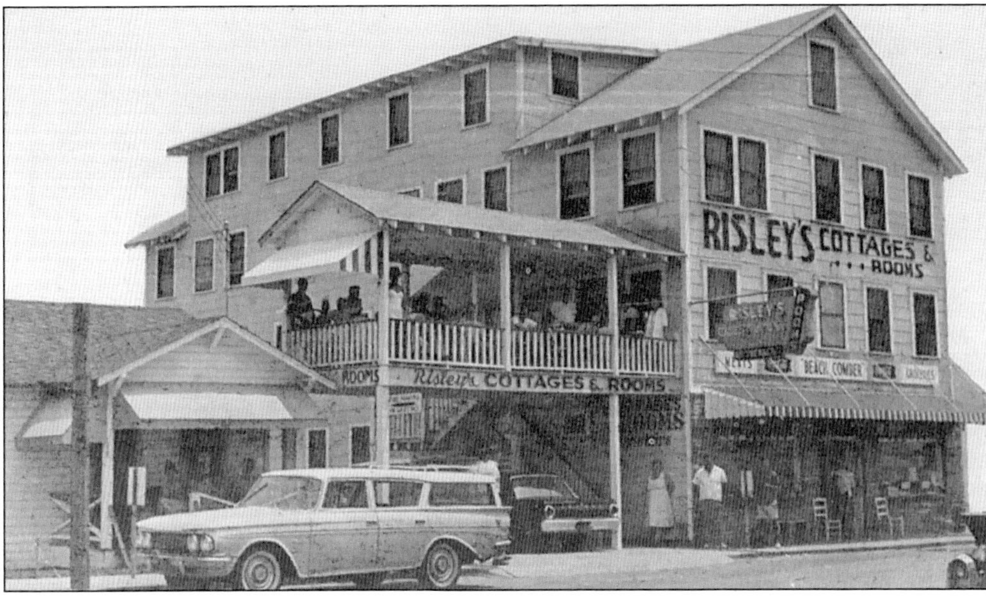

Risley's Cottages and Rooms, *c.* 1961. In 1935, Eugene and Margaret Harper Risley built three cottages on Harper Avenue, one block from the ocean. A larger building was constructed on the corner in 1940, giving the boarding house 17 additional rooms. When it opened, rooms were rented for the nightly rate of $2.50 per person, four people to a room. From 1940 to 1945, a restaurant occupied the corner structure. After the restaurant closed, a grocery store was located in the building, until it was razed in 1976. (Courtesy of Eugene F. Risley Jr.)

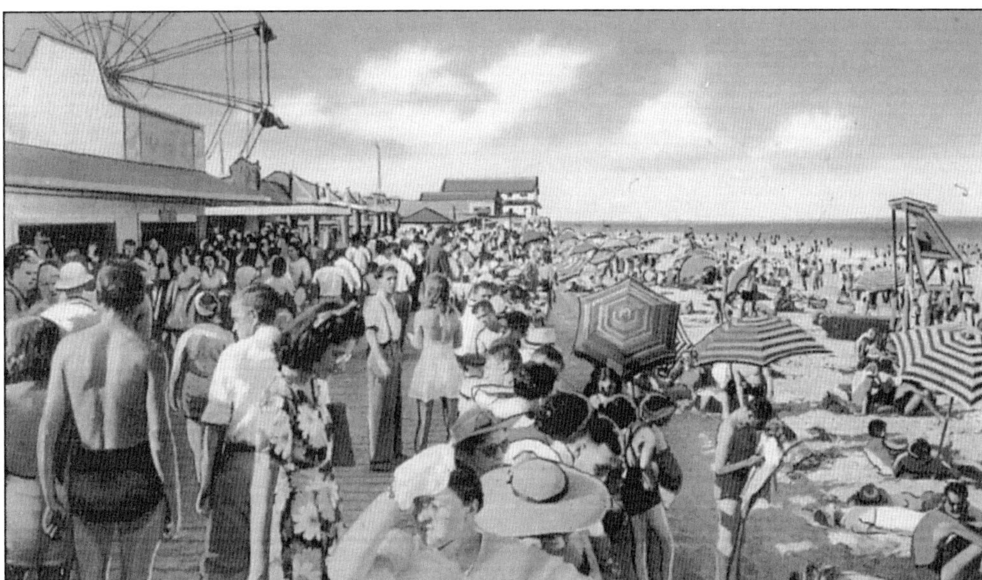

The Boardwalk, *c.* 1942. During summer weekends, the boardwalk is crowded with tourists. Bowling alleys, bingo parlors, and other concessions are part of the fun of visiting the beach. The boardwalk has been a part of Carolina Beach since its very early days, and gives the beach its nickname: "the Atlantic City of the South."

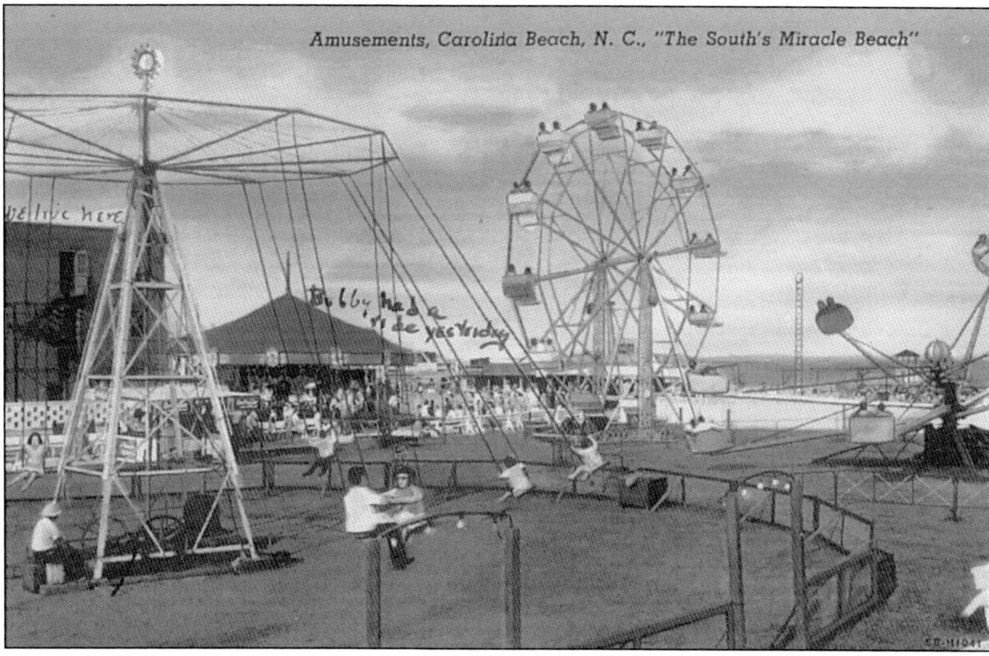

AMUSEMENTS, CAROLINA BEACH, NORTH CAROLINA, C. 1940S. Rides such as Ferris wheels, the octopus, swings, and bumper cars thrill visitors from far and wide. Faison Amusement Company operated one of the first parks. Shortly after WW II, the Kaus Amusement Company built the Blue Water Court between the boardwalk and Woddy Hewett Avenue.

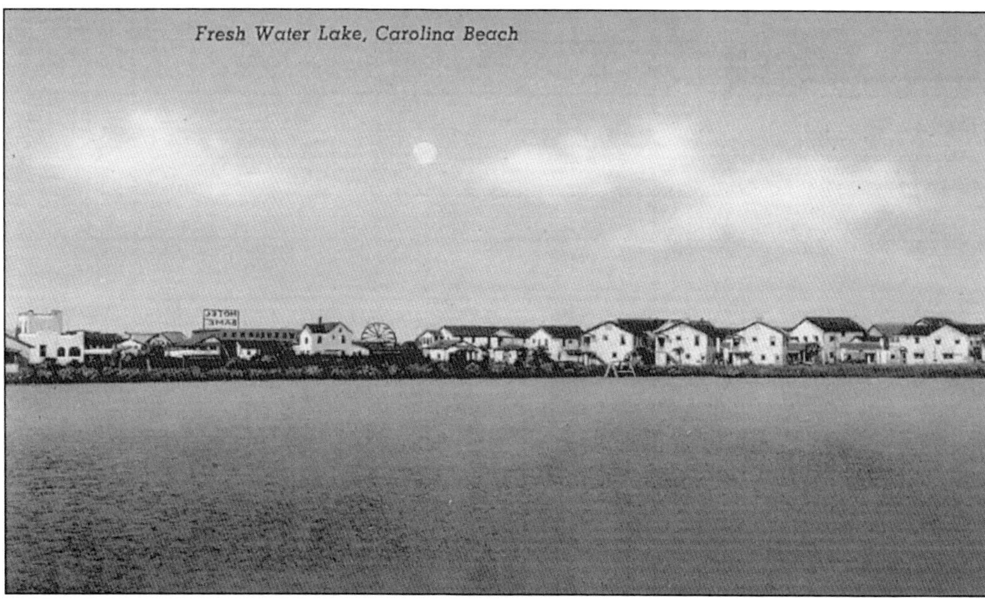

FRESH WATER LAKE, CAROLINA BEACH, C. 1940S. It is quite unusual to have a freshwater lake within less than a thousand feet of the Atlantic Ocean. In the early 1940s, Charles B. Parmele donated the lake to the Town of Carolina Beach. Located on Highway #421, a natural spring is the source of the lake's water, which is known to have alligators in it from time to time.

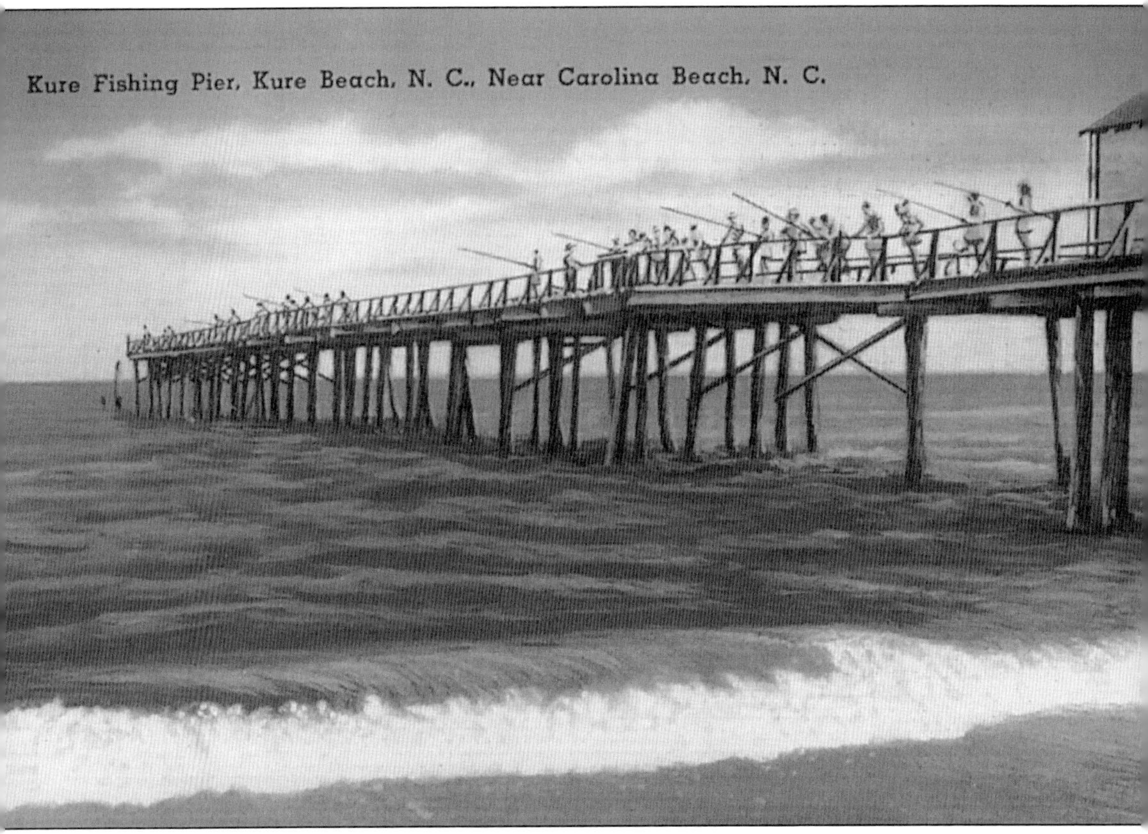

KURE FISHING PIER, C. 1942. Located 2 miles south of Carolina Beach on Highway #421, Kure Beach was named for Hans A. Kure (1851–1914), a native of Denmark, who was an early beach developer. Kure's son, Lawrence Christian, built the first wooden fishing pier in 1920. This pier was the second one erected on the North Carolina coast. Over the years, hurricanes and northeasters have damaged or destroyed it, the last time in 1996 by Hurricane Fran. Each time, the pier has been repaired or rebuilt to accommodate the thousands of fishermen who have lined its rails during fishing season.

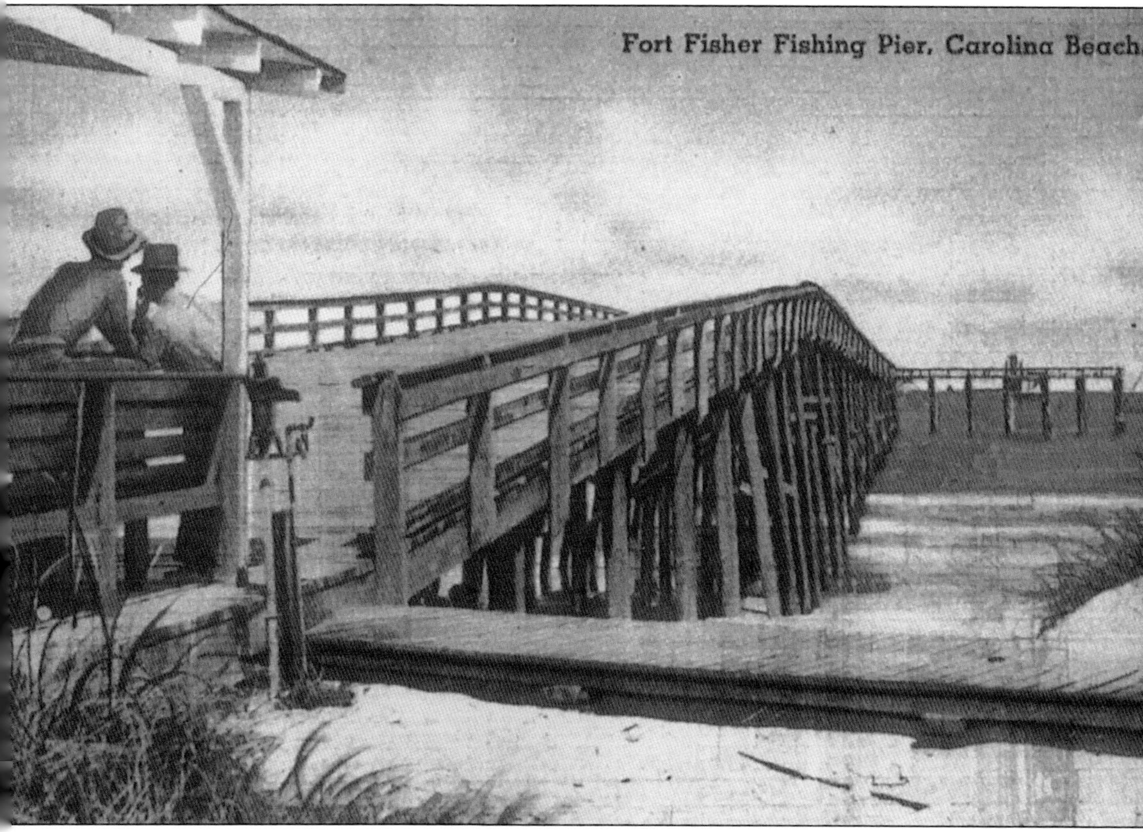

FORT FISHER FISHING PIER, C. 1942. By the late 1930s, brothers Louis B. and Thomas R. Orrell had purchased most of the land south of the Fort Fisher gates. In 1939, they constructed a fishing pier, which was about a thousand feet in length. The end "T" of the pier was directly over the wreck of the blockade runner *Modern Greece.* A restaurant and a bait and tackle concession were located on the pier at its entrance. Nearby were 12 small fisherman's cottages. In 1954, the fury of Hurricane Hazel completely destroyed the pier, leaving about three pilings standing.

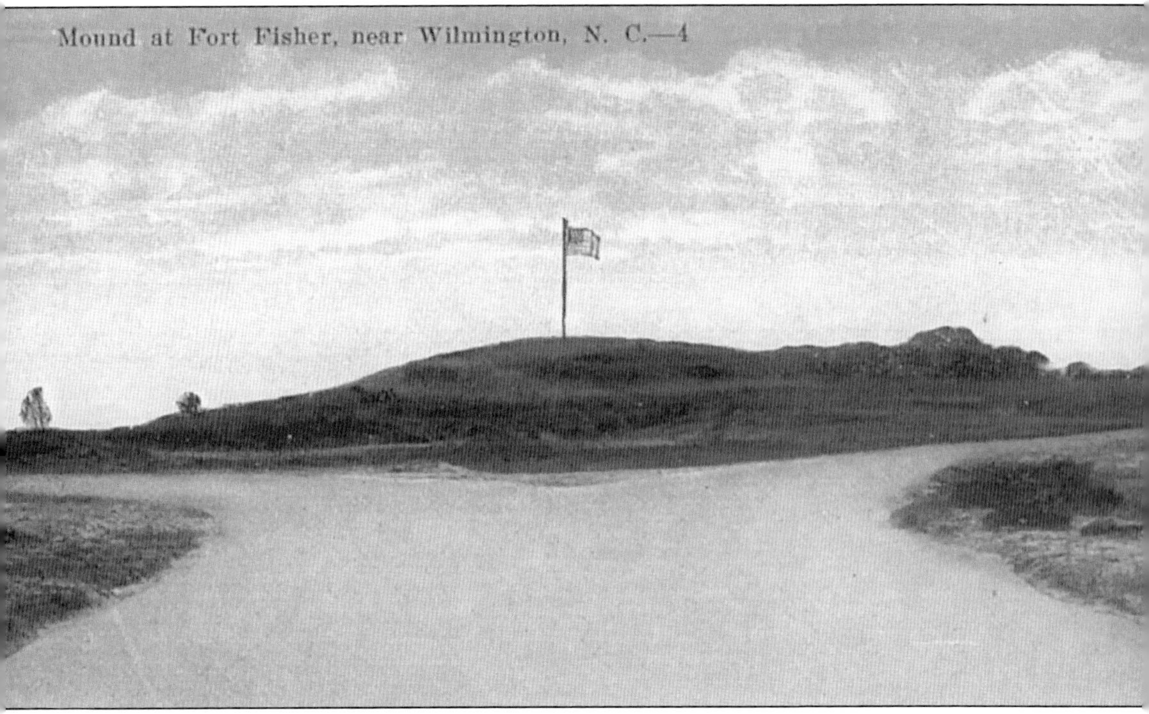

MOUND AT FORT FISHER, C. 1910. Located at the southern tip of Federal Point peninsula, Fort Fisher protected the Port of Wilmington during the Civil War. The famous Confederate fort was named for Colonel Charles F. Fisher, who was killed in the first battle of Manassas. Constructed of sand and massive timbers, earthen mounds were part of the fortifications. In 1864–1865, it was the scene of two of the largest Union naval bombardments of the Civil War. The Union capture of Fort Fisher sealed the fate of the Confederacy. Unfortunately, erosion has claimed all of the oceanfront mounds.

Six

River and Rail Connections

First, there was the Cape Fear River. Most of the early settlements along the Atlantic coast were near or on a river. From Colonial days, ships came into port bringing much wanted goods from afar. They returned with locally produced material, such as naval stores and lumber. The river was the highway into the interior. Fayetteville was an inland port, to which sailboats and later steamers made daily trips. Because roads from the South were over low marshy land, it was much faster to take a boat down the river to Southport than to go by horse and wagon. Land transportation did not catch up with river traffic until the 1920s, when two bridges were constructed across the Cape Fear and the Northeast Cape Fear Rivers.

Railroads brought development to the interior. The Wilmington & Weldon Railroad was organized in 1839. Burgaw in Pender County received a railroad connection the next year. It was not until 1911 that the Wilmington, Brunswick & Southern Railroad was completed to Southport. Thanks to river and rail connections, our neighbors in Pender and Brunswick Counties have close ties to the port city.

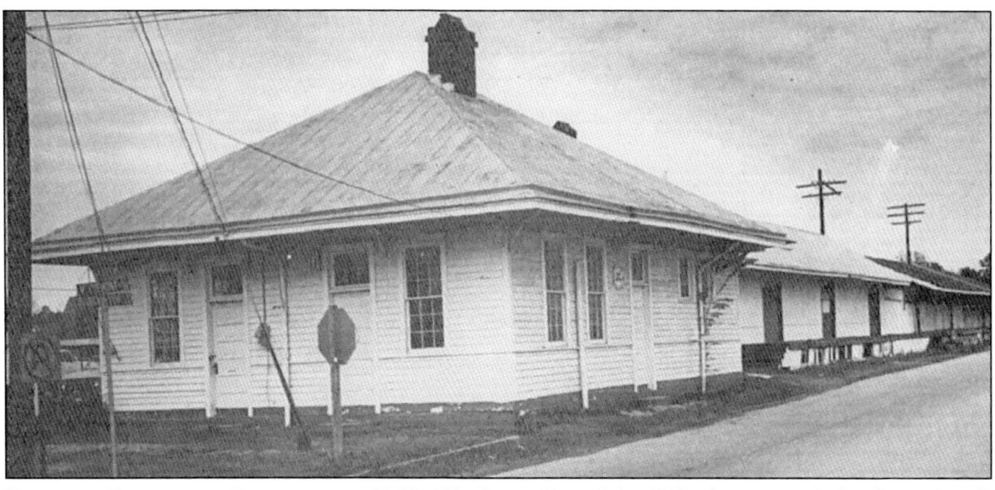

Burgaw Railroad Station, *c.* 1960. The last spike of the Wilmington & Raleigh Railroad, which was to evolve into the Wilmington & Weldon Railroad, was driven on March 7, 1840. On this railroad, a station was established at Cypress Grove, later called Burgaw Depot. Burgaw was a named for an American Indian tribe who lived along Burgaw Creek. (Courtesy of Tom Bradshaw.)

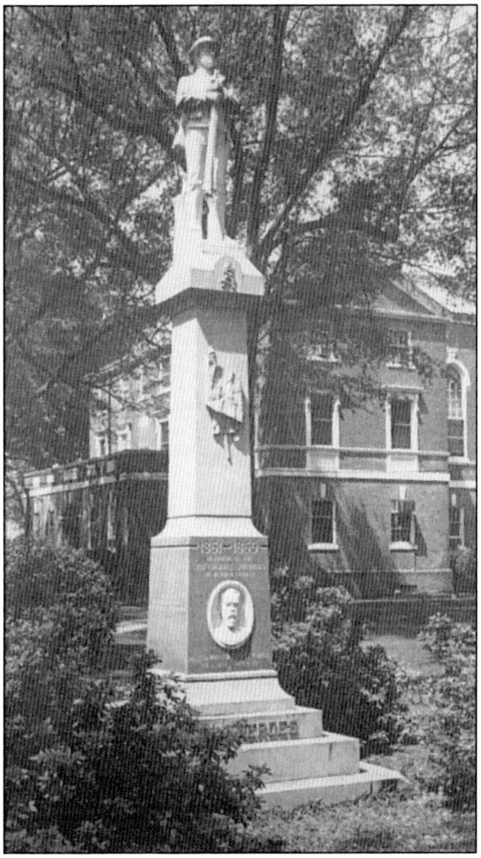

MONUMENT OF GENERAL WILLIAM DORSEY PENDER, C. 1960. On February 16, 1875, a new county was formed from New Hanover County by the North Carolina Legislature. It was named for Confederate General William Dorsey Pender (1834–1863), a native North Carolinian who died from wounds received at the Battle of Gettysburg. Given by the Pender County Chapter, United Daughters of the Confederacy, the monument was unveiled on May 27, 1914. It occupies a prominent spot on the courthouse grounds. (Courtesy of Tom Bradshaw.)

PENDER COUNTY COURTHOUSE. Burgaw was designated the county seat in 1877 because of its central location The first Pender County Courthouse and Jail was built in 1885. It was constructed in the middle of a large square in the center of town. In 1935, the original building was demolished and a new courthouse, shown here, was built on the same site. The red-brick courthouse was dedicated on November 7, 1937. (Courtesy of Pender County Historical Society.)

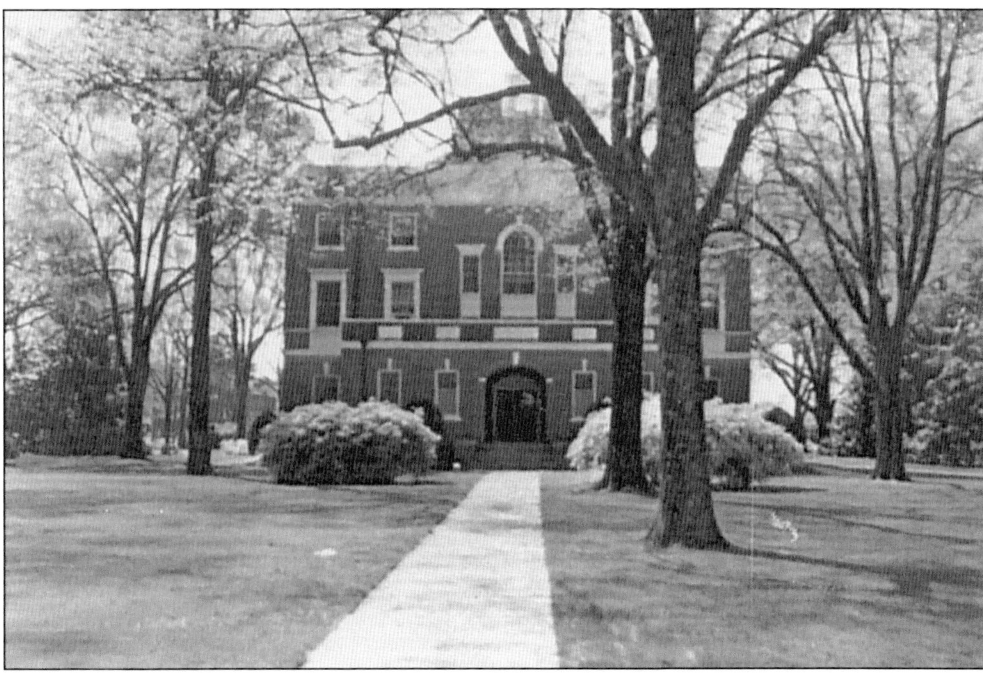

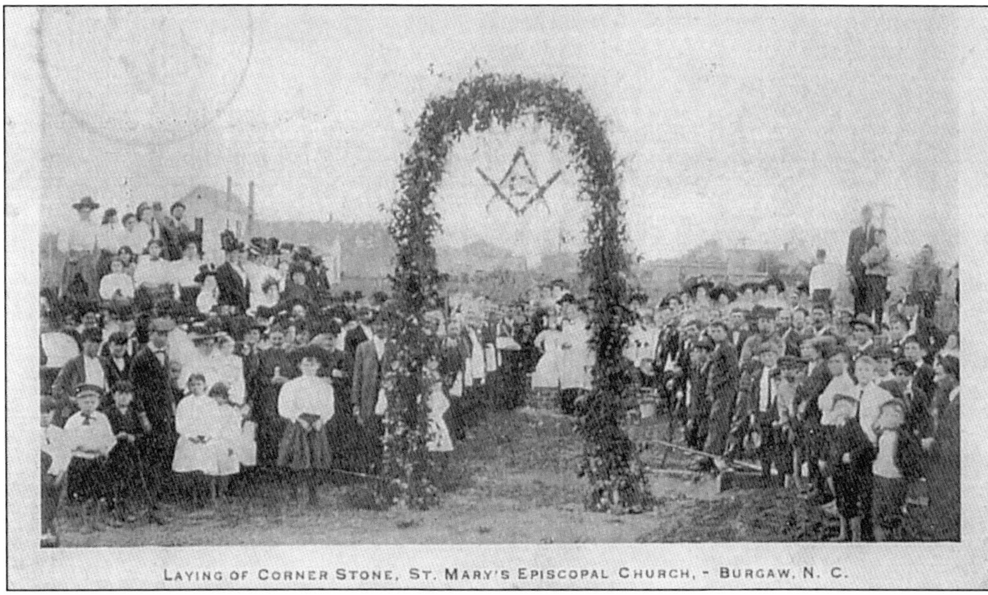

LAYING OF CORNERSTONE OF ST. MARY'S EPISCOPAL CHURCH, *c.* 1910. On November 24, 1908, the cornerstone of St. Mary's Episcopal Church on Wilmington Street in Burgaw was laid with elaborate ceremonies. The brick church was 30 by 50 feet and was a mission of the Wilmington Episcopal Diocese. In 1978, a new church was built on an adjacent lot and the old structure was razed. (Courtesy of Pender County Historical Society.)

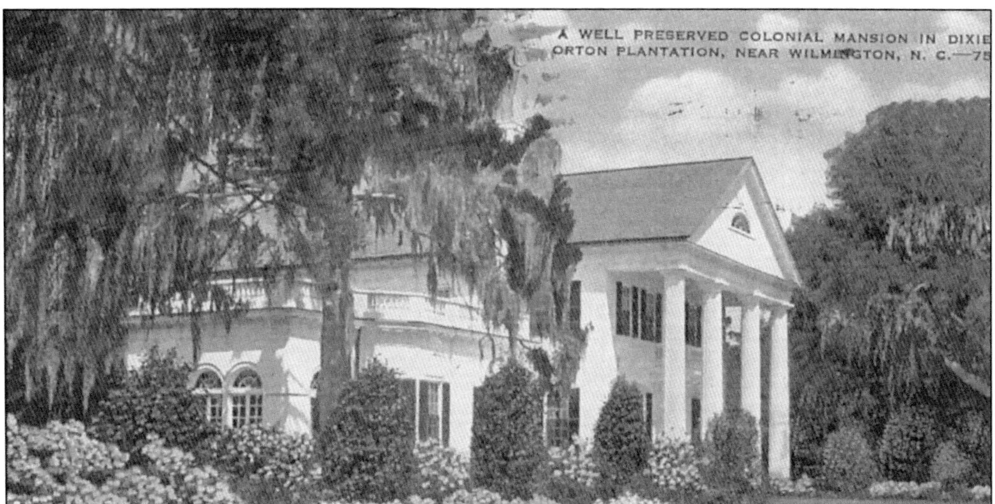

ORTON PLANTATION, *c.* 1940. Located on the western bank of the Cape Fear River, the center portion of the mansion at Orton Plantation was built about 1725 by "King" Roger Moore (*c.* 1694–1751). It remained in the Moore family for three generations. Later, the property was owned by other prominent residents, including General Benjamin Smith, who was a governor of North Carolina. Dr. James Sprunt (1846–1924) and his wife, Luola Murchison Sprunt (1858–1916), purchased the old rice plantation from the estate of his father-in-law, Colonel Kenneth M. Murchison (1831–1904), in 1904. The Sprunts added the Colonial Revival wings to the house.

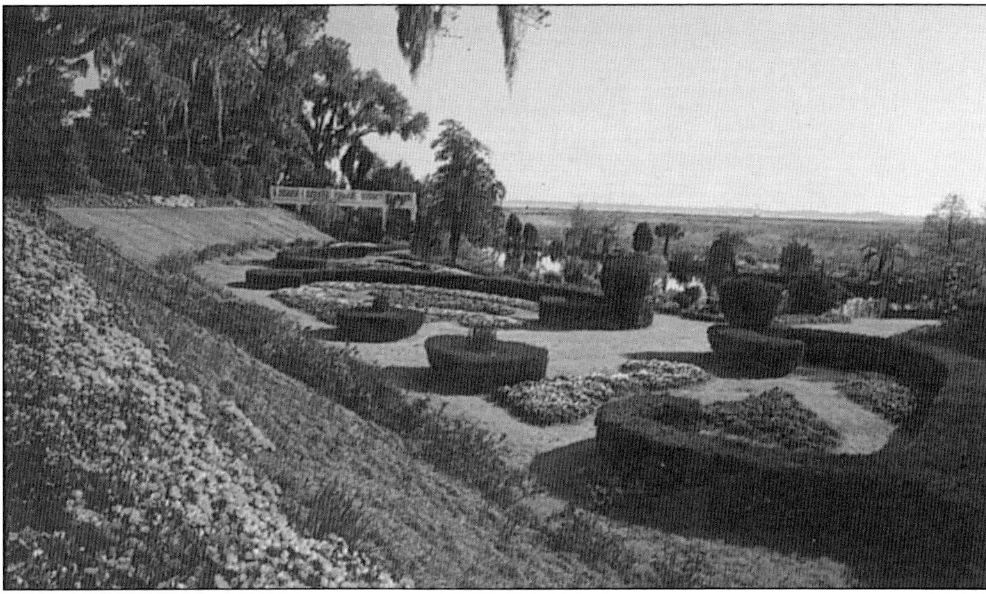

SCROLL GARDEN, ORTON PLANTATION, C. 1955. After the Sprunts purchased the plantation in 1904, they began an ambitious landscaping plan, which created lovely formal gardens around the old mansion. A profusion of camellias, azaleas, and other flowering plants were planted on the property. Shown here is the scroll garden, with the old rice fields and the Cape Fear River in the background. (Courtesy of Hugh Morton.)

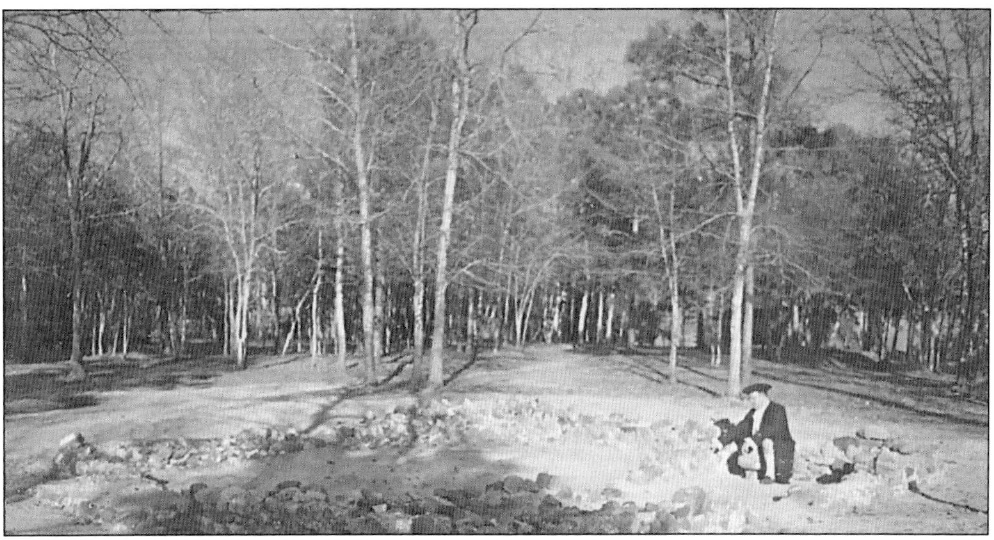

BRUNSWICK TOWN, C. 1960. The first permanent settlement on the Cape Fear River, Brunswick Town was founded in 1725. The town flourished for a time and was included in New Hanover County, when it was formed in 1729. After the hurricane of 1769, which caused much destruction, most of the settlers left for the new settlement of Newton or Wilmington, 16 miles up the river. Only the ruins of St. Philip's Anglican Church, an adjacent graveyard, and the excavated foundations of a few buildings remain. Shown here, noted local historian Bill Reaves, dressed in colonial attire, is seated among the ruins of the Colonial town.

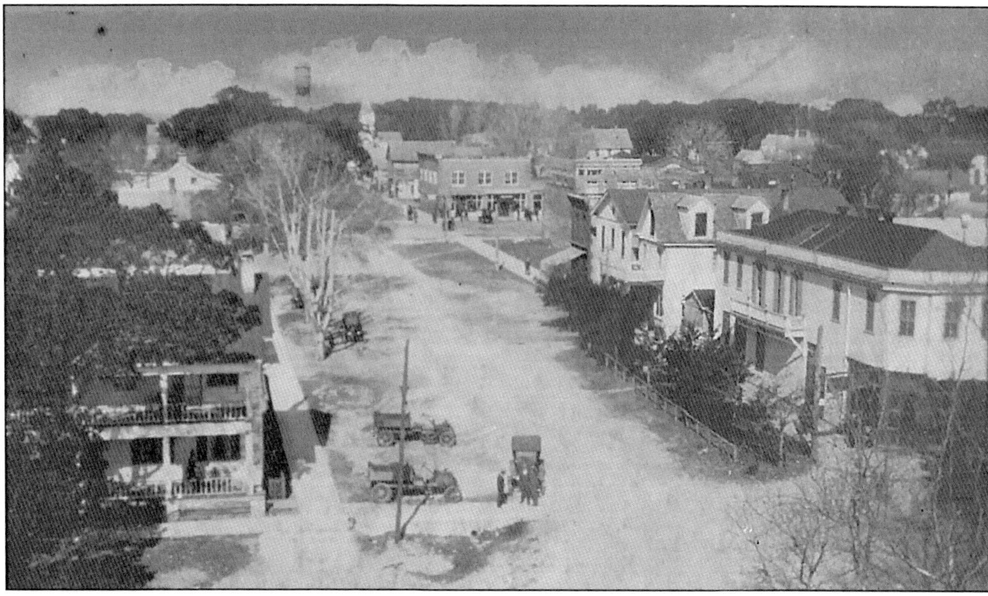

Howe Street, Southport North Carolina, c. 1920. Chartered in 1792, the Town of Southport was formerly known as Smithville for General Benjamin Smith (1751–1826). The name was changed in 1887 to recognize that it was the most southerly seaport in North Carolina, located on the western side of the Cape Fear River near its mouth. This scene is of Howe Street from the corner of Bay Street. The large structure at right was the Miller Hotel, owned by Leonhardt Miller, a native of Germany. Once the social center of town, the building was razed *c.* 1955. On the left corner, the Carolina House, a boarding house, has also been demolished.

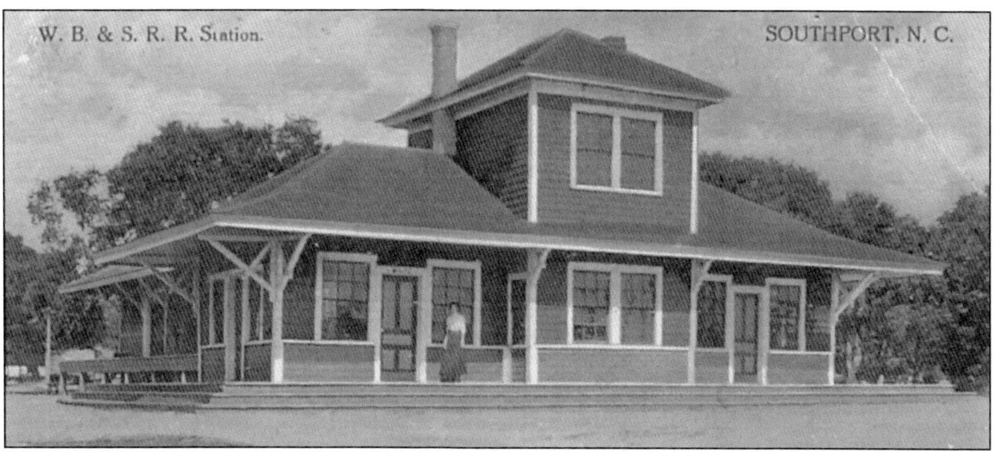

Wilmington, Brunswick & Southern Railroad Depot, c. 1912. On November 23, 1911, a grand celebration greeted the arrival of a train into Southport from Wilmington, inaugurating the first railway service in town history. The trip took 2 hours and 36 minutes. The depot was located on the corner of Moore and Rhett Streets near the old Smithville Burying Grounds. By the 1930s, the popularity of automobiles and the construction of better roads made the railroad to Southport unprofitable. Passenger service was maintained until 1933, and freight service stopped in 1938. In April 1940, an explosion of ammonia at the depot destroyed the building.

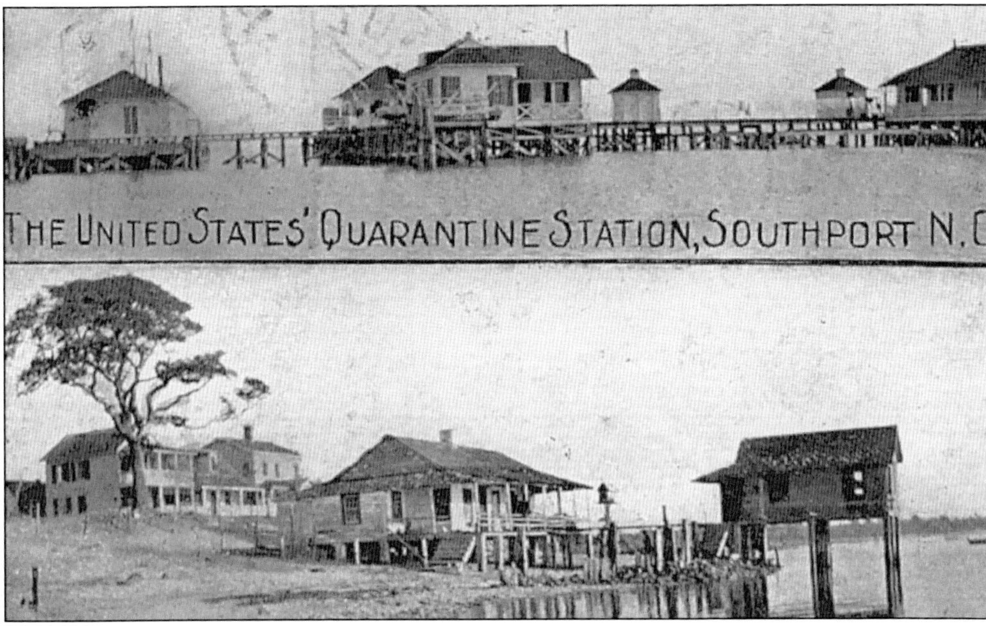

U.S. QUARANTINE STATION AND A FISHERMAN'S COTTAGE, *c.* 1907. The upper panel of this postcard is the Quarantine Station, built on a pier in the Cape Fear River in 1895–1896. Every vessel coming into port had to stop at the station. If there was anyone with a contagious disease on board, the infected individual had to be taken from the ship and placed in quarantine. The ship would then be sprayed with sulfur to fumigate it before continuing up river to the port of Wilmington. The lower panel is a fisherman's cottage on the river.

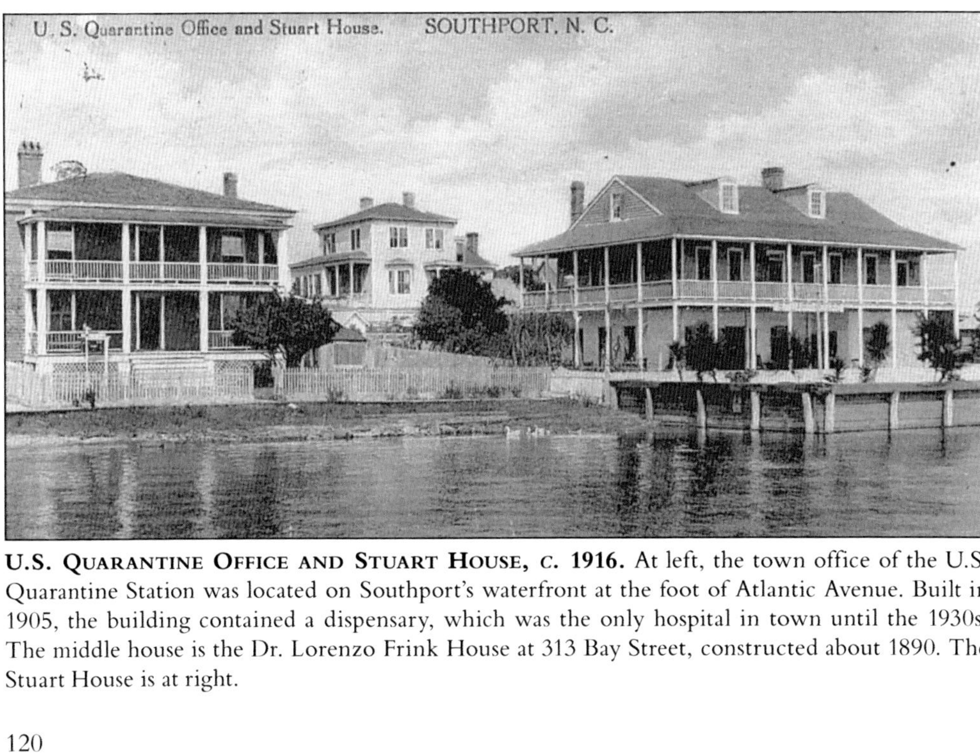

U.S. QUARANTINE OFFICE AND STUART HOUSE, *c.* 1916. At left, the town office of the U.S. Quarantine Station was located on Southport's waterfront at the foot of Atlantic Avenue. Built in 1905, the building contained a dispensary, which was the only hospital in town until the 1930s. The middle house is the Dr. Lorenzo Frink House at 313 Bay Street, constructed about 1890. The Stuart House is at right.

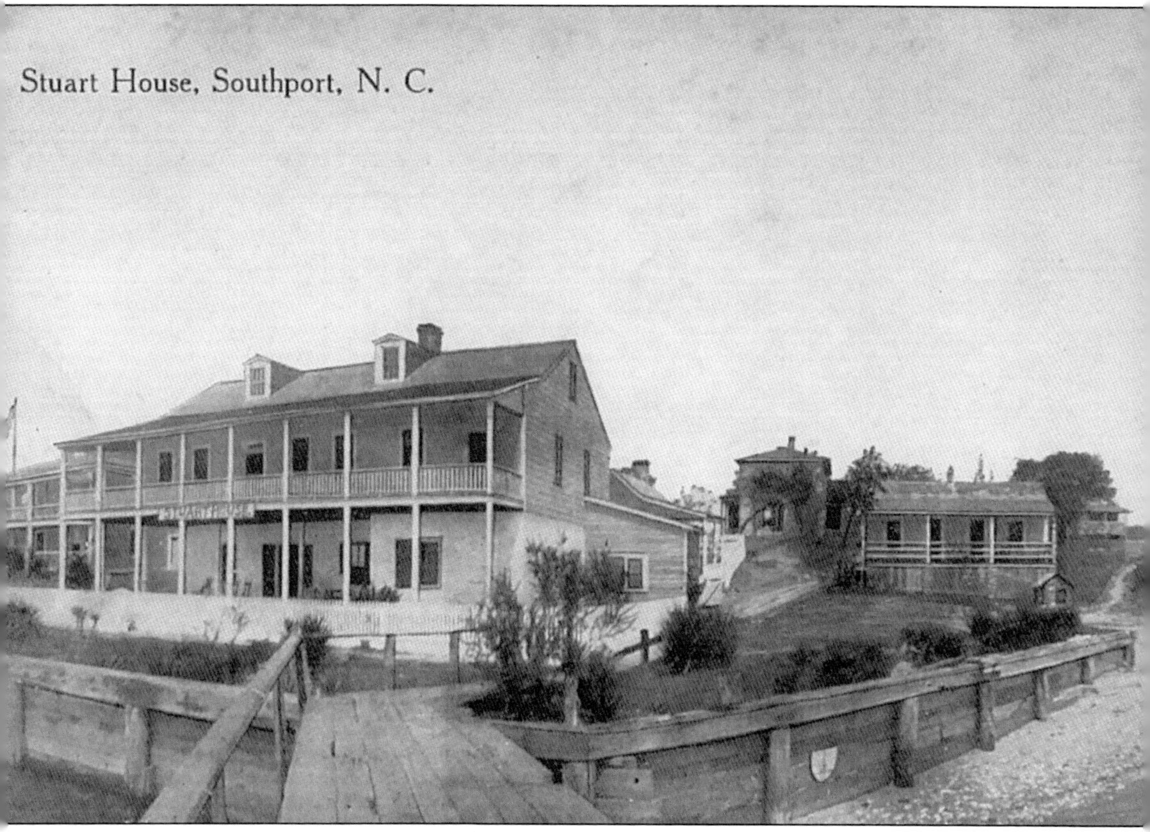

THE STUART HOUSE, C. 1908. Mary Elizabeth Garland Bensell was a widow with five children when she established a boarding house on the Smithville waterfront in 1843. Shortly thereafter, she married Dr. Charles Henry Stuart, a native of Scotland and a doctor at Fort Johnston. Their only child was Miss Kate Stuart (1844–1929), who inherited the boarding house after her mother's death. She played hostess to lawyers, businessmen, judges, and other prominent people from all over the state. A strong believer in education, she operated a school for a time. In 1879, fully clothed in a long skirt and petticoats, Miss Kate jumped into 18 feet of water to rescue the small daughter of a Clyde Line steamer captain. Afterwards, she was known as "The Heroine of Smithville." A tireless and tenacious supporter of her native town, she was the only woman member of the Chamber of Commerce, embracing such civic causes as obtaining a railroad for the town and against moving the Brunswick County seat of government from Southport. The Stuart House was one of the many victims of Hurricane Hazel in 1954.

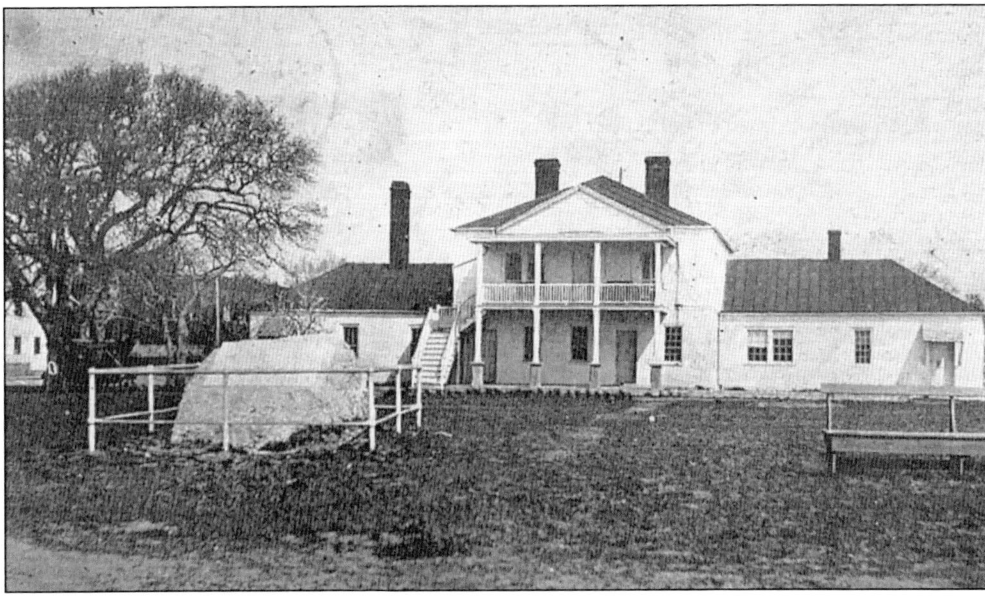

THE GARRISON, FORT JOHNSTON, C. 1916. Named for Colonial Governor Gabriel Johnston, Fort Johnston was built in 1745 to ward off a Spanish attack of Brunswick Town and is the oldest fort in the Cape Fear area. The garrison was built on East Bay Street between 1805 and 1809 as officers' quarters. The Southport Library occupied the east wing of this building at one time. Today it is the home of the commanding officer of Sunny Point Military Ocean Terminal.

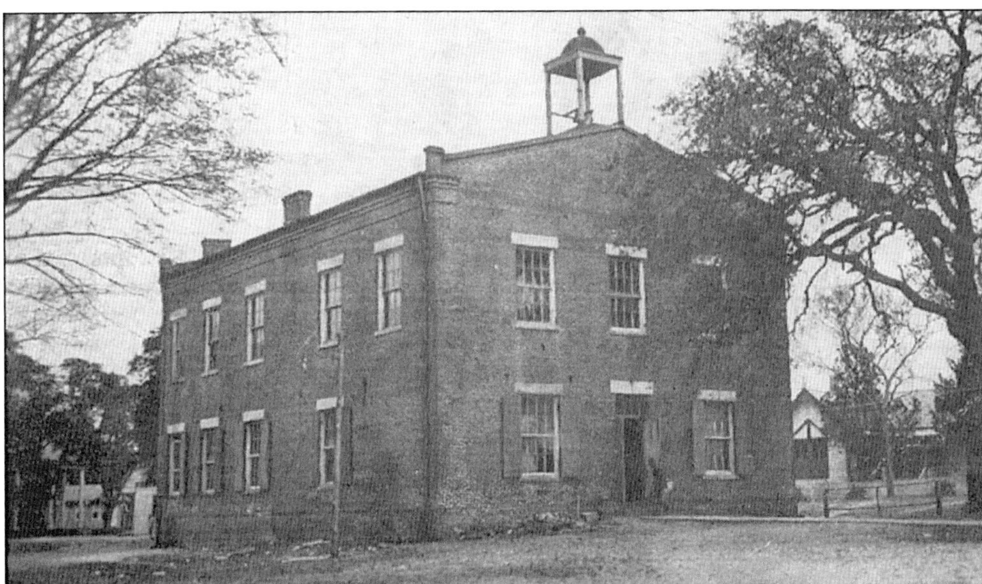

BRUNSWICK COUNTY COURT HOUSE, C. 1916. Smithville became the county seat of Brunswick County in 1808. Located on East Moore Street, the courthouse was built in 1854 and was probably the second one on the same site. In 1922, a porch was added to the structure. Note the cupola on top of the building, which originally contained a bell. The structure is now the Southport Town Hall.

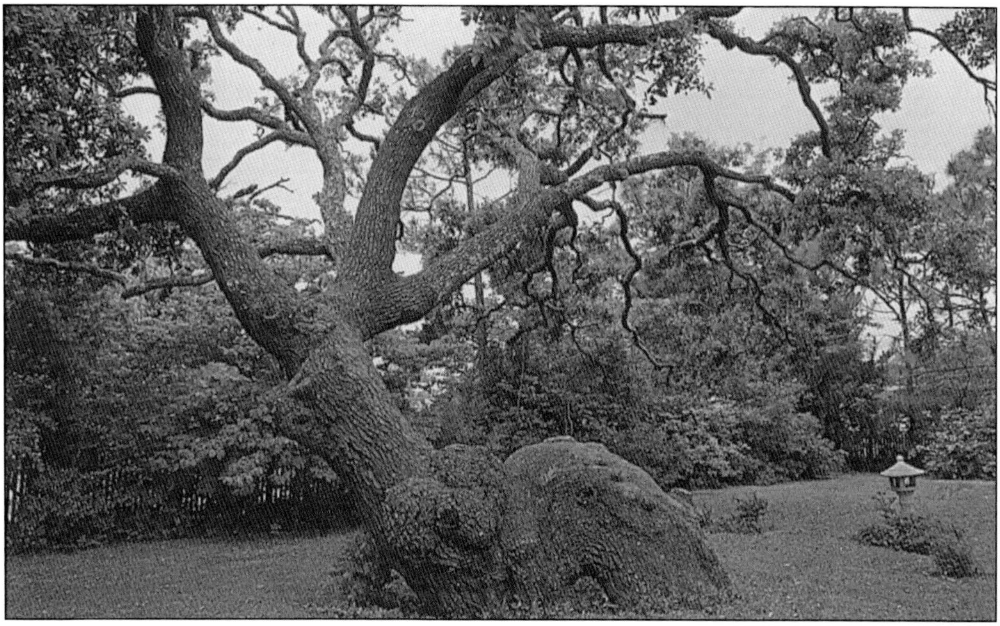

INDIAN TRAIL TREE, C. 1955. Located in Keziah Memorial Park, the Indian Trail Tree has been estimated to be more than 800 years old. A marker in the park reads as follows: "Indians may have bent the young tree to mark the trail to their fishing grounds. The tree took root a second time thus developing the unusual formation." *Ripley's Believe It or Not* brought the tree to the nation's attention in the 1950s. (Courtesy of Hugh Morton.)

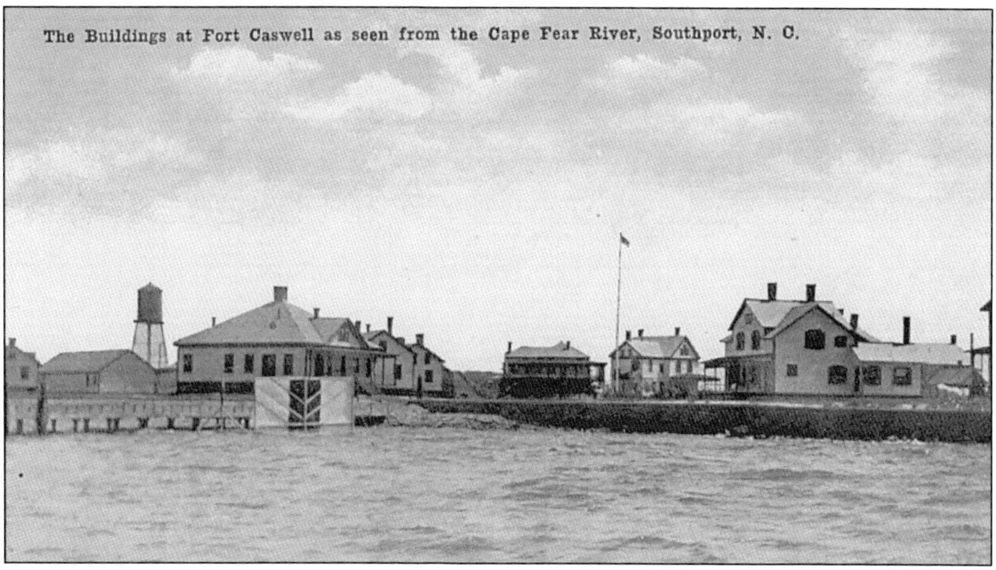

FORT CASWELL C. 1918. Across the bay from Southport is Fort Caswell, which dates from 1826. It was named for Revolutionary War Colonel Richard Caswell, who later became the first governor of the State of North Carolina. The fort was utilized in WW I as an army training facility. The Wilmington Light Infantry trained here before being deployed to France. During WW II, the fort was an anti-submarine Navy patrol base. The property was sold to the North Carolina State Baptist Convention in September 1949.

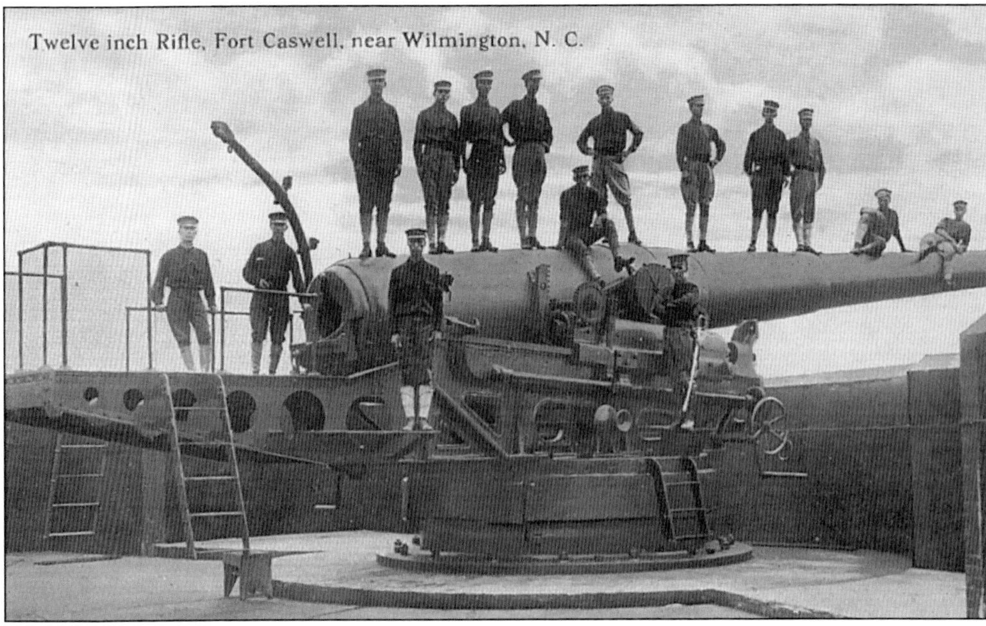

FORT CASWELL, C. 1918. While training for foreign duty in 1917–1918, soldiers fired big guns within the confines of the fort. Author and local historian Mrs. Susie Carson wrote in the *Pelican Post*, "Notices were given to the citizens of Southport when the guns were to be fired. Townspeople removed pictures and mirrors from their walls and dishes from shelves because when the guns went off, the houses shook violently and mirrors, dishes, and pictures crashed to the floor. The noise from the guns was deafening."

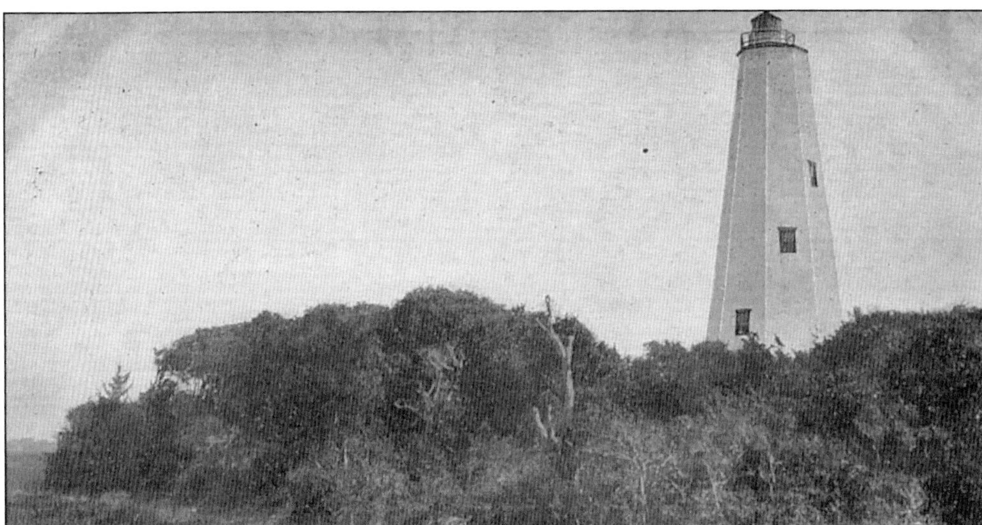

BALD HEAD LIGHTHOUSE, C. 1914. When the lighthouse was constructed in 1817, it was located on Smith Island, which was named for Thomas Smith, who acquired it in the early eighteenth century. The island is now called Bald Head, a name originally applied only to the round sandy area on its southwestern edge. "Old Baldy" warned vessels away from the dangerous Frying Pan Shoals and provided a beacon for ships entering the river channel. The 110-foot structure is the state's oldest lighthouse.

Selected Bibliography

Block, Susan Taylor. *Cape Fear Lost.* Charleston, SC: Arcadia Publishing, 1999.

Bloodworth, Mattie. *History of Pender County, North Carolina.* Richmond, VA: 1947.

Carson, Susan S. *Joshua's Dream: A Town with Two Names.* Southport, NC: 1992.

Cashman, Diane. *Centennial History of the Cape Fear Country Club, 1896–1996.* Wilmington: 1996.

Conser, Walter H. Jr. *Sacred Spaces: Architecture and Religion in Historic Wilmington.* Wilmington, 1999.

Fales, Dr. Robert M. *Wilmington Yesteryear.* Wilmington: 1984.

Hall, Lewis Philip. *Land of the Golden River, I.* Wilmington: 1975.

———. *Land of the Golden River, II & III.* Wilmington: 1980.

Hutteman, Ann Hewlett. "Catalog of the Louis T. Moore Photograph Collection." North Carolina Room, New Hanover County Public Library, 2000.

———. *One Hundred Golden Summers: A History of the Hanover Seaside Club, 1898–1998.* Wilmington: 1999.

King, Irving H. *The Coast Guard Under Sail: The Revenue Cutter Service.* Annapolis, MD: 1989.

Landon, Charles S. *The North Carolina State Ports Authority.* Durham, NC: 1963.

Lounsbury, Carl. *The Architecture of Southport.* Southport, NC: 1986.

Massengill, Stephen E. and Robert M. Topkins. *A North Carolina Postcard Album, 1905–1925.* Raleigh, NC.

Pelican Post, Oak Island, NC. October 1997; Winter 2000.

Reaves, William M. *History of Burgaw, NC: Pender County Centennial Edition.* Wilmington: 1979.

Reaves, William M. Newspaper Files. North Carolina Room, New Hanover County Public Library.

Russell, Anne. *Carolina Yacht Club Chronicles.* Wilmington: 1993.

Shaffer, Edward T.H. *Carolina Gardens: the History, Romance and Tradition of Many Gardens of Two States Through More Than Two Centuries.* New York: 1939.

Smith, Everard. *Victory on the Home Front: The USO in New Hanover County, North Carolina, 1941–1946.* Wilmington: 1999.

Sprunt, James. *Chronicles of the Cape Fear River.* Wilmington: 1916.

Stick, David. *North Carolina Lighthouses.* Raleigh, NC: 1980.

Tetterton, Beverly and Glenn. *The North Carolina Fact Book I and II.* Wendell, NC: 1999.

Watkins, Greg. *Wrightsville Beach: A Pictorial History.* Wrightsville Beach: 1997.

Wilmington City Directories, archived at the North Carolina Room, New Hanover County Public Library.

Wilmington Star-News, archived at North Carolina Room, New Hanover County Public Library.

Wrenn, Tony P. *Wilmington, North Carolina: An Architectural and Historical Portrait.* Charlottesville: 1984.

Interviews: Eugene F. Risley Jr. Carolina Beach.
Susan S. Carson. Southport.

Index

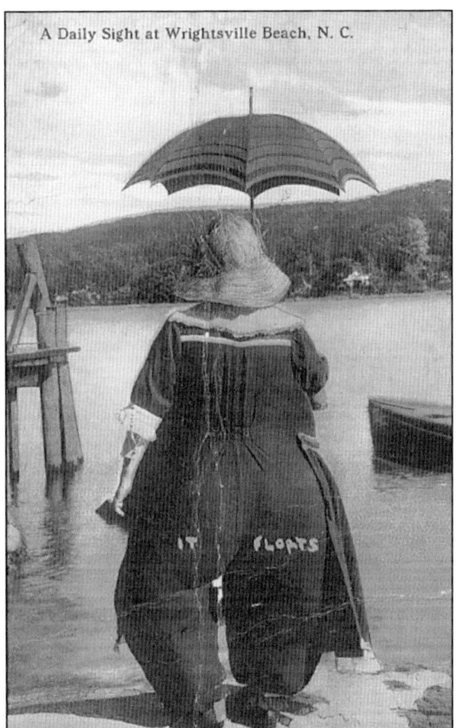

"A Daily Sight at Wrightsville Beach, North Carolina," 1917.